STATE LIBRARY
REGIONAL CENTER
CALDWELL, OHIO

I0998569

WITHDRAWN

OCT 31 1967

WITHDRAWN

GREAT LIVES OBSERVED

Gerald Emanuel Stearn, *General Editor*

EACH VOLUME IN THE SERIES VIEWS THE CHARACTER AND ACHIEVE-
MENT OF A GREAT WORLD FIGURE IN THREE PERSPECTIVES—
THROUGH HIS OWN WORDS, THROUGH THE OPINIONS OF HIS CON-
TEMPORARIES, AND THROUGH RETROSPECTIVE JUDGMENTS—THUS
COMBINING THE INTIMACY OF AUTOBIOGRAPHY, THE IMMEDIACY
OF EYE-WITNESS OBSERVATION, AND THE COMPARATIVE OBJECTIV-
ITY OF MODERN SCHOLARSHIP.

GEORGE RUDÉ, *the editor of this volume in the Great Lives
Observed series, is Professor of History and head of the de-
partment at the University of Stirling, Scotland. A Fellow of
the Royal Historical Society, he was the winner in 1955 of the
Society's Alexander Prize. Among his published works are:* The
Crowd in the French Revolution; Wilkes and Liberty: A Social
Study of 1763 to 1774; Revolutionary Europe, 1883-1815; The
Crowd in History: A Study of Popular Disturbances in France
and England, 1730-1848; *and* The Eighteenth Century, 1715-
1815.

Forthcoming volumes in the Great Lives Observed series

Hitler, *edited by George Stein*

Jesus, *edited by Hugh Anderson*

Lincoln, *edited by James P. Shenton*

Luther, *edited by Paul A. Lee*

Franklin Delano Roosevelt, *edited by Gerald D. Nash*

Mao, *edited by Jerome Ch'en*

John Calhoun, *edited by Margaret L. Coit*

Churchill, *edited by Martin Gilbert*

GREAT LIVES OBSERVED

Robespierre

Edited by GEORGE RUDÉ

[He] was his own executioner.
—J. N. McMANNERS

STATE LIBRARY OF OHIO
65 S. FRONT ST.
COLUMBUS, OHIO 43215

68- 33091

A SPECTRUM BOOK

PRENTICE-HALL, INC., ENGLEWOOD CLIFFS, N.J.

State Library Service Center
Region I
1445½ NORTH SCOTT STREET
NAPOLEON, OHIO   43545

Copyright © 1967 by PRENTICE-HALL, INC.,
Englewood Cliffs, New Jersey.

A SPECTRUM BOOK

All rights reserved.
No part of this book may be reproduced
in any form or by any means
without permission in writing from the publishers.

Current printing (last number):

10 9 8 7 6 5 4 3 2 1

Library of Congress Catalog Card Number 67-18696

Printed in the United States of America

Contents

PART ONE

ROBESPIERRE LOOKS AT THE WORLD

1

2

3

4

5

v

13
Robespierre in Retrospect 121

Bertrand Barère: "A True Republican" (1832), *121* Filippo Buonarotti: "The Victim of Immorality" (1837), *122* Madame de Stael: "Hypocritical" (1818), *126* Napoleon at St. Helena: "Scapegoat of the Revolution" [As Reported by the Count de las Cases (December 15, 1815), *128* As Reported in Gourgaud's Journal (December 16, 1816), *129*]

PART THREE
ROBESPIERRE IN HISTORY

14
French Historians of the 19th Century 131

Adolphe Thiers (1824-5), *132* Eugène Sue (1857), *134* Alphonse Aulard (1901), *136*

15
French Historians of the 20th Century 140

Albert Mathiez: Robespierre and Religion (1910), *141* Georges Lefebvre: Robespierre's Political Ideas (1933), *147* Albert Soboul: Robespierre and the Popular Movement (1964), *152*

16
English Historians and Robespierre 157

Thomas Carlyle (1837), *158* Lord Acton (1895-9), *161* J. M. Thompson (1935), *164* George Rudé (1958), *170*

GREAT LIVES OBSERVED

ROBESPIERRE

Introduction

The French Revolution of 1789 is generally accepted as having been one of the great cataclysmic events and turning points in the history of modern times. Only the Russian and the Chinese revolutions of this century can compare with it in terms of the social convulsions and fundamental political changes that they brought about. And at the very center of this event, during its most significant and hectic years, stood Maximilien Robespierre, who, more than any other man, may be said to have been its guiding spirit, its very incarnation. At times, the names of other contenders for this title have been put forward: Mirabeau as the great tribune of the first National Assembly; Danton as the embodiment of revolutionary national defense; Marat or Saint-Just as the archexponent of the Terror; and even Carnot, the great organizer of the Republic's military victories. But none of these held the center of the stage for so long; none left their mark, as Robespierre did, on each phase of the Revolution from its inception in May 1789 to the drama of Thermidor (July 1794) when his fall and execution have appeared to many to bring it virtually to an end.

It is all the more remarkable that the image we have of this man, who left so deep an imprint on a world-historical event, should be so blurred and confused. Indeed, it is almost no exaggeration to say that in England and North America he is scarcely known at all as an historical figure except to students of the French Revolution. There has been only one valuable biography of him in the English language. Even his native France, which prides itself on the respectful homage that it pays to the more illustrious of its sons, has strenuously denied him any formal public recognition. On the centenary of the Revolution in 1889, Danton was given a statue in the heart of Paris, but not Robespierre; and even his bicentenary went by without any national act of commemoration.

One reason for this neglect is, no doubt, that Robespierre's name evokes, even today, strong political passions; having become, as the man of the Terror and the great democrat of "the Year II," a hero with the Left, he has been coldshouldered by the Center and the Right, who view his memory with varying degrees of horror, aversion or contempt. Even in his lifetime, it is true that he aroused similarly divided loyalties, particularly during his last months when he was loved and revered by many, hated and feared by others. But due to the circumstances of his fall and execution, the memory of him that was handed down to posterity was almost exclusively one-sided. His executioners—the strangely assorted "men of Thermidor"—saw to this; on the whole, their determined efforts to obliterate the whiter image in favor of the blacker were remarkably successful. The remains of Mirabeau and Marat found a temporary sanctuary in the Panthéon, the revolutionaries' Valhalla; but those of Robespierre were flung into a common grave, a flood of pamphlet literature was let loose to revile his memory, and he became the scapegoat for every atrocity ascribed to the Terror and its practitioners. His supporters were hounded, silenced and proscribed; and the picture of him that emerged was of a thin-lipped, prim, humorless, mean and petty tyrant and *buveur de sang,* dedicated to the cult of the guillotine and aspiring to a personal dictatorship. So he has seemed a more suitable subject for an historical Grand Guignol than for a niche in the gallery of the great. This picture has stuck in the minds of many; and, though shorn of some of its grosser absurdities, it still survives in many a history textbook.

In France, the picture has been somewhat modified since Albert Mathiez began, about forty years ago, to rescue Robespierre from his "Chamber of Horrors" and give him respectability; in any case, France's own political experience has been such as to ensure, once the issues involved had been widely discussed, that many Frenchmen would be found who would appreciate the problems and choices facing Robespierre and his associates in the grim and dangerous months of 1793 and early 1794. How far could they have acted otherwise without exposing the Revolution to its enemies from without, let alone to those from within? Such dilemmas and choices have not faced Americans since at least Washington's time (and then the issues were really quite different) and have not faced Englishmen since the days of Cromwell and the Long Parliament; and "Terror" has grown into a dirty word in the Anglo-Saxon political vocabulary. It is perhaps this more than any other consideration that has inhibited English and American historians from giving Robespierre his due as an historical figure. (Even J. M. Thompson, who wrote the best and most perceptive biography of Robespierre in English, found it difficult to reconcile the liberal of 1789-92 with the "terrorist" of 1793-4.)[1]

This book will not make any conscious attempt to whitewash its subject, to gloss over his irritating mannerisms, or to excuse his prim pedantry and petulant, even vindictive, outbursts. Nor will it hold a brief for all his actions. But, by giving the reader a brief account of his career, discussing some of the problems that confronted him, and present-

[1] See pp. 164-169.

ing him through his own speeches and the varying opinions held of him by contemporaries and historians, it may be possible to lend greater credibility to the image, the dilemmas, the actions and the ideas of an important Frenchman.

Maximilien Marie Isidore de Robespierre was born at Arras on May 6, 1758, the son and grandson of lawyers.[2] After three years' schooling in his native town, he was sent with a scholarship to the Collège Louis-le-Grand in Paris to study Classics and Law under Oratorian teachers; among his schoolmates was Camille Desmoulins, the later revolutionary journalist whom he was to send to the guillotine with Danton. Maximilien became the "star" classical scholar of his year and, ironically in view of later events, was chosen to deliver a Latin address of welcome to the young Louis XVI when the King passed through the capital after his coronation at Rheims in 1775. Returning to Arras, he adopted his father's profession and built up a modest practice as a "poor man's" lawyer; he also dabbled in literature, dedicated a political tract to "the nation of Artois," and joined the local debating society, the Rosati. So it was with a certain reputation as a lawyer, politician and man of letters that he was elected as one of eight deputies to represent the Third Estate (commons) of Arras at the Estates General when it was summoned to meet at Versailles in May 1789. He went to live in Paris, first at an address in the Rue Saintonge, in the Marais quarter, and later (in July 1791) in the house of Maurice Duplay, master cabinetmaker, at no. 366, Rue Saint-Honoré, which lay conveniently close to the Jacobin Club and the National Assembly. These two were soon to occupy almost all his waking hours, and he did not leave Paris again except for a brief visit to Arras in October 1791.

Soon after his arrival at Versailles, Robespierre joined the newly formed Breton Club, at first composed of the deputies of Brittany but soon developing into a national "pressure group" drawing in the most active elements of all the provincial delegations. Little known to the wider public at this time, his name was at first recorded in the journals as "Robes-pierre," "Robesse-Pierre," and even as "Roberts-piesse" or "Robespienne," or more simply as "Robert Pierre." But, after a hesitant start, he made a certain mark as a frequent contributor to the debates. His first recorded speech, on June 6, was an exposure of the lack of charity among bishops; and, six weeks later, he was chosen as one of

[2] I am indebted to the Editors of *History Today* for permitting me to reproduce in the following pages a substantial part of my article "Robespierre," which appeared in that journal in May 1958.

fifty deputies who accompanied the King on a visit to Paris after the fall of the Bastille. In October, the King was compelled, after a new insurrection, to make his permanent residence in the capital; and in the "Constituent" Assembly which followed him there, Robespierre quickly acquired a reputation as a spokesman of the Left and as a consistent democrat and liberal. It was in keeping with these views that he protested against martial law in October 1789, championed the Nancy mutineers in October 1790, and made speeches on the National Guard, in favor of adult suffrage, against the death penalty and against political professionalism in April and May of 1791.

In July of that year, there took place the first great crisis in Robespierre's political career. The King had attempted to flee the country in June; and when he was brought back under strong military escort to the capital, Robespierre, with others, demanded that he be deposed and that the Executive be constituted "by other means." Accordingly, from the rostrum of the Jacobin Club (as the Breton Club had been renamed since its removal to Paris), he supported the more "plebeian" Cordeliers Club's call for a petition and demonstration in the Champ de Mars. But, before the demonstration could take place, the Constituent Assembly had decided to accept the fiction that Louis had been the victim of an aristocratic *coup* and should be retained in office. Robespierre, either from deference to the Assembly once it had made its wishes known or from fear of an intrigue to replace Louis by his cousin the Duke of Orleans, persuaded the Jacobins, among whom he now enjoyed a remarkable ascendancy, to withdraw their support. So the Cordeliers Club went ahead on their own. Martial law was declared, and Lafayette's National Guard fired on an unarmed crowd, leaving fifty dead on the Champ de Mars. Numerous arrests followed; other leading democrats, including Danton, went into hiding; but Robespierre, though strongly suspect as an acknowledged leader of the Left, was merely threatened and went off quietly to live at Maurice Duplay's. Yet he retained his popularity in the streets of Paris; and when the Constituent Assembly, having completed its work, dissolved itself in September, it was Robespierre, along with Pétion (soon to be elected the city's mayor) who was garlanded by Parisian crowds as a hero of the day.

The second crisis in his political career followed soon after and revealed once more how little he was inclined to sacrifice political beliefs to the transitory glamor of popular appeal. Robespierre, like all other deputies to the old Constituent Assembly, was debarred—by a "self-denying ordinance" of his own promotion—from sitting in the Legislative Assembly that took its place; so, for the coming year, he transferred his main political activities to the Jacobin Club. And it was here that he won considerable unpopularity by the part that he played in the great debate on peace and war. War with Austria and Prussia was already imminent. The Court Party favored it, believing it would undo the work of the Revolution and restore the throne to its former authority. The War Minister, Narbonne, favored it, hoping that it would pave the way for a strong military government. For other reasons, it was favored by Jacques-Pierre Brissot and his Left group of *Brissotins* (soon to be renamed "Girondins"): they thought that a "revolutionary" war with the Austrians and Prussians would discredit their rivals, the constitutional monarchists, bring their friends into office and, by means of "armed missionaries," persuade France's neighbors to come under her political control almost without firing a shot. Such views also found favor among the militants in the Paris clubs. Alone among the leaders of the Left (with occasional support from Marat), Robespierre strongly resisted this mood and challenged Brissot's assumptions in a number of powerful speeches. War, he argued, would play into the hands of the Court, expose France to a military dictatorship, and prejudice the Revolution's achievements before there had been time to complete them. Moreover, he insisted, to count on a friendly reception being given to France's "armed missionaries" was to foster illusions and to court disaster. But Brissot and the war party won; war was declared on Austria in April 1792, and Robespierre slipped into a period of popular disfavor.

Yet the mood of national elation did not last long, and Robespierre's fears soon appeared to be justified by the defeats, desertions and treachery in the highest places that rapidly followed. Yet, in the long run, it was the monarchy, and not the Revolution, that proved to be the war's principal victim. When the King, having been compelled by events to appoint Girondin Ministers, took an early opportunity to dismiss them, he was met by a storm of popular protest; the Tuileries Palace itself was invaded by men and women of the *faubourgs* (suburbs), and Louis was publicly humiliated. The demand for the King's abdication quickly gained the majority of the Paris Sections (electoral districts). The lead in this campaign had at first been taken by the Girondins, while Robespierre and his Jacobin followers had played a waiting game; in fact, in mid-July, Robespierre was still stressing the need for a popularly elected National Convention, rather than an armed insurrection, to amend the Constitution and settle the future of the monarchy. But the Girondins, alarmed by the popular ferment that they had themselves unleashed, now drew back in support of the King. They had not bargained for a Republic that should be at the mercy of the votes and weapons of the hitherto "passive" citizens, or *sans-culottes* ("lower orders"). So the leadership of the movement passed to the Jacobins. Robespierre himself was not a member of the "correspondence" committee that organized the uprising, though he was in close touch with its leaders and joined its offspring, the Revolutionary Commune, after the event. On August 10, Louis was driven from the Tuileries and, soon after, a National Convention was summoned in the place of the now discredited Legislative Assembly. To this new Assembly Robespierre was returned, before Danton and Marat, at the head of a long list of Jacobin deputies for Paris.

The struggle between Girondins and Jacobins was now transferred to the Convention and was resolved only with the expulsion of the Girondin leaders nine months later. In each of the crises that marked it, Robespierre played a leading part—first, as the defender of the Paris Commune, whose zeal for revolutionary justice had alarmed the Assembly's majority; next, as the advocate of the King's speedy condemnation. Louis should be brought before the Convention, Robespierre urged, and be sentenced to execution as a traitor: strictly, there was no need for a trial, as he had already been found guilty by the sovereign people. The Girondins, while agreeing to a trial, favored a stay of execution and—failing that—a referendum; but they were outvoted, and Louis was executed on January 21, 1793.

A further crisis arose in March over the conduct of the war. In the fall, the new Republic had cleared its eastern frontiers by its victories of Valmy and Jemappes. But General Dumouriez had since been driven back from the Netherlands and, failing to persuade his army to march on the Convention, had deserted to the enemy. Mutual recriminations followed in the Assembly. The Girondins, as close associates of the general, were the more exposed; but, to defend themselves, they turned the attack against Danton, who had been sent to parley with Dumouriez on the eve of his desertion. The attempt failed; but there emerged from it, partly on Robespierre's initiative, two of the most important institutions of the Revolution—the Revolutionary Tribunal and the Committee of Public Safety.

Meanwhile there had been food riots in the Paris grocery shops, and Robespierre, who—like his fellow Jacobins and the Girondins—failed to see what they were really about, condemned them as an aristocratic provocation. But when, soon after, a demand arose, fostered by the extreme democrats (or *Enragés*) for a drastic "purge" of the Convention, Robespierre and the Jacobins were able to turn this movement, as well as the food crisis, to their own political advantage by directing popular fury against the Girondin leaders. From April, a flood of resolutions from the Parisian Sections demanded the expulsion of the Girondins from the Assembly. Once more, a central revolutionary committee was formed to direct operations, and thousands of *sans-culottes* were recruited to the National Guard at the rate of two francs for each day spent under arms. In the bloodless uprising that followed on May 31 to June 2, the Convention was compelled to "surrender" twenty-nine Girondin deputies, and the Jacobins emerged as the dominant party in the Assembly.

Again, Robespierre took no direct part in the insurrection; yet his was the guiding voice and his the brain that inspired it. Long an ardent defender of the inviolability of the National Assembly and of the unrestricted freedom of speech and the press, he had been brought by his experience of war and revolution to shed his liberal ideas. The Revolution, he now believed, could be saved, and its internal and external enemies be defeated, only if, with the aid of the armed *sans-culottes,* a strong central government were set up to restrain both the "selfish rich" and the remnants of aristocracy. The program is nowhere exactly spelled out, but it can be deduced from both his speeches at this time and from a memorandum later found among his papers:

> What we need [he wrote] is a single will . . . This rising must continue until the measures necessary for saving the Republic have been taken. The people must ally itself with the Convention, and the Convention must make use of the people.

Such words served as a program of action for the insurgents of June 1793 and laid the foundations for the Revolutionary government that followed a few months later. Yet it took the experience of four more months of spreading civil war (Lyons, Bordeaux, Caen, Toulon, Marseilles and the peasants of the Vendée had all rebelled against the government in Paris), of further military defeats, rising food prices, and administrative anarchy in the provinces before the Assembly could be persuaded to abandon the hallowed precepts of the "philosophers" and entrust a government from their own midst with full executive powers.

So a Revolutionary government gradually emerged (formally constituted in December), deriving its mandate from the Assembly but resting firmly on the twin pillars of the Committees of Public Safety and General Security. This government was able, for over nine months, to establish a more or less "single will" in the direction of affairs—in striking contrast to the chaos over which the preceding Girondin majority had presided—and to win a considerable body of support among the Parisian *sans-culottes,* whose militants held office in the local committees of the Sections and in the Commune itself. Robespierre joined the Committee of Public Safety on July 27, 1793 and, for a year, was its most active, experienced, and respected member, while still retaining his position in the Convention and Jacobin Club. He and his colleagues administered the country by despatching "representatives on mission"—forerunners of Napoleon's Prefects—to supervise and supplement the work of the Departments; checked the course of inflation, which under the Girondins had assumed disastrous proportions; crushed the internal rebellion; drafted numerous laws relating to education, industry, peasant holdings, the civil code and public assistance; raised, fed and equipped the Republic's armies; and generally "organized" the victories, culminating in that of Fleurus (June 26, 1794), which finally drove the invaders from French soil.

More attention has, of course, been paid by writers of both history and romance to the other, less constructive side of the Committee's work: its dealings with the internal enemies of the Republic. During the so-called "Reign of Terror," some 18,000 fell victim to the guillotine, and perhaps another 25,000 were shot or killed by other means—the great majority in those western, southern and eastern frontier regions that were most affected by war and civil war; in Paris itself, where the Revolutionary Tribunal operated, executions amounted to little over 2,700.[3] For the executions in Paris the members of the two Committees were jointly responsible. The most spectacular trials before the Tribunal were those of Danton and the "Indulgents," who had challenged the government from the Right, and of Hébert and a group in the Cordeliers Club, who had challenged it from the Left. In this extermination of opposing "factions," whose operations he saw as a mortal danger to government based on "a single will," Robespierre played a principal part.

Yet, within four months of Danton's death, the Revolutionary government had fallen apart and Robespierre himself had perished on the guillotine. On June 4, he had been elected president of the Convention by a record majority; four days later, he seemed to be at the height of his popularity when he presided over the colorful pageant designed by the artist David and devoted to the Cult of the Supreme Being. Yet, behind the scenes, dangerous divisions, both of policy and personality, had already begun to appear in the relations between the two Com-

---

[3] D. Greer, *The Incidence of the Terror during the French Revolution* (Cambridge: Harvard University Press, 1935).

mittees and within the Committee of Public Safety. Robespierre was accused of setting himself up as a "pontiff" of the new cult and of aiming to form a Triumvirate with his close colleagues, Couthon and Saint-Just. These charges were taken up by a group of deputies, including Fouché, Barras and Tallien, whose terroristic excesses and financial extortions in the provinces had marked them out for public censure and proscription by "the Incorruptible." The great body of moderates in the Assembly too, on whose support Robespierre had been able to count in his war against the "factions," had, since the victory of Fleurus, begun to cool towards a régime of Terror and "tightened belts." Their defection proved decisive; in the dramatic session of 9th Thermidor (July 27, 1794), Robespierre was refused a hearing, and he and his brother Augustin, with other close supporters, were placed under arrest.

Yet, even now, the fortunes of the Robespierrists might have been retrieved if they had been able to count on the support of the Paris Sections and their armed force, the National Guard. But the *sans-culottes* had been estranged by recent government measures. In September 1793, after popular demonstrations at the Convention, the Assembly had imposed a ceiling on the price of food and other necessities (law of the General Maximum); but, more recently, the pressure of merchants and producers had persuaded the Committee to relax controls and allow prices to rise in order to create higher profit margins. Besides, after the "purge" of Hébert's group in April, many of the local clubs and societies, seen as a possible focus of opposition to government, had been closed down; thus many militants had been reduced to political silence. In addition, the Robespierrist Commune had, four days before the political crisis came to a head, published a new schedule of wage rates which, had it operated, would have halved the earnings of a great many Parisian workers. There were protest meetings at the City Hall on 9th Thermidor itself; and when the Commune summoned the battalions of the National Guard to rally in support of the arrested leaders, the response was half-hearted. Robespierre and his companions escaped from their jailers and gathered at the City Hall; but they failed—either from legalistic scruple or from a lack of purpose—to direct an effective counterstroke against the Convention; their armed supporters gradually melted away and joined their enemies.

That night, Robespierre and his handful of supporters were declared "outlaws" by the Assembly. In the early hours of 10th Thermidor (July 28), an armed force under Barras appeared at the City Hall and, meeting no opposition, carried them off for formal identification by the Revolutionary Tribunal. A few hours later, they were hustled to the Place de la Révolution (the present Place de la Concorde) for execution. Among twenty-two victims, Robespierre was the last to mount the scaffold. He left an estate of a little over $300. With him perished not only a man or a group but a system. The democratic Republic of the Year II gave way to the property owners' Republic of Thermidor and the Directory. The "single will" remained in abeyance until Bonaparte, five years later, restored it on the new foundation of a military dictatorship.

Chronology of the Life of Robespierre

1758	(May 6). Born at Arras, son of Maximilien Barthélemy François de Robespierre, an *avocat*.
1766-1769	At school at the Collège d'Arras.
1769-1781	At school at the Collège Louis-le-Grand in Paris.
1781-1789	Practicing law at Arras.
1788	(August). First published work: "A la Nation Artésienne."
1789	(April). Elected deputy to the Estates General at Versailles for the Third Estate (commons) of Arras. Comes to live in the Rue Saintonge in Paris.
	(May). Joins the Breton Club (the later Jacobin Club) at Versailles.
	(June 6). First recorded speech in the National Assembly.
	(July 14). Fall of the Bastille. On the 17th, Robespierre accompanies King to Paris.
	(October 21). Protests against martial law.
1789 (October)—1791 (September)	Active as spokesman for Left in Constituent Assembly in Paris.
1790	(August). Protests against severe measures taken against mutinous Nancy garrison.
	(October). First magistrate of district court at Versailles.
1791	(April). Speech on the *marc d'argent* (the right to vote) read at the Cordeliers Club.
	(May). Speeches against re-election to new Assembly of deputies of the Constituent and against death penalty.
	(June). Public prosecutor to Criminal Tribunal of Department of Paris.
	(June 21). Demands deposition of Louis XVI at Jacobin Club.
	(July 17). "Massacre" of Champ de Mars. Robespierre goes to live at Maurice Duplay's at 366, Rue Saint-Honoré.
	(September 30). Receives popular ovation in Paris.
	(October). Triumphal—and final—visit to Arras.

1791 (December)	
—1792	
(February)	Speeches against Brissot's "revolutionary" war.
1792	(April 20). French declaration of war against Austria.
	(mid-July). Leads Jacobin campaign for removal of King and election of a National Convention by male adult suffrage.
	(August 10). Member of General Council of Paris Revolutionary Commune. Louis driven from Tuileries by battalions of National Guard.
	(September). Elected deputy for Paris to National Convention.
	(November-December). Letters and speeches on the "trial" of the King.
	(December 2). Speech on the regulation of food supplies.
1793	(January 21). Execution of Louis XVI.
	(February 24). Condemns Paris grocery riots.
	(April 24). Speech on property rights and a new Declaration of the Rights of Man.
	(June 2). Expulsion of Girondin deputies from Convention. Robespierre proposes government "of a single will."
	(July 27). Appointed to Committee of Public Safety.
	(September 29). Convention adopts Law of *Maximum Général*, imposing a general control of prices and wages.
	(December 25). Speech on the principles of Revolutionary Government.
	(November 23). Condemns antireligious excesses of "Hébertists."
1794	(March 25). Execution of Hébert and associates.
	(April 5). Execution of Danton, Desmoulins and the "Indulgents."
	(May 7). Speech on the Cult of the Supreme Being.
	(June 10). Heads procession at inaugural festival of Supreme Being.
	(July 26). Last speeches in National Convention and Jacobin Club.
	(July 27, 28). Refused hearing in Convention, arrested and executed.

ROBESPIERRE LOOKS AT THE WORLD

In this section, we present extracts from some of Robespierre's principal speeches on the main events of the day. They were delivered, variously, in the Constituent Assembly (1789-91); the Jacobin Club, and the National Convention (September 1792-July 1794). In translation, an attempt has been made to retain the style and flavor of the original French text.

1

On the Right to Vote (March 1791)[1]

This is the most important of several speeches made by Robespierre in the Constituent Assembly in support of male adult suffrage as one of the "imprescriptible rights" of the citizen. The exact date of its delivery is not known, as it was not reported in the official journal, Le Moniteur; but it was printed some time in March 1791 and read in the Cordeliers Club on April 20.

Like other democrats, Robespierre believed that the Assembly had seriously departed from both the letter and the spirit of the Declaration of the Rights of Man by denying the franchise to a considerable portion of the population. By a law of October 1789, the Assembly had, on the proposal of the Abbé Sieyès, decreed a system of election by two stages and divided citizens into "active" (voting) and "passive" (nonvoting). "Active" citizens were those who paid a direct tax equivalent to the value of three days' unskilled labor; these might vote in the primary assemblies for the "electors" who, at the second stage, alone had the right to elect the deputies to the legislative assembly. To qualify as an "elector" (limited to one in ten of all "active" citizens), one had to pay a

---

[1] From *Oeuvres de Maximilien Robespierre* (Paris: Presses Universitaires de France, 1950), VII, 161-6, 170-80; trans. G. Rudé. Reproduced in English translation by permission of the publisher.

tax equivalent of ten days' wages; while a deputy had to pay a tax at least equal to a silver mark (marc d'argent), or about 54 francs. The law was amended in August 1791, considerably reducing the property qualification required of deputies but substantially increasing that required of "electors." [2]

Robespierre's demand for male adult suffrage was not achieved (and then with some exceptions) until the elections to the National Convention in September 1792. After his fall, a return was made to a restricted franchise, based on property qualifications, by his successors in October 1795.

Why are we gathered in this legislative assembly? Doubtless to restore to the French nation the exercise of imprescriptible rights that belong to every citizen. This is the main purpose of every political constitution. If it fulfills this obligation, it is just and free; if it fails to do so, it is nothing but a conspiracy against mankind.

You recognized this truth yourselves, and in a striking manner, when you decided, before beginning your great work, that a solemn declaration must be made of the sacred rights that serve as the immutable foundations on which it rests.

> All men are born and remain free, and are equal at law.
> Sovereignty derives from the nation as a whole.
> The law is the expression of the general will. All citizens have the right to contribute to its making, either directly by themselves or through their freely elected representatives.
> All citizens are admissible to every public office, and no distinction is made between them except in respect of their virtues and talents.

These are the principles that you have enshrined. It will now be readily seen which are the measures that I wish to combat; it is enough to test them against these immutable laws of human society.

1. Can the law be termed an expression of the general will when the greater number of those for whom it is made can have no hand in its making? No. And yet to forbid such men as do not pay a tax equal to three days' wages the right even to choose the electors whose task it is to appoint the members of the legislative assembly—what is this but to

---

[2] There have been numerous estimates made, both by contemporaries and historians, of the number or proportion of Frenchmen who were disqualified as voters, as "electors" or as deputies by these provisions. For a discussion, see R. R. Palmer, *The Age of the Democratic Revolution* (Princeton, N.J., 1959, 1964), I, 522-8.

deprive a majority of Frenchmen of the right to frame the laws? This provision is therefore essentially unconstitutional and antisocial.

2. Can men be said to enjoy equal rights when some are endowed with the exclusive right to be elected members of the legislative body or of other public institutions, others merely with that of electing them, while the rest are deprived of all these rights at once? No. Yet such are the monstrous distinctions drawn between them by the decrees that make a man active or passive, or half active and half passive, according to the varying degrees of fortune that permit him to pay three days' wages in taxes, ten days, or a silver mark. All these provisions are, then, essentially unconstitutional and antisocial.

3. Are men admissible to all public posts, and is no distinction made except such as derive from their virtues and talents, when an inability to pay the required tax excludes them from every public office regardless of the virtues and talents that they may possess? No. All these provisions are therefore essentially unconstitutional and antisocial.

4. And again, is the nation sovereign when the greater part of the persons composing it is deprived of the political rights from which sovereignty derives its essence? No. And yet you have just seen that these same decrees deny them to the majority of Frenchmen. What would remain of your Declaration of Rights if these decrees were allowed to continue? It would become an empty formula. What would the nation become? A slave; for it is freedom to obey laws of which one is oneself the maker, but it is slavery to be compelled to submit to the will of another. What would your constitution become? One fit for an aristocracy. For aristocracy is that state in which one part of the citizens is sovereign and the rest is subject. And what kind of an aristocracy? The most intolerable of all: an aristocracy of the Rich.

All men *born* and *domiciled* in France are members of the body politic termed the French nation; that is to say, they are French citizens. They are so by the nature of things and by the first principle of the law of nations. The rights attaching to this title do not depend on the fortune that each man possesses, nor on the amount of tax for which he is assessed, because it is not taxes that make us citizens: citizenship merely obliges a man to contribute to public expenditure in proportion to his means. You may give the citizens new laws, but you may not deprive them of their citizenship.

The upholders of the system that I am denouncing have themselves realized this truth; for, not daring to challenge the title of citizen in those whom they condemn to political disinheritance, they have confined themselves to destroying the principle of equality inherent in that title by drawing a distinction between active and passive citizens. Trusting in the ease with which men may be governed by words, they have sought to lead us off the scent by using this new expression as a cover for the most flagrant violation of the rights of man.

But who can be so stupid as not to perceive that such a phrase can neither invalidate the principle nor solve the problem? For, in the idiom of these subtle politicians, it is exactly the same thing to declare that certain citizens shall not be active as to say that they shall no longer exercise the rights attaching to the title of citizen. Well, I shall ask them once more by what right they may thus strike their fellow citizens and constituents with paralysis and reduce them to inactivity; and I shall not cease protesting against this barbaric and insidious phrase which, if we do not hasten to efface it, will disgrace our language and our code of laws, so that the word "liberty" itself may not become meaningless and laughable.

What need I add to such self-evident truths? Nothing in regard to the representatives of a nation whose wishes and opinions have already anticipated my demand; but I still must reply to the contemptible sophisms by means of which the prejudices and ambitions of a certain class of men seek to buttress the disastrous doctrine that I here denounce. It is to them only that I now wish to speak.

The people, men of no property . . . the dangers of corruption . . . the example of England and of other nations reputed free: these are the arguments that are being used to confound justice and to combat reason.

One single sentence should be an adequate reply: the people, that great multitude whose cause I plead, have rights whose origin is the same as yours. Who has given you power to take them away?

The general interest, you say! But is anything of general interest except what is just and honest? And has not this universally valid maxim a particular relevance to the social order? And if the object of society is the good of all and the preservation of the rights of man, what must one think of those who wish to base it on the power of a few and on the abasement and total degradation of the rest of the human race? What sort of men are these self-inflated politicians who loudly applaud their own genius when, as the result of laborious subtleties, they have at length succeeded in substituting their own ephemeral fantasies for the unchanging principles that the eternal lawgiver himself has engraved in the hearts of men!

England! Well, what matters England to you? What matters her vicious constitution, which may well have appeared free to you when you were reduced to the basest servitude but which can only be acclaimed today from ignorance or empty repetition? The free nations! Where are they to be found? What does history tell you of those whom you honor with this name? Are they not agglomerations of men more or less divorced from reason and nature, more or less enslaved, subjected to governments who climbed to power through chance, ambition or violence? Is it then slavishly to emulate the errors and injustices which have so long degraded and oppressed the human race that eternal justice has summoned you, the only men so summoned since the creation of the world, to reestablish on earth the rule of justice and liberty, having at your command the richest fruits of intelligence that have ever enlightened the government of men and placed in the almost miraculous set of circumstances that it has thought to assemble, in order to invest you with full powers to restore to man his happiness, his virtue and his elementary dignity?

Do those men realize the responsibility of this sacred mission who answer our just complaints with a curt and cold: "With all its vices, our constitution is still the best that has ever existed"? Have 26 million men entrusted you with the fearful charge of safeguarding their destiny in order that you may lightheartedly leave in this constitution fundamental vices that undermine the foundations of the social order? Perhaps you will say that the reform of a great number of abuses and the enactment of several useful laws are so many concessions to the people that dispense you from the obligation of doing more for them? No; all the good that you have done was a duty rigorously imposed. To fail to do the good that you still have to do would be a distortion of justice; the evil that would result would be an act of treason against the nation and humanity. And more: if you do not do everything for liberty, you will have done nothing. There are not two ways of being free: one must be so entirely or one becomes once more a slave. Leave one solitary resource to despotism, and you will soon restore its power. Aye, already it seeks to seduce and to enthrall you; give an inch and it will hold you fully in its sway. O you who glory in having lent your names to a great change and are not too much concerned if it is sufficient to assure the happiness of mankind, do not be deceived: the chorus of praise that astonishment and shallow thinking have provoked will soon die away; and posterity, comparing the greatness of your obligations and the immensity of your resources with the fundamental vices of your work will say of you with indignation: "They could have made men free and happy, but they did not wish to. They were unworthy of the task."

But, you will say, shall the people, those who have nothing to lose, have the same rights of citizenship as we? Those who have nothing to lose! How false and unjust such language, begotten of delirious pride, appears in the sight of truth!

These men of whom you speak are apparently men who live and subsist and yet have no means of living or subsisting! For if they have such means, they have, I think, something to lose or to preserve. Yes, the rough clothing that covers me, the humble retreat where I buy the right to withdraw and to live in peace; the modest wage on which I feed my wife and my children: these are, I admit, not estates, country mansions, or coaches-and-pairs. They are perhaps *nothing* in the eyes of luxury and opulence; but they are something to humanity. They are a sacred property, as sacred no doubt as the glamorous domains of the rich.

I will say more. My liberty, my life, the right to obtain protection or revenge for those who are dear to me, the right to cast off oppression and to freely exercise all the faculties of my mind and spirit: are not all these beneficent properties, the first that nature has bestowed on man, placed, like your own, under the protection of the laws? And yet you say that I have no interest in these laws; and you wish to deprive me of the share that is my due, as it is yours, in the administration of the commonwealth, and for no other reason than that you are wealthier than I! Ah! if the scales were no longer to remain evenly balanced, should they not be weighted in favor of the citizens of lesser fortune? Have not the laws been framed and the public authority been established to protect the weak against injustice and oppression? It is, then, to flout all the principles that govern society to entrust them entirely to the rich.

But the rich and the men of power have reasoned otherwise. By a strange abuse of words they have confined the general notion of property to their own selected categories. They have termed themselves the only men of property; they have claimed that men of property alone are worthy of the name of citizen; they have named their private interest the general interest, and, to ensure the success of this claim, they have arrogated to themselves the sole exercise of public power. And we— O frailty of mortal man!—we who aspire to instruct them in the principles of equality and justice, we are preparing, in our blindness and folly, to build our constitution on such absurd and cruel prejudices.

But what is, after all, the rare merit in paying a silver mark or such other tax on which you make such exalted privileges dependent? If you make a larger contribution to the public treasury than I, is it not because society has favored you with greater pecuniary advantages? And, if we wish to press the point further, what is the source of that extreme inequality of fortunes that concentrates all wealth in the hands of a few? Is it not the result of bad laws, of bad government and of all the vices of corrupted societies? Now, why should those who are the victims of these abuses be doubly punished for their misfortune by the loss of their dignity as citizens? I do not dispute your right to enjoy the unequal portion that you have received, since this inequality is a necessary or an incurable evil; but do not take from me, at least, the imprescriptible rights of which no manmade law is entitled to deprive me. Permit me even at times to be proud of an honorable poverty, and do not seek to humiliate me by arrogantly presuming to monopolize the title of sovereign while leaving me none other than that of subject.

But the people, you say, are prone to be corrupted!

Ah! cease, I pray you, cease to profane the moving, sacred name of people by linking it with this notion of corruption. Who is he that, among men equal in rights, dares to declare his fellows unworthy to exercise theirs in order to despoil them to his own advantage? And indeed, if you allow yourselves to base such a sentence on a mere suspicion of corruptibility, what a terrible power you are arrogating to yourselves to judge humanity! And where will your proscriptions end?

But should they fall on those who do not pay the silver mark or on those who pay a far larger sum? For in spite of all your prejudice in favor of such virtues as come with wealth, I venture to believe that you will find as many among the poorest citizens as among the wealthiest! Do you honestly believe that a hard, laborious life engenders as many vices as one of comfort, luxury and ambition? And have you less faith in the probity of our artisans and peasants, who, according to your formula, will hardly ever be active citizens, as you have in that of tax-farmers, courtiers, and those whom you call great lords, who, following the same formula, would be so six hundred times over? Once and for all, I wish to avenge those whom you call the *people* for these sacrilegious slanders.

But are you capable of knowing and appreciating men—you who, since your powers of reasoning developed, have judged them only according to the absurd ideas of despotism and feudal pride; you who, accustomed to the strange jargon then invented, thought it natural to degrade the greater part of the human species by the use of terms such as *canaille* and *populace;*[3] you who have told the world that there were men without *birth,* as if any living man had not been born; that some men were *nothing* (who were really men of worth) and others men of *respectability* and *distinction,* who were in fact among the most vile

[3] English equivalents: "riff-raff," "scum," "mob."

and corrupt of all mankind? Of course, you may not be called upon to render to the people all the justice that is its due. For myself, I call to my witness all those whose nobility of soul and feeling has brought them close to the people and made them worthy to know and to love equality; they will say that, in general, there is nothing so just and good as the people when not angered by excessive oppression; that it is grateful for the least mark of concern that you show it, for the slightest good that you do it, even for the ill that you fail to do it; that it is among the people that you find, behind a reputedly coarse exterior, frank and upright souls and a good sense and energy that you would long seek in vain within the class that despises it. The people demands only what is necessary, it merely wants justice and tranquillity; the rich lay claim to everything, they invade all others' rights and aim at universal domination. Social abuses are the handiwork and province of the rich, they are the scourge of the people. The interest of the people is the general interest, that of the rich is a particular interest; and yet you wish to give the people no voice in government and make the rich all-powerful!

Will you now answer me with those time-worn accusations which have continuously been leveled at the people ever since it shook off the yoke of despotism, as if the people as a whole could be charged with a few local and particular acts of vengeance carried out at the beginning of an unexpected revolution in which, suddenly awakening from a long oppression, it was in a state of war with all its tyrants? Nay, was there ever a time that gave more striking proof of the people's natural goodness than that [July 1789] when, armed with irresistible might, it stopped suddenly of its own accord and laid down its arms at the summons of its representatives? O you that are so relentless toward suffering humanity and so indulgent toward its oppressors, turn over the pages of history, scan them carefully, count the crimes of the tyrants, and then judge between them and the people.

Nay, more. From the very efforts made by the enemies of the Revolution to degrade the people in your esteem and to degrade yours in the people's, by suggesting to you measures intended to stifle its voice or to weaken its energy, or to lead its patriotism astray, by hiding your decrees from it in order to prolong its ignorance of its rights; from the unwavering patience with which it has borne all its misfortunes in the expectation of a happier state of things; from this we learn that the people is the sole support of liberty. Who, then, could tolerate the idea of seeing it despoiled of its rights by the very revolution that is due to its courage and to the tender and generous devotion with which it defended its representatives! Is it to the rich and to the great that you owe this glorious insurrection that saved France and yourselves? Were not the soldiers who rallied to the service of the nation at arms men of the people? And to what class did their leaders belong, those who would have led them against you? . . . Did the people then take up arms to help you to defend its rights and its dignity, or was it to give you power to encompass its destruction? Did it aid you to break the yoke of feudal aristocracy in order to fall back under the yoke of an aristocracy of wealth?

Up to now, I have adopted the language of those who seem to mean by the word "people" a class of men set aside from their fellows and to whom they attach a certain label of contempt or inferiority. It is now time that I express myself more precisely, in recalling that the system we condemn disfranchises nine-tenths of the nation[4] and that it even excludes from the lists of those it terms active citizens vast numbers of men who, even in the bad old days of pride and prejudice, were honored and distinguished for their education, their industry, even for their fortunes.

Such is, in fact, the nature of this institution that it provides for the most ridiculous anomalies; for, while taking wealth as the measure of the rights of citizenship, it departs from this very rule by attaching them to what are called direct taxes, although it is evident that a man who pays substantial indirect taxes may enjoy a larger fortune than one who is subjected to a moderate direct tax. But who would have thought it possible that the sacred rights of man should be made to depend on the changing nature of financial systems, on the variations and diversities that our system presents in the different parts of the same State? What sort of system is it where a man who is a citizen in one part of France ceases to be one either in part or in whole if he moves to another and where a man who is one today will no longer be one tomorrow if he should suffer an adverse turn of fortune!

What sort of system is it in which an honest man, despoiled by an unjust oppressor, sinks into the class of the *helots* while his despoiler is raised by this very crime into the ranks of the citizens; in which a father, as the number of his children increases, sees with a growing certainty that he will not be able to leave them this title owing to the constant diminution of his divided inheritance; in which every father's son throughout half our land recovers his fatherland only at the point where he loses his father! . . . In short, what is the worth of my much

[4] This figure, though widely believed by democrats at the time, is an exaggeration.

vaunted right to belong to the sovereign body if the assessor of taxes has the power to deprive me of it by reducing my contribution by a cent and if it is subject at once to the caprice of man and the inconsistency of fortune? . . .

2
On Capital Punishment

The first of the two speeches that follow was made in the Constituent Assembly on May 30, 1791. Here we see Robespierre as the liberal statesman arguing in support of the total abolition of the death penalty on liberal and humanitarian grounds; at this stage, he makes no exceptions to a general rule.

In contrast, in the second speech, delivered in the National Convention in December 1792, he is arguing that not only is the death penalty justified in the case of Louis XVI but that the King has already been condemned by the revolutionary action of the sovereign people. The case has been picked on to argue that Robespierre, as in his changing attitude to war and peace, was inconsistent and allowed his principles to be subverted by the demands of political expediency. The reader must judge this for himself, but he will note that, in both cases, Robespierre's case is a political one, not one that appeals to moral absolutes. In the first case, the State will be strengthened (he argues) rather than weakened by showing clemency to the ordinary murderer or common-law criminal; in the second, the new Republic will be seriously injured if a crime of such magnitude is allowed to go unpublished and if a criminal of such political importance is permitted to survive.

Later, when far less important offenders than Louis were sentenced to death by the Revolutionary Tribunal, the same basic argument of salus reipublicae suprema lex *was invoked to justify their execution.*

ON THE ABOLITION OF THE DEATH PENALTY (MAY 30, 1791)[1]

The news having reached Argos that citizens had been condemned to death in the city of Athens, people flocked into the temples to beseech the gods to persuade the Athenians not to harbor such cruel and distressing thoughts. I have come to beg not the Deity but the legislators, who should be the voice and the interpreters of the eternal laws bequeathed by the gods to mortal man, to efface from our penal code the bloody laws that sanction judicial murder, laws which are repugnant to the Frenchmen's new way of life and to their new constitution. I

[1] From H. Morse Stephens, *The Principal Speeches of the Statesmen and Orators of the French Revolution 1789-1795* (Oxford, 1892), II, 299-304; trans. G. Rudé.

wish to prove to them: first, that the death penalty is fundamentally unjust; secondly, that it is not the most effective of penalties and that, far from preventing crimes, it increases them.

If, outside civil society, a ferocious enemy comes to threaten my life or if, repulsed a score of times, he yet returns to ravage the field that my hands have tilled, since I can only match his strength with mine, I must either perish or kill him; and, if I do so, the law of natural defense will justify and approve my deed. But in civil society, where the force of all can be arrayed against one, what principle of justice will it invoke in putting him to death? What necessity can society plead for dispensing with it? A conqueror who puts his captured enemies to death is called a barbarian! A man who cuts the throat of a child that he can disarm and chastise is thought to be a monster. An accused man whom society condemns is for it nothing more than a conquered and powerless foe; in its presence, he is weaker than a child in that of a grown man.

And so, in the eyes of truth and justice, the scenes of death that society commands with so much ceremony are nothing but cowardly murders, solemn crimes committed according to legal procedures, not by individuals but by the nation at large. Do not be astonished at the cruelty, the extravagance of some of these laws. They are the work of a few tyrants; they are the chains with which they fetter the human race; they are the arms with which they subject them; they have been written down in letters of blood. "It is not permitted to put a Roman citizen to death." Such was the law passed by popular acclaim; but Sulla conquered and said: "All who have borne arms against me are worthy of death." Octavius and the companions of his crimes confirmed this law.

Under Tiberius, it was a capital offense to have praised Brutus. Caligula condemned those to death who were sacrilegious enough to undress before the Emperor's image. When tyranny had invented the crime of *lèse-majesté,* in cases where men had committed deeds which were either insignificant or heroic, who would have dared to suggest that their penalty should be other than death without himself incurring a charge of *lèse-majesté?*

When fanaticism, the monstrous progeny of ignorance and despotism, invented in turn the crime of divine *lèse-majesté,* when in its madness it conceived the notion of avenging God himself, was it not obliged to offer him blood and to put him on a level with the monsters who claimed to be cast in his image?

The death penalty is necessary, say the upholders of the barbarous old ritual; without it there is no sanction powerful enough to arrest crime. Who has told you so? Have you counted all the means whereby the penal laws can inflict pain on the human system? Alas, short of actual death, how much physical and moral agony may a man not suffer!

The will to live yields to pride, the most imperious of all the passions that possess the soul of man; the most terrible punishment that can be inflicted on man as a social being is to be publicly disgraced, which is the supreme mark of public execretion. When the legislator may strike the citizen in so many places and by so many means, why should he feel reduced to resorting to the penalty of death? Punishments are not intended to torture the guilty, but to deter men from committing crimes from a fear of the consequences.

The legislator who prefers death and other atrocious penalties to the milder means that he has at his disposal outrages the sensibility of the public and deadens moral sentiment among the people he governs; he is like an unskilled tutor who, from his frequent resort to cruel punishment, brutalizes and degrades the spirit of his pupil; moreover, in seeking to overstretch the springs of government, he weakens them and wears them out.

The legislator who maintains this penalty is one who renounces the salutary principle which recognizes that the most effective means of repressing crime is to make the penalty fit the passion that engendered it and to punish the passion, as it were, in itself. He confuses every principle, he disturbs every relationship, and he deliberately thwarts the objects of the penal laws.

The death penalty is necessary, you say? If that is so, why have so many nations been able to do without it? By what chance have these nations come to possess the greatest wisdom, happiness and freedom? If the penalty of death is the most suited to prevent great crime, it must follow that crime has been less frequent among the peoples who have adopted it and been the most lavish in its use. But the opposite is the truth. Take the example of Japan. Nowhere have the death penalty and torture been so lavishly applied; and nowhere have crimes been so frequent and so atrocious. It would appear that the Japanese have set out to vie in ferocity with the barbarous laws that scourge and afflict them. Did the republics of Greece, in which punishments were moderate and the death penalty was either rarely used or was completely unknown, present a picture of more crime and less virtue than countries governed by laws of blood? Do you believe that Rome was stained by more crimes when, in the days of its glory, the Portian law had abolished the severe penalties imposed by the kings and decemvirs than it was at the time of Sulla, who revived them, or of the emperors who carried their severity to an excess that was worthy of their infamous tyranny? Has Russia been convulsed since the autocrat who rules her entirely suppressed the death penalty, as if she had wished, by this act of humanity and enlightenment, to atone for the crime of maintaining millions of men under the yoke of despotism?

Listen to the voice of reason and justice; it cries out to us that human judgments are never sure enough for society to be able to put to death a man who has been condemned by fellow men who share his fallibility. Even if you imagine the most perfect judicial system, even if you find the most upright and the most enlightened judges, you will still have to allow place for error or prejudice. Why deny yourselves the means to correct them? Why condemn yourselves to the impossibility of holding out a helping hand to those unjustly sentenced? What is the use of vain regrets or of the illusory reparation that you make to an empty shadow or of lifeless ashes? To deny a man the possibility to expiate his crime by repentance or virtuous deeds, pitilessly to shut him off from any return to virtue and self-esteem, to hasten to force him into his tomb while he is freshly stained by his crime; all this is to my mind the most horrible refinement of cruelty.

The legislator's first duty is to form and to preserve public morality, which is the source of all liberty and of all social well-being. When, in pursuit of a particular goal, he departs from this basic and general aim, he commits the most vulgar and the most disastrous of errors.

The laws must, therefore, always afford peoples the purest model of reason and justice. If for the august severity and the moderate calm that should distinguish them they substitute anger and vengeance; if they shed human blood that they have the power to prevent and that they have no right to shed at all; if they display before the people scenes of cruelty and corpses bruised by torture, then they pervert in the citizens' minds all idea of what is just and unjust, and they give rise within society to terrible prejudices which engender others in their turn. Man is no longer so sacred a concern, his dignity is rated of lesser worth when public authority sets little store by his life. The idea of murder inspires far less terror when the law itself sets the example of it for all to see. Horror of crime diminishes when its only punishment is by another crime. Beware of confusing the efficacy of punishment with its excessive severity: the one is fundamentally opposed to the other. Moderate laws win the support of all; savage laws provoke a general conspiracy.

It has been observed that in free countries crimes have been more rare and penalties less severe; the one follows logically from the other. Free countries are those in which the rights of man are respected and in which, in consequence, the laws are just. Wherever they outrage humanity by their excessive rigor, they afford the proof that in such countries the dignity of man and the rights of the citizen are unknown or are not respected and that the legislator is but a master in command of slaves, whom he pitilessly punishes according to his fancy. I conclude that the death penalty must be repealed.

ON THE ACTION TO BE TAKEN AGAINST LOUIS XVI
(DECEMBER 3, 1792) [2]

The Assembly has been unwittingly dragged away from the real point at issue. It is not a question of conducting a trial. Louis is not an accused person; you are not judges; you are not, and you cannot be, anything else but statesmen and representatives of the nation. It is not a question of your passing a sentence for or against a man, but of taking a measure of public security and of performing an act of national policy. A dethroned king in a Republic is good for only two things: either to disturb the peace of the State and to overthrow liberty, or to confirm both peace and liberty. Now, I maintain the course of your deliberations has run directly counter to this latter aim. . . .

Louis was King; then the Republic was founded. The important question that is occupying you can be decided by these same few words. Louis was dethroned for his crimes. Louis denounced the French people as rebels. He called in the armies of his fellow tyrants, and the victory of the people decided that he alone was the rebel. Louis cannot be judged; he is already judged. He is condemned, or if he is not, the sovereignty of the Republic is not absolute. To propose a trial for Louis XVI, in whatever form, is to retrace our steps towards royal and constitutional despotism. It is a counterrevolutionary idea, since it puts the Revolution itself on trial. If Louis can still be the subject of a trial, Louis can be absolved, he can be judged innocent. . . . Citizens, take care. You are being deceived by false notions. You are confusing the rules of civil and positive law with the principles of the law of nations. You are confusing the mutual relationships of citizens with the relationship of a nation with an enemy conspiring against it. You are confusing the situation of a people in revolution with that of a people with a settled government. You are confusing a nation punishing a public official with one that is destroying the government itself. . . .

When a nation has been found to have recourse to the right of insurrection, it returns to a state of nature with regard to the tyrant. How can the latter invoke the social pact? He has destroyed it. . . . It is a

[2] From H. Morse Stephens, *op. cit.*, II, 358-66; trans. W. J. Gardner and G. Rudé.

gross contradiction to suppose that the Constitution can preside over this new state of affairs. It would be to suppose that the Constitution itself has survived. What are the laws which now replace it? The laws of nature, that which is the basis of society itself: the safety of the people. The right of punishing the tyrant and the right of dethroning him are the same things. They do not take different forms. The trial of the tyrant is insurrection; his judgment is the fall of his power; his punishment is what the liberty of the people demands.

We have let ourselves be led into error by foreign examples that have nothing in common with us. Cromwell had Charles I tried by a court under his control, and Elizabeth had Mary of Scotland condemned in the same way. These methods are natural to tyrants sacrificing their equals, not to the people, but to their own ambition and seeking to mislead the opinions of the populace by shams. It was not then a question of principles or of liberty but of trickery and intrigues. But the people! What other law can they follow save that of justice and reason backed by their own supreme power?

We treat as legitimate acts what any free people would have regarded as the greatest of crimes. We ourselves incite the citizens to baseness and corruption. One day we may be giving civic crowns to Louis' defenders; for if they defend his cause, they have the right to hope for its triumph; otherwise, you would be performing a ridiculous comedy in the eyes of the world. And we dare speak of Republic! We invoke procedures because we have no principles; we pride ourselves on our moderation because we lack all energy; we display a false humanity because feelings of true humanity are foreign to us; we revere the shadow of a king because we are without compassion for the weak and oppressed.

Bring Louis XVI to trial! But what is this trial but the appeal of insurrection to some court of law or assembly? When a king has been destroyed by the people, who has the right to revive him and to make of him a new pretext for disorder and rebellion? And what other consequences might flow from such an action? By giving a platform to the champions of Louis XVI you reawaken all the quarrels of despotism with liberty; you accord the right to blaspheme against the Republic and against the people, for the right to defend the former despot carries with it the right to say anything that may promote his cause. You will rouse all the factions; you will reanimate and rekindle the dormant embers of royalism. One will be free to take sides for or against. What will be more legitimate and more natural than to repeat and spread abroad the maxims that his defenders will be able to profess aloud at your bar and from your very rostrum? What sort of Republic is it whose founders invite its enemies to come in from every side in order to attack it in its cradle? . . .

It is a great cause, it has been said, that must be judged with a slow and measured circumspection. It is you who make a great cause of it. Nay, more: it is you that make a cause of it at all. What is there great in it? Is it the complications? No. Is it the person concerned? In the eyes of freemen, there is none so vile; in the eyes of humanity, there is none more guilty. He can impress only those who are more cowardly than himself. Is it the usefulness of its result? All the greater is the reason to hasten it. A great cause would be the draft of a law in the people's interest, or the cause of a humble citizen oppressed by despotism. What is the motive for these eternal delays that you recommend to us? Do you fear to wound the feelings of the people? as if they feared anything other than the weakness or ambition of its mandatories? as if the people were a vile herd of slaves, stupidly attached to the stupid tyrant that it has proscribed, desiring, at whatever price, to wallow in baseness and servitude! You speak of opinion. Is it not your duty to guide it and to give it strength? If it is misled or becomes perverted, who should be blamed for it but you? Do you fear to incur the displeasure of the foreign kings who are leagued against us? You will not tell me that the way to defeat them is to appear to fear them and that the way to confound the criminal conspiracy of the European despots is to respect the person of their accomplice! Do you fear the peoples of other countries? If so, you still believe in their innate love of tyranny. Why then do you aspire to the glory of liberating the human race? What contradiction leads you to suppose that the nations that were not astonished by our proclamation of the rights of humanity will be appalled by the punishment of one of its most cruel oppressors? Or, it has been said, you fear the verdict of posterity? Yes, posterity will indeed be astonished by your weakness and inconsequence; and our descendants will laugh at both the presumption and the prejudices of their fathers.

It has been said that it would take genius to go to the roots of this question. I maintain that all that is needed is good faith: it is far less a matter of seeking enlightenment than of not deliberately seeking to be blinded. Why should what appears clear to us at one moment appear so obscure at another? Why should that which the good sense of the people so easily resolves be changed into an almost insoluble problem for its delegates? Have they the right to have a general will and a wisdom different from those prescribed by universal reason?

I have heard the defenders of inviolability advance a theory so bold that I would almost have hesitated to utter it myself. They have said that if the people had put Louis XVI to death on August 10, they would have committed a virtuous act. But such a view can have no other basis than the crimes of Louis XVI and the rights of the people. Has, then, a lapse of three months altered his crimes or the people's rights? If at that time he was saved from public indignation, it was no doubt solely in order that his punishment, when solemnly pronounced by the National Convention in the name of the nation, might make a deeper impression on the enemies of mankind; but now to raise doubts as to his guilt or to the propriety of bringing him to justice is to betray the solemn pledge given to the people of France. There are perhaps those who, either to prevent the Assembly from assuming a character worthy of itself, or to refuse to give the nations an example to inspire in them a love of republican principles, or for even less honourable motives, would weep no tears if a private hand were to usurp the duties of public justice. Citizens, beware of this trap; any man who dared to give such counsel would merely serve the enemies of the people. Whatever happens, Louis' punishment will serve no purpose unless it bear the solemn character of an act of public vengeance.

How should the people be concerned about the wretched person of the last of our kings? Representatives, what concerns them, and what concerns you, is that you should carry out the duties that their confidence imposes on you. You have proclaimed the Republic, but have you given it substance? We have not yet enacted a single law that is worthy of that name; we have not yet remedied a single abuse inherited from despotism. Remove the names, and tyranny is still entirely with us; moreover, we have factions more vile and charlatans more immoral, and we are threatened by new outbreaks of disorder and civil war. We are a Republic, and Louis still lives! and you still place the person of the King between ourselves and liberty! Let us beware, by an excess of scruple, of becoming criminals; let us beware that, by showing too great an indulgence for the culprit, we do not put ourselves in his place.

A new problem arises. To what punishment shall we sentence Louis? The death penalty is too cruel. No, says another, to live is more cruel; I demand that he should live. Advocates of Louis, is it from pity or from cruelty that you wish him to escape the penalty for his crimes? For myself, I abhor the penalty of death that your laws so liberally impose, and I have neither love nor hatred for the King; it is only crime that I hate. I demanded the abolition of the death penalty in the Assembly that you still call the Constituent Assembly; and it is not my fault if the first principles of reason appeared to that Assembly to be moral and political heresies. But if you never thought to invoke them on behalf of so many wretches whose crimes are not so much theirs as those of the government, what prompts you now to remember them in order to plead the cause of the greatest of all criminals? You ask for an exception to the penalty of death for the one man in whose case it would be justified! Yes, the death penalty in general is a crime, and for this one reason: that, according to the indestructible laws of nature, it can be justified only in cases where it is necessary for the security of the person or the State. Now, public security never warrants that it be invoked in respect of ordinary common-law offenses, because society can always prevent them by other means and render the culprit harmless to injure her further. But when a king is dethroned in the midst of a Revolution whose laws are still in the making, a king whose very name draws the scourge of war onto a nation in tumult, neither prison nor exile can destroy the influence that his existence continues to exert on the public welfare; and this cruel exception to the ordinary laws that justice prescribes can be imputed only to the nature of his crimes. It is with regret that I utter this baneful truth. . . . But Louis must die in order that our country may live. Among a people at peace, free and respected both within and without its borders, one might heed the advice that you are given to be generous. But a people whose liberty, after so much sacrifice and struggle, is still in dispute; a people whose laws are still inexorable only for the weak and the poor; a people which is still divided by the crimes of tyranny; such a people desires to be avenged; and the generosity that we are called upon to display would be too much like that of a band of brigands sharing out their spoil.

I propose that you adopt a decree forthwith to determine Louis' fate. As for his wife, you will send her before the courts, like all other persons charged with similar crimes. His son will be kept in the Temple until peace and public liberty have been assured. In his own case, I demand that the Convention *declare him, forthwith, to be a traitor to the French nation and a criminal against humanity;* I demand that he be made a great example of before the whole world in the very place where, on August 10, the generous martyrs of liberty perished. I demand that this memorable event be consecrated by the erection of a monument, destined to nourish in the hearts of the peoples the love of their rights and the hatred of tyrants; and in the souls of tyrants a wholesome terror of popular justice.

3

On War and Peace
(December 18, 1791)[1]

This is the first of three great speeches made by Robes-
pierre in the Jacobin Club between December 1791 and February
1792 on the widely debated question of whether France should
allow herself to be drawn into war with Austria and Prussia. The
speech reproduced here was delivered on December 18, 1791 as a
direct reply to one made on the 9th by Jacques-Pierre Brissot,
deputy for Eure et Loir and main spokesman for a Left group
within the Assembly (later called "Girondins"), who were insisting
that a "revolutionary war" fought by France against the "tyrants"
of Europe would bring her solid political advantages. Robespierre
deals with all their arguments in this and his subsequent speeches.
Again, it will be observed that he presents his case in strictly
political terms; he is not concerned with moral absolutes, but with
the situation at hand, in which he sees war as being a desperate
measure that could only injure the young Revolution and play
into the hands of the Court and the aristocracy.

To war! cry the Court and the Ministry and their countless partisans. To war! The cry is taken up by large numbers of good citizens,
prompted by a generous impulse and more prone to yield to the enthusiasm of patriotic feeling than to reflect soberly on the mechanism of
revolutions and on the intrigues of their rulers. Who will dare to resist
the compulsion of this cry? No one, unless it be those who are convinced
of the need for mature deliberation before embarking on a step so
fateful for the safety of the State and the future of the Constitution,
those who have observed that it is to the precipitation and enthusiasm
of a moment that have been due the measures which, by promoting the
plans and increasing the power of our enemies, have been the most
disastrous and the most comprising to our liberties; those who know
that the part that it behooves all true lovers of their country to play is

[1] From *Oeuvres de Maximilien Robespierre* (Paris: Presses Universitaires de France,
1953), VIII, 47-52, 58-64; trans. G. Rudé. Reproduced in English translation by permission of the publisher.

to sow in one season in order to reap in another and to seek in experience the triumph of truth.

I do not come here to applaud momentarily popular opinions, nor to flatter those in authority; neither do I come to preach a doctrine of cowardice, nor to advise a fainthearted policy of weakness and inertia. But I come to expose a deep-rooted conspiracy, with which I think I am somewhat familiar. I, too, want war but in a way demanded by the national interest: let us first destroy our enemies within and then march against the enemy without, if any still remains.

The Court and the Ministry want both war and the execution of the plan they propose to you. The nation will accept the war if it is the necessary price of liberty; but it wants, if possible, both liberty and peace and it rejects any plan for a war whose object might be to destroy liberty and the Constitution, even if it is put forward under the pretext of defending them.

What is the war that we are faced with? Is it a war of one nation against other nations or of one king against other kings? No: it is a war of the enemies of the French Revolution against that revolution. Are the most numerous, the most dangerous, of those enemies at Coblentz? No: they are in our own midst. Is it reasonable to fear that we might find some of them in the Court and in the Ministry itself? I do not propose to answer this question; but since war would entrust to the Court and the Ministry the supreme command of the forces of the State and the control of the future of our liberty, we must agree that the mere possibility of such a disaster must be carefully weighed in the course of our deliberations. . . .

War is always the first object of a powerful government which wishes to increase its power. I shall not speak to you of the opportunity that a war affords for a government to exhaust the people and to dissipate its treasure and to cover with an impenetrable veil its depredations and its errors; I shall speak to you rather of what touches even more directly the most precious of our interests. It is in time of war that the executive power displays the most redoubtable energy and that it wields a sort of dictatorship most ominous to a nascent liberty; it is in time of war that a people neglects all discussion concerning its civil and political rights in order to devote itself entirely to external matters and that it withdraws its attention from its lawgivers and magistrates in order to focus all its aims and hopes on its generals and ministers, or rather on the generals and ministers of the executive power. It is to meet the eventuality of war that nobles and officers have devised those articles of a new but too little known law which, as soon as France is declared to be in a state of war, will hand over the policing of our frontier towns to the military commanders and, in favor of their laws, will silence those that protect the citizens' rights.

It is in time of war that the same law empowers them to impose *arbitrary* punishment on their soldiers. It is in time of war that the habit of unquestioning obedience and the natural enthusiasm that military success inspires make the soldiers of the nation become the soldiers of the monarch and his generals. In times of factionalism and trouble, army leaders become the arbiters of their country's destiny and tip the balance in favor of their own chosen party. If they are Caesars or Cromwells, they seize the authority themselves. If they are spineless courtiers, incapable of doing good yet powerful to promote evil, they return to surrender their authority to their masters and aid them to assume arbitrary power, on condition that they may become their first servants. . . . War was the cause of Sparta's loss of liberty as soon as she bore her arms far beyond her frontiers. War, skillfully provoked and directed by a perfidious government, was the reef on which the liberty of many a free people has been wrecked.

This is not the argument employed by those, eager to embark on war, who appear to look upon it as the source of every good, for it is far easier to yield to enthusiasm than to consult the oracle of reason. Thus one already sees the tricolor flag planted on the palaces of emperors, sultans, popes and kings: these are the very expressions of a patriotic writer[2] who is a devoted partisan of the cause I here denounce. Others assure us that no sooner have we made war than we shall see every throne crumble simultaneously before us. For myself, having seen the slow progress of liberty in France, I confess I cannot yet believe in the liberty of people besotted and enslaved by despotism. I believe as ardently as any man in the miracles that may be achieved by the courage of a great people which bestirs itself to conquer the freedom of the world; but when I consider the actual circumstances in which we find ourselves, when in place of the people I see the Court and the servants of the Court, when I hear all this prating of universal freedom by men corrupted by the rottenness of Courts, men who, in their own countries, never cease to slander and to persecute her; then I demand that one should at least stop to reflect on a matter of such importance.

If the Court and the Ministry have an interest in war, then, as you will see, they have neglected nothing to bring it to us. . . .

Before proposing to make war it was their duty not only to make every effort to prevent it, but to use every means at their disposal to

[2] Brissot.

keep the peace within; and yet disturbances are breaking out all over the country, and it is the Court, it is the Ministry, which is provoking them.

Are not our seditious priests the auxiliaries and allies of the rebels in exile? The impunity which they have enjoyed, the encouragement they have received, the malevolence with which the constitutional clergy[3] has been abandoned and persecuted have lighted the torch of fanaticism and discord. A decree, prompted by the need for internal security, would have suppressed these men who disturb the public peace in the name of the Almighty; but you cover them with your protective shield; with one hand you offer a declaration of war, and thus you provoke all at once a war that is both foreign, civil and religious.

What more certain proof can one have of a conspiracy conceived by the enemies of our liberty? Having expounded this conspiracy, I will now explain its real object to you with greater precision.

Do they wish to plunge France into bloodshed in order to reestablish the old régime with all its deformities? No, they know well enough that such an undertaking would be too difficult to realize; and the leaders of the ruling faction have no desire to revive those abuses of the old régime which they found harmful to their interests. In the present state of affairs, such changes as they want are only those that correspond to their personal aims and ambitions. . . . Now, since they rally openly under the standard of the Court and the Ministry, since it is the Court and the Ministry that inspire them, cajole them and employ them, it is therefore clear that the Court and the Ministry wish, if not to overthrow, at least to change the Constitution. Now, what can this change be unless it be along the lines that I have already suggested to you? But can you imagine that the Court would embrace a measure as decisive as a declaration of war without relating it to the realization of the plan that it holds so dear? No. The Court is setting a trap for you in proposing this measure: this trap is so evident that every patriot who has opted for the course that I am rejecting has felt the need for an assurance that the Court was not seriously disposed to war and, having proposed it, was seeking the means to avoid it.

But, in all that I have said so far, if I have not convinced you that the opposite is the truth, does it not suffice to consider all the methods that it uses to direct public opinion towards this course? Does it not suffice to hear all this simultaneous baying for war by all the ministers and all the journalists in their pay and to read the lavishly circulated pamphlets

[3] Those priests who, since November 1790, had taken an oath of loyalty to the Constitution.

directed against those who hold a contrary view? Does it not suffice to
remember that, within the National Assembly itself, the Minister of
War[4] accused patriots who oppose the war in such terms as make it impossible for the Ministry not to want it? The Court has always wanted
it, and still wants it; but it wished to await a favorable moment for its
declaration and to present it to you under conditions most convenient
to itself. It was necessary to wait until the *émigrés* had swelled the rebel
forces and until the foreign powers had had time to concert their
activities in this regard. It was also necessary to defeat the rigorous decree which might have discouraged and dried up the flood of emigration;
but at the same time care had to be taken that they should not attack
our frontiers first, for after the complaints that had come in from every
side of the conduct of the former Minister of War, and after the most
recent mark of favor shown to the *émigrés,* the nation would have laid
this invasion at the Ministry's own door; it would have seen through the
veil of deception and in the fury of its indignation it would have found
the energy to accomplish its salvation. It was necessary to appear, at that
point, to arouse by means of a lying proclamation the nation's anger
against those very men whom they were protecting from the just severity
of the laws. It was necessary to have both the war and the nation's
confidence, which alone would assure them of the means of guiding that
war, without fear of discovery, in the direction desired by the Court. But
to allay any suspicions that so sudden a change and so seemingly contradictory a mode of conduct might arouse, a wise policy demanded that
the Assembly should be requested to take the decisive step. The first
stage in this plan was realized when "ministerial" deputies persuaded
the Legislative Assembly to send, against its own best interests, a message
to the King, which departed from its principles and unwittingly entered
into those of the Court.[5] The Assembly also wished that the citizens
themselves should appear to anticipate its own wishes; and while it
refused arms to the National Guards, it did everything possible to make
the war a popular cause: it went into the most detailed preparations to
arouse the enthusiasm which it required; witness the false rumors that
it has spread about, and witness the orators ostentatiously summoned, at
this moment of tension, to the bar of the Assembly.

And now, to reply directly to a certain patriotic representative,[6] what
precautions do you propose in order to avert these dangers and to com-

[4] The Comte de Narbonne.
[5] A reference to the Assembly's message of November 29, 1791, requesting the King
to order the Electors of Treves and Mainz to eject the French *émigrés* from their
territories.
[6] He is addressing Brissot.

bat this alliance? None whatever. All that you have said to reassure us amounts to one single phrase: "No matter! Liberty will triumph in spite of all." But there is no suggestion here that you have the task to ensure that triumph by confounding the plots of its enemies! *Mistrust, you say, is a terrible evil.* But I would suggest that it is far less terrible than the blind confidence that has caused us so much trouble and embarrassment and is leading us to the edge of the precipice. Patriotic representatives, do not malign mistrust; leave such a treacherous doctrine to the cowardly intriguers who have used it in order to cover up their treasonable activities. Let the brigands who wish to invade and profane the temple of liberty have the task of engaging the dreaded dragons that guard its entrance. . . . Mistrust, whatever you may say, is the protector of the rights of the people: it is to the love of liberty what jealousy is to passion. Newly elected representatives, learn at least from the experience of three years of intrigue and treachery: remember that if your forerunners had felt the need for this virtue, your task would have been far easier to accomplish. Without it, you too are destined to become the plaything and the victim of the most vile and depraved of men, and beware that, of all the qualities required to save liberty, this be not the only one that you lack.

If we are betrayed, adds the same patriotic deputy, *the people will be there.* Yes, no doubt; but you will not be unaware that the insurrection you propose is a rare, uncertain and drastic remedy. The people was there in all the free countries when, in spite of its rights and its omnipotence, clever men, having lulled it to sleep for a while, enslaved it for centuries to come. It was there in July last when its blood flowed freely in the heart of this capital;[7] and *at whose order?* The people is there; but you, its representatives, are you not there, too? And what are you doing there if, instead of foreseeing and confounding the plans of its oppressors, you merely abandon it to the terrible right of insurrection and to the unknown outcome of the overthrow of states? I know that such a fortunate set of circumstances may arise in which a thunderbolt, hurled by its hands, may crush the traitors; but the people must at least have had time to recognize their treachery. You must not therefore exhort it to close its eyes, but to keep them wide open; you must not blindly subscribe to every proposal of its enemies and hand over to it the task of directing the course and determining the outcome of a crisis that will decide its ruin or its salvation. That, however, is what you are doing in adopting the war plans proposed to you by the Ministry. Do you know of a people which has conquered its liberty while at the same

---

[7] On July 17, 1791, on the occasion of the "massacre" of the Champ de Mars.

time supporting a foreign, civil and religious war directed by the very despotism that had provoked that war and whose authority it was seeking to restrain? . . . Did the Americans have to combat fanaticism and treachery within while fighting without an army concerted against them by their own government? And does it follow that because they triumphed after a hard struggle over the despot who made war on them when supported by a powerful ally, led by Washington and favored by the errors of Cornwallis; does it follow from this that they would have triumphed if they had been ruled by George III's ministers and led by his generals? . . .

If we are to be deceived or betrayed, you say, it is better to declare war than to wait for it to come. In the first place, this is not the real issue that I wish to resolve, for my object is not simply to wait for the war, but to prevent it. But as I wish to destroy the whole basis of your argument, I shall prove in a few words that to wait for war would be a surer guarantee of liberty than to adopt the Ministry's proposals.

In the case of an anticipated act of treason there is, as you have foreseen, only one resource left to the nation: that is a sudden and salutary explosion of anger by the people of France; but this would only be assured by an invasion of our country, since then the French, suddenly aroused from their lethargic trust, would display marvels of energy and courage to defend their freedom against their foes. The government and the aristocracy have understood this well enough, and they are determined to exorcize the storm that such a display of patriotism would let loose on them; they have realized that the Ministry and the Court must appear to wish to direct themselves the thunderbolt against our enemies so that the executive power, having once more become an object of enthusiasm and veneration, might freely and untrammeled execute the sinister design of which I have spoken. Then any enlightened and energetic citizen who might dare to cast suspicion on a minister or on a general will be denounced by the ruling faction as an enemy of the State; then the traitors will repeatedly demand, in the name of public safety, that blind obedience and disastrous moderation which, up to now, have saved all conspirators from being brought to justice. Then everywhere the voice of reason and of patriotism will be silenced in the face of military despotism and the audacity of the factions. . . .

To conclude. This is not the moment to declare war. Before all else, this is a moment to manufacture arms, in every place and at every hour; to arm the National Guards; to arm the people, if only with pikes; to adopt severe measures, and not such as have been adopted up to now, so that it will not be left to ministers to neglect with impunity what the security of the State demands; to uphold the dignity of the people and to defend its too long neglected rights. It is the moment to pay faithful attention to our financial resources, which are still steeped in mystery, instead of wasting them further on a reckless war, to the prosecution of which our revolutionary paper money itself would be an obstacle if we carried it beyond our frontiers; it is the moment to punish the guilty ministers and to persist in our determination to repress the seditious clergy.

If, in spite of reason and the public interest, war proved to be inevitable, we should at least spare ourselves the disgrace of conducting it according to the initiative and precepts of the Court. We should have to begin by indicting the last Minister of War, so that his successor should understand that the eye of the people is firmly fixed upon him; we should have to begin by bringing the rebels to trial and confiscating their possessions, so that our soldiers should not appear as armed warriors enlisted in the service of the King to fight an opposing faction, but as executors of our national justice bent on punishing the guilty. But if, when you go to war, you appear merely to be adopting the ministers' intentions; if, at the first sight of the head of the executive power, the nation's representatives prostrate themselves before him and acclaim with premature and servile applause the first agent that he offers to them; if they set the nation an example of frivolity, idolatry and credulity; if they induce in her the dangerous illusion that the prince or his agents are liberators; then how can you hope that the people will be more vigilant than those whom it has entrusted with its safety, more devoted than those whose duty it is to be devoted in its service, and more wise than those whom it appointed for their wisdom? . . .

I have little hope that my words will have the power to carry conviction at this moment; and I do not desire that bitter experience should prove me right. But if that should be, I shall have at least one consolation: I shall be able to call my country to witness that I shall not have contributed to her ruin.

4

On the Control of Food Supplies

One of the most intractable problems the Revolution-aries had to face was the assurance of an adequate supply of food, particularly to the big cities such as Paris. The opening months of the Revolution were attended by an acute bread shortage and rising prices, and there were riots all over the country. There were further disturbances in Paris in January-February 1792 and in the Beauce and the Orléanais in February-March and again in Novem-ber-December of that year. The first of the speeches reproduced here was made in the National Convention on December 2, while the second outbreak in the Beauce was still in progress.

The deputies to the Convention, like their predecessors in the earlier Assemblies, were essentially economic liberals and resisted the growing popular demands to impose controls on prices and supplies. Basically, Robespierre shared the views of the majority and, as he shows here, was loath to interfere "unnecessarily" with the freedom of the market; yet he conceded that food (particularly bread) was not a commodity like any other and should, in all cir-cumstances, be readily available to every citizen. Thus, where neces-sary, special measures should be taken to ensure a free and ade-quate distribution, involving stern police action against hoarders and speculators; but he makes no suggestion as yet of even a partial control of prices. This, however, was to come later; one reason for the defeat of the Girondins by the Jacobins was undoubtedly that the latter were more willing, when necessity demanded, to accept the sort of general control of prices and supplies that eventually emerged in the Maximum Law of September 29, 1793.

The other two short speeches were made in the Jacobin Club at the time of the Paris riots of February 25-26, 1793, when large crowds compelled grocers to reduce the price of sugar, coffee and candles in every quarter of the city. It is evident that Robespierre's attitude on this occasion is far less sympathetic to the rioters than before. The reasons are (a) that he considered sugar and coffee to be semiluxury commodities and not basic necessities like bread; (b) that he had convinced himself (possibly for that very reason) that the riots had been provoked by aristocratic elements; and (c) that, like all other political leaders of the Left—with the exception of the small group of Enragées *led by Jacques Roux—he thought it ridiculous, if not degrading, for the "men of 1789," who had taken the Bastille, to be so actively concerned with "paltry merchandise"! The point betrays the ambivalent attitude of Robespierre and his associates towards the economic problems of the poor. On such basic issues as bread and wages even the most radical among the Jacobins were never quite able to shake off their middle-class prejudices.*

ON FOOD SUPPLIES (DECEMBER 2, 1792) [1]

To speak to the representatives of the people about the means of providing for their subsistence is not only to speak to them of the most sacred of their interests; for they are so close to one another that one might say that they are one.

It is not only the cause of the poorer citizens that I wish to plead, but that of the landowners and merchants as well.

I shall confine myself to recalling to your mind principles that are evident enough but which seem to have become forgotten. I shall only place before you simple measures that have already been suggested; for I have less a mind to devise brilliant theories than to return to the basic notions of common sense.

In every country in which nature is generous in its provision of the elementary means of subsistence, shortage can be attributable only to the vices of administration or of the laws themselves; and bad laws and bad administration are themselves the result of false principles and of bad social habits.

It is a fact generally recognized that the soil of France produces far more than is required to feed its inhabitants and that the present shortage is an artificial shortage. The consequences of this fact and of the principle that I have enunciated may be distressing, and this is hardly the moment for you to take comfort from them. Citizens, it is your duty to assure the triumph of true principles and to give the world just laws. It would be unbecoming for you to allow yourselves to become bogged, like servile imitators, in the rut of tyrannical prejudice dug by your predecessors; or, rather, you are setting out along a new path which none have trodden before you. At the least, you must submit to a severe examination all laws enacted under the royal despotism or inspired by the aristocracy, whether noble, clerical or bourgeois; and up to now you have inherited none other. The most impressive authority that has been

[1] *Sur les subsistances* (Paris, 1792); trans G. Rudé.

quoted to us is a certain minister of Louis XVI, whose policies were challenged by another of that same tyrant's ministers.[2] I have seen the growth and development of the laws passed by the Constituent Assembly with regard to the grain trade; they were no different from those of their forerunners. They have not changed up to this moment, because the interests and prejudices that lay behind them have not changed. At the time of that Assembly, I saw events take place that have been repeated since: I saw the aristocracy denounce the people; I saw hypocritical intriguers impute their own crimes to the defenders of liberty, whom they termed agitators and anarchists. I saw an insolent minister, whose virtue was then deemed to be above reproach, elicit the applause of a nation that he was ruining; and, in the midst of these criminal intrigues, I saw tyranny emerge armed with martial law, and with all the solemnity of law, bathe itself in the blood of starving citizens.[3] Millions handed over to the minister whose accounts might not be challenged; bounties voted to the greater profit of the leeches battening on the people; unrestricted freedom of trade, and bayonets to keep the people quiet or to quell their pangs of hunger; such was the much vaunted policy of the first legislators of our Revolution.

The value of bounties may be debated; freedom of trade is necessary up to the point where homicidal greed begins to misuse it; the use of bayonets is an atrocity; so the system is fundamentally incomplete, because it fails to go to the roots of the problem.

The mistakes that have been made in this regard appear to me to arise from two principal causes:

1. The authors of the system have treated those commodities most necessary to human existence merely as ordinary merchandise and have made no distinction between trade in wheat and, say, in indigo; they have spent more time talking about the grain trade than they have about the people's needs; and by omitting this factor from their calculations, they have, in practice, falsely applied principles which, in themselves, are self-evident. It is this mixture of truth and falsehood which has given a plausible appearance to an erroneous system.

2. Still less have they adapted them to the stormy conditions that revolutions bring in their train; and their vague theories, even if they were adequate in ordinary circumstances, would be quite unsuited to the emergency measures which are called for in moments of crisis. They

[2] A reference to Necker's criticisms of Turgot's free-trade policies, which precipitated the grain riots of 1775.

[3] On July 17, 1791, martial law was invoked by Bailly and Lafayette to shoot down demonstrators in the Champ de Mars in Paris.

have counted for a great deal the profits of merchants and landowners, but the lives of human beings they have counted as almost nothing. And why? Because it was the ministers and the men of wealth and social position who wrote and who ruled; if this had fallen to the people, the system would no doubt have been considerably amended!

Common sense tells us, for example, that such commodities as are not essential to subsistence may be left to unlimited commercial speculation; the momentary shortage which may ensue is, in such cases, a tolerable inconvenience; and, generally, it may be assumed that the unrestricted freedom of this trade will redound to the greater profit of both the State and the individual. But where human lives are concerned we are not justified in taking such a risk. It is not imperative that I should be in a position to buy expensive cloth; but it is imperative that I should have the means to buy bread for my children and myself. The merchant may be allowed to store in his warehouse the merchandise that panders to luxury and vanity until he finds the right moment to sell it at the highest price; but no man has the right to stock quantities of wheat while his neighbor is dying of hunger.

Which is the first object of our polity? To guarantee the imprescriptible rights of man. And which is the first of these rights? That of existence. The first social law is, therefore, that which assures every member of society of the means of existence; all others are subordinated to it; property has only been founded and protected to give it greater strength; and the very basis of property is to ensure the means to live. It is not true that property can ever be in conflict with the right to live.

Food that is necessary for man's existence is as sacred as life itself. Everything that is indispensable for its preservation is the common property of society as a whole. It is only the surplus that is private property and can be safely left to individual commercial enterprise. Any commercial speculation that I engage in to the danger of my neighbor's life is not a business dealing; it is an act of brigandage and a form of fratricide.

If we adopt this principle, what is the problem to be resolved when we legislate on food supplies? It is to assure to all members of society the right to enjoy that share of the fruits of the earth that is necessary for their existence, to guarantee a fair price for their labor to the landowners and cultivators, and to leave the surplus to the freedom of the market.

I challenge the most scrupulous defender of property to dispute these principles unless he is prepared to declare openly that he means by this word the right to despoil and to murder his fellow human beings. How then has it been possible to claim that any restriction, or rather any regulation, affecting the sale of wheat was a threat to property and to disguise this barbarous system under the spacious title of the freedom of trade? Do not the authors of this system see that they are adopting a hopelessly contradictory attitude?

Why are you compelled to agree to place a ban on the foreign export of grain whenever there is not a complete abundance within the country? You yourselves regulate the price of bread; do you regulate that of the spices or luxury products from the Indies? Why all these exceptions unless they be evidence of a concern for the very principles that I have been formulating? There is more: the government sometimes places limited controls even on the trade in luxury goods; and this is in accordance with sound commercial practice. So why should there be an exception in the case of trade in the necessities of life?

Doubtless, if all men were just and virtuous, if greed were never tempted to plunder the substance of the people; if, responsive to the promptings of nature and reason, the rich all looked on themselves as the housekeepers of society or as the brothers of the poor; if such were the case, one might recognize no other law but the most unlimited freedom. But if it is true that avarice may speculate on want and tyranny on popular despair, if it is true that every passion may declare war on suffering humanity, why should not laws be framed to repress these abuses? Why should they not be made to arrest the hand of the death-dealing monopolist as they would that of the common murderer? Why should they not concern themselves with the people's livelihood after having so long concerned themselves with the pleasures of the great and the omnipotence of despots?

Now, which are the means whereby we may remedy these abuses? It has been said that they are impracticable, but I maintain that they are as simple as they are infallible. It is said that even a genius would be unable to find a solution; but I maintain that they will injure neither the interests of trade nor the rights of property.

We must protect the distribution of grain in every corner of the Republic; but we must also take the necessary precautions to ensure that that distribution takes place. And my complaint is precisely this: that the distribution itself is faulty. For the scourge of the people and the source of scarcity lie in the obstacles that, in the name of unrestricted freedom, are placed in the way of distribution. Is there a proper distribution of the nation's food when greedy speculators keep it stocked in their granaries? Does it become distributed when it accumulates in the hands of a small number of millionaires, who withhold it from the market in order to increase its price through scarcity and who coldly calculate how many families must perish before supplies have been withheld long enough to satisfy their avarice? Is it distributed when it is merely transported across the regions that produced it before the eyes of the poor, who suffer the torments of Tantalus, in order to be buried in the unknown storehouse of some manipulator of the public's want? Is it distributed when the poor man starves in the midst of plenty for lack of a gold coin or a piece of paper of sufficient value to buy himself a meager share?

A proper distribution is that which places all commodities of first necessity within reach of every mortal man and which brings abundance and life into every cottage. Does the blood properly circulate when it is blocked in the brain or in the chest? It circulates when it flows freely throughout the whole body: food is the lifeblood of the people, and its free circulation is no less necessary to the health of the body politic than that of blood to the life of the human body. Aid, therefore, the free circulation of grain by preventing every harmful impediment. How may this object be attained? By denying to men of greed the motive or the means to hinder it. Now, there are three factors that favor such obstruction: they are secrecy, unrestricted freedom, and the certainty of escaping punishment. . . .

Now, [to deal with secrecy] I propose two simple remedies: the first is to take such steps as are required to determine the quantity of grain produced by every region and that harvested by every owner or cultivator. The second is to compel every merchant to sell his grain in the market and to forbid any transportation of purchased grain by night. . . .

I have said that the other causes of the disastrous activities of monopoly were unrestricted freedom and the certainty of escaping punishment. What surer means to encourage cupidity and to absolve it from all restraint than to lay down the principle that the law has no right to keep an eye on it or to impede its operations in any way at all, or than to maintain that the only rule applied to it is that it may act with the fullest impunity? Nor is this all; for such are the lengths to which this principle has been carried that it is now almost established that speculators are beyond the law; that monopolists are public benefactors, and that in the disputes that arise between them and the people it is always the people that are wrong. Either monopoly can commit no crime, or else its crime is a reality; and if it is a fantasy, how is it that from time immemorial this fantasy has been believed? Why did we experience its effects from the first moment of our Revolution? Why do reliable reports and incontrovertible facts continually denounce its criminal activities? If it is a reality, by what strange privilege does it alone have the right to be protected? What limits would the pitiless vampires who speculate on public destitution set to their crimes if every kind of protest were invariably met by bayonets and the categorical command to believe that all speculators are pure and public benefactors? Unrestricted freedom merely serves to excuse, protect and perpetuate similar abuses. How could it possibly prevent them? Of what are people complaining? Is it not of the ills caused by the present system or at least of the ills that it has been unable to avert? And what remedy is now proposed? The present system. I denounce to you the murderers of the people, and you reply: "Leave them alone." From this system society is the consistent loser; the grain merchant alone is favored. . . .

I realize that when one examines the circumstances in which this or that riot, provoked by a real or an artificial shortage of corn, breaks out, one sometimes detects the trace of an outside influence. Ambition and intrigue thrive on the promotion of disorder: sometimes such interested parties stir up the people in order to find a pretext for shooting them down and for making freedom itself appear dangerous to weak and selfish men. But it is no less true that the people are naturally upright and peaceful; their intentions are always pure; and ill-disposed persons can rouse them only if they can present them with a compelling motive and one that is legitimate in their eyes. Such men exploit their dissatisfaction far more than they arouse it; and when they lead the people into misguided actions in relation to food supplies, it is only because oppression and poverty lend credence to their fears. When the people are happy, they are never turbulent. Whoever knows the French people knows that it is not in the power of a madman or of a bad citizen to excite them, without reason, against the laws that they cherish, and still less against the representatives that they have chosen and the freedom that they have conquered . . .

And you, legislators, remember that you are not the representatives of a privileged caste but of the French people. Do not forget that the source of all order is justice; that the surest guarantee of social peace is the happiness of the citizens; and that the prolonged convulsions that tear nations apart are but the struggle of prejudice against principle, of self-interest against the public interest, and of the pride and the passions of powerful men against the rights and the needs of the weak.

ON THE PARIS FOOD RIOTS OF FEBRUARY 25-26, 1793 [4]

On February 25, 1793

As I have always loved humanity and have never sought to flatter any man, I shall speak the truth. This is a plot directed against the patriots themselves. The intriguers are determined to bring the patriots to their ruin. The people have been rightly filled with indignation. I have said before, in the midst of persecution and without the support of others, that the people are never wrong. I dared to proclaim this truth at a time when it was not yet recognized; it has been vindicated by the later course of the Revolution.

The people have so often heard the law invoked by those who wished to enslave them that they have grown to distrust such talk.

The people are still persecuted by the rich, who are still what they always were: hard and merciless. (*Applause.*) The people see the insolence of those who have deceived them; they see how wealth has accumulated in their hands; conscious of their own wretchedness, they do not feel the need to take such measures as will carry the Revolution through to its goal; and when one speaks to them in the language of reason, they follow but the promptings of their own anger against the rich and allow themselves to be led along false paths by men who capture their confidence in order to destroy them.

For this there are two causes, of which the first is the natural disposition of the people to seek the means to alleviate their wretched condition. This in itself is a natural and legitimate disposition: the people believe that, in default of protective laws, they have the right to take their own measures to satisfy their needs.

But there is another cause, which lies in the treacherous designs of the enemies of freedom, of the enemies of the people, who are convinced that the only way to open our doors to the enemy without is to arouse popular alarm concerning our food supplies and to make the people suffer the consequences of the resultant commotion. I have, myself, been a witness of these disturbances. Along with decent citizens, we have seen strangers and men of wealth clad in the honorable garb of the *sans-culottes*. We have heard them say: "They promised us abundance after the King's death, and we have been more wretched than ever since that poor King died." We have heard them protest, not against the intriguing and counterrevolutionary section of the Convention, which now sits where

[4] From two speeches made in the Jacobin Club, the first on February 25 and the second on March 1, 1793. (*Oeuvres de Maximilien Robespierre*, IX, 274-6, 286-8; trans. G. Rudé.)

once sat the aristocrats of the Constituent Assembly, but against the Mountain, against the deputies of Paris and the Jacobins, whom they present as hoarders and speculators.

I am not saying that the people are guilty, nor that their agitation is a crime. But when the people rise, should they not have an object worthy of themselves? Should they be merely concerned with paltry merchandise? They have gained nothing from it, for the sugar loaves have been carried off by the lackeys of the aristocracy; and even if they have gained something, what disasters have they not reaped to offset this slender advantage? Our enemies wish to terrify all who have any property by persuading them that our system of liberty and equality is subversive of all order and security.

The people, indeed, must rise: not to seize sugar, but to exterminate the brigands. (*Applause*.) . . .

On March 1, 1793

. . . Aristocracy, seconded by hypocrisy, raises its menacing head once more. The *émigrés* join with the intriguers to rob us of our happiness and liberty. The people triumph, but they suffer; they remain calm, but they are insulted and slandered by those who wish to rouse them for their own destruction. The moment when the vile champions of royalty should be hiding their shame is the one that they choose to display their greatest audacity.

In spite of Pitt's gold, in spite of the maneuvers and intrigues of the protectors of the tyrant, in spite of Le Pelletier's assassination,[5] the people had surrounded the tyrant's scaffold with an impressive calm. But the horde of strangers, *émigrés* and scoundrels wished to make one last effort. Pitt himself had announced that disturbances would break out in Paris within a week. A deputy whom I shall not name told us that Louis Capet's death would bring great calamities in its train.

There is a momentary shortage of bread at the bakers', due as much to panic buying as to the intrigues of those who have caused it; "Fayettists" and aristocrats, masquerading as patriots, were spread about in the societies and groups. A petition was presented at the Convention whose style betrayed the authors of this perfidious conspiracy. Groups of women began to assemble on the pretext of protesting against the high price of soap.[6] Our alarm grew when citizens in the public gallery, misled by the sinister perversity of our enemies, called us speculators and hoarders. Thanks to our own zeal and vigilance, these slanders were

---

[5] A Jacobin leader assassinated in January 1793.

[6] There was a demonstration of this kind in the Assembly on February 24.

silenced and calm was restored; but that the recent events are closely linked with sinister designs is proved by the fact that the Jacobins of Paris were said to be the instigators of disturbance. We shall not demean ourselves by justifying our conduct; but, in order to indicate the true cause of the insurrection, we shall place certain important facts before you.

Among the women demonstrators were the servants of known aristocrats; there were even aristocrats in person disguised as *sans-culottes:* several were arrested and handed over to the courts. A certain Descombief [7] was arrested near the meeting hall of the Jacobin Club, which he had had the temerity to enter. Some miscreants were even heard to raise the wanton and sacrilegious cry of *Long live Louis XVI.* I must tell you, too, that the warehouses of the large hoarders were left untouched,[8] that the shops of patriots received a particular and unmerited attention, and that the "Fayettist" and aristocratic shopkeepers displayed a quite unnatural joy and self-composure.

In the Faubourg St. Marcel, not a single shopkeeper or merchant was disturbed. The efforts of the agitators who went into the Faubourg St. Antoine were fruitless: they failed completely to rouse the population of that quarter.[9] That is the true people of Paris. They cast down tyrants; they do not invade grocers' shops. (*Applause.*) The people of Paris have overthrown despotism, but they have not laid siege to the counting houses of the Rue des Lombards.

How vile are these petty impostors who slander the people because they fear them! But, my friends and brothers, when they tell you that the Jacobins are the authors of the recent events, answer that they can only be attributed to those who have sought to oppress the defenders of liberty, to those who have given protection to the *émigrés;* to those who set themselves up as the champions of tyranny, who voted for the appeal against Louis' sentence of death, who insulted the memory of Michel Le Pelletier; and to those who fomented the insurrection that broke out in the city of Lyons, the home and birthplace of the virtuous Roland, where aristocrats have defiled the emblems of liberty and murdered patriots. (*Cries of indignation.*) Several have been thrown into the river; news of this has reached me today . . . Tell them that liberty, in spite of every sort of perfidy, will triumph over all the arts of intrigue and

[7] Possibly J. F. Descombiès, a former naval officer later sentenced to death by the Revolutionary Tribunal in May 1794.

[8] This statement is not borne out by the police records relating to this affair.

[9] There were, in fact, extensive disturbances in at least two of the three Sections of the Faubourg St. Antoine: for the losses suffered by 25 grocers in the Quinze-Vingts Section alone, see Archives de la préfecture de police, Aa220, fos. 240-41.

aristocracy. But our task is to advance liberty by half a century throughout the world. To achieve this aim, let us combine our efforts in order to protect feeble minds against the poisoned tracts of the partisans of despotism; for never shall the Jacobins be found guilty of injuring the cause of freedom, which they have sworn to defend with their dying breath. If you doubt this fact, come to see the Jacobins, come to be instructed in their midst; and the men of ill will shall tremble as they trembled before the federal battalions whom they had themselves summoned to the capital.[10] (*Applause.*)

[10] A reference to the part played in the overthrow of the monarchy by the National Guards of Marseilles, Brest and other cities, originally brought to Paris to attend the anniversary ceremony of July 14, 1792.

5
On Property (April 24, 1793)[1]

Another basic problem frequently confronting the Revolutionaries was that of property rights. How far should private property be considered inviolate, and how far was it proper for the State to intervene in order to remove abuses or even to ensure a more equitable distribution of goods? The Declaration of Rights of 1789 had quite explicitly stated that "property is a sacred and inviolable right" and had laid down no limitations to its free exercise. This continued to be the prevailing notion, though not shared by a few minority groups, until the fall of the monarchy and the political and economic crisis of 1793 compelled the Jacobins to reconsider the question in preparing a second Constitution to replace that of 1791.

Robespierre took an active part in this debate and presented his views to the Convention in a speech of April 24, 1793. Like his fellow Jacobins, he believed that the right of property should be more closely defined and limited, if need be, to satisfy the claims of the State in times of emergency and to ensure that its exercise by some did not infringe the rights of others—in particular, those of the poorer citizens. So the Constitution, when it emerged in June of that year, gave the State the obligation to provide education for all and work or relief for the needy. Robespierre wanted to go further: he proposed a progressive tax on incomes and that a clear distinction be drawn between property rights that were "justly" and those that were "unjustly" exercised; only the former should be protected by the State. His views, however, were not accepted, and these provisions were omitted from the Constitution of 1793.

Later, Robespierre and Saint-Just put forward, in the Laws of Ventôse (March 1794), a plan for the confiscation of the property of political "suspects" and its distribution among the poor. (The law was never implemented.) But Robespierre was no socialist. He was as horrified as anyone by the suggestion of an "Agrarian Law" (or equal division of goods); and he would certainly have lent no

[1] Introductory speech from H. Morse Stephens, *op. cit.,* II, 366-70; trans. G. Rudé. Proposed Declaration of Rights from J. Hall Stewart, *A Documentary Survey of the French Revolution* (New York, Crowell-Collier & Macmillan, Inc., 1951), pp. 430-34. Reprinted by permission of the publisher.

See also, Georges Lefebvre on Robespierre's political ideas on page 147.

support to Babeuf's plan of 1796 to transfer all property to the State.

First, I shall propose to you a few articles that are necessary to complete your theory on property; and do not let this word "property" alarm anyone. Mean spirits, you whose only measure of value is gold, I have no desire to touch your treasures, however impure may have been the source of them. You must know that the agrarian law, of which there has been so much talk, is only a bogey created by rogues to frighten fools. I can hardly believe that it took a revolution to teach the world that extreme disparities in wealth lie at the root of many ills and crimes, but we are not the less convinced that the realization of an equality of fortunes is a visionary's dream. For myself, I think it to be less necessary to private happiness than to the public welfare. It is far more a question of lending dignity to poverty than of making war on wealth. Fabricius' cottage has no need to envy the palace of Crassus. I would as gladly be one of the sons of Aristides, reared in the Prytaneum at the cost of the Republic, than to be the heir presumptive of Xerxes, born in the filth of courts and destined to occupy a throne draped in the degradation of the peoples and dazzling against the public misery.

Let us then in good faith pose the principles that govern the rights of property; it is all the more necessary to do so because there are none that human prejudice and vice have so consistently sought to shroud in mystery.

Ask that merchant in human flesh what property is. He will tell you, pointing to the long bier that he calls a ship and in which he had herded and shackled men who still appear to be alive: "Those are my property; I bought them at so much a head." Question that nobleman, who has lands and ships or who thinks that the world has been turned upside down since he has had none, and he will give you a similar view of property.

Question the august members of the Capetian dynasty.[2] They will tell you that the most sacred of all property rights is without doubt the hereditary right that they have enjoyed since ancient times to oppress, to degrade, and to attach to their person legally and royally the 25 million people who lived, at their good pleasure, on the territory of France.

But to none of these people has it ever occurred that property carries moral responsibilities. Why should our Declaration of Rights appear to contain the same error in its definition of liberty: "the most valued

[2] The French royal family.

property of man, the most sacred of the rights that he holds from nature"? We have justly said that this right was limited by the rights of others. Why have we not applied the same principle to property, which is a social institution, as if the eternal laws of nature were less inviolable than the conventions evolved by man? You have drafted numerous articles in order to ensure the greatest freedom for the exercise of property, but you have not said a single word to define its nature and its legitimacy, so that your declaration appears to have been made not for ordinary men, but for capitalists, profiteers, speculators and tyrants. I propose to you to rectify these errors by solemnly recording the following truths:

1. Property is the right of each and every citizen to enjoy and to dispose of the portion of goods that is guaranteed to him by law.

2. The right of property is limited, as are all other rights, by the obligation to respect the property of others.

3. It may not be so exercised as to prejudice the security, or the liberty, or the existence, or the property of our fellow men.

4. All holdings in property and all commercial dealings which violate this principle are unlawful and immoral.

You also speak of taxes in such a way as to establish the irrefutable principle that they can only be the expression of the will of the people or of its representatives. But you omit an article that is indispensable to the general interest: you neglect to establish the principle of a progressive tax. Now, in matters of public finance, is there a principle more solidly grounded in the nature of things and in eternal justice than that which imposes on citizens the obligations to contribute progressively to state expenditure according to their incomes—that is, according to the material advantages that they draw from the social system?

I propose that you should record this principle in an article conceived as follows:

"Citizens whose incomes do not exceed what is required for their subsistence are exempted from contributing to state expenditure; all others must support it progressively according to their wealth."

The Committee[3] has also completely neglected to record the obligations of brotherhood that bind together the men of all nations, and their right to mutual assistance. It appears to have been unaware of the roots of the perpetual alliance that unite the peoples against tyranny. It would seem that your declaration has been drafted for a human herd planted in an isolated corner of the globe and not for the vast family of nations to which nature has given the earth for its use and dwelling.

I propose that you fill this great gap by adding the following articles.

[3] The Constitutional Committee of the National Convention.

They cannot fail to win the regard of all peoples, though they may, it is true, have the disadvantage of estranging you irrevocably from kings. I confess that this disadvantage does not frighten me, nor will it frighten all others who have no desire to be reconciled to them. Here are my four articles:

1. The men of all countries are brothers, and the different peoples must help one another according to their ability, as though they were citizens of a single state.

2. Whoever oppresses a single nation declares himself the enemy of all.

3. Whoever makes war on a people to arrest the progress of liberty and to destroy the rights of man must be prosecuted by all, not as ordinary enemies, but as rebels, brigands and assassins.

4. Kings, aristocrats and tyrants, whoever they be, are slaves in rebellion against the sovereign of the earth, which is the human race, and against the legislator of the universe, which is nature.

A PROPOSED DECLARATION OF THE RIGHTS OF MAN AND CITIZEN

The representatives of the French people, assembled in National Convention, recognizing that human laws which do not derive from the eternal laws of justice and of reason are only the outrages of ignorance or despotism against humanity; convinced that forgetfulness and contempt of the natural rights of man are the sole causes of the crimes and misfortunes of the world, have resolved to set forth in a solemn declaration these sacred and inalienable rights, in order that all citizens, being able constantly to compare the acts of the government with the aim of every social institution, may never allow themselves to be oppressed and degraded by tyranny, in order that the people always may have before their eyes the bases of their liberty and welfare; the magistrate, the rule of his duties; the legislator, the object of his mission.

Accordingly, the National Convention proclaims in the presence of the Universe, and before the eyes of the Immortal Legislator, the following declaration of the rights of man and citizen.

1. The aim of every political association is the maintenance of the natural and inalienable rights of man and the development of all their attributes.

2. The principal rights of man are those of providing for the preservation of his existence and his liberty.

3. These rights appertain equally to all men, whatever the difference in their physical and moral powers.

4. Equality of rights is established by nature; society, far from impairing it, guarantees it against the abuse of power which renders it illusory.

5. Liberty is the power which appertains to man to exercise all his faculties at will; it has justice for rule, the rights of others for limits, nature for principle, and the law for a safeguard.

6. The right to assemble peaceably, the right to manifest one's opinions, either by means of the press or in any other manner, are such necessary consequences of the principle of the liberty of man that the necessity of enunciating them presumes either the presence or the recent memory of despotism.

7. The law may forbid only whatever is injurious to society; it may order only whatever is useful thereto.

8. Every law which violates the inalienable rights of man is essentially unjust and tyrannical; it is not a law at all.

9. Property is the right of each and every citizen to enjoy and to dispose of the portion of goods that is guaranteed to him by law.

10. The right of property is limited, as are all other rights, by the obligation to respect the rights of others.

11. It may not be so exercised as to prejudice the security, or the liberty, or the existence, or the property of our fellow men.

12. All holdings in property and all commercial dealings which violate this principle are unlawful and immoral.

13. Society is obliged to provide for the subsistence of all its members, either by procuring work for them or by assuring the means of existence to those who are unable to work.

14. The aid indispensable to whosoever lacks necessities is a debt of whosoever possesses a surplus; it appertains to the law to determine the manner in which such debt is to be discharged.

15. Citizens whose incomes do not exceed whatever is necessary for their subsistence are exempted from contributing to public expenditures; all others must support them progressively, according to the extent of their wealth.

16. Society must favor with all its power the progress of public reason and must place education within reach of all citizens.

17. The law is the free and solemn expression of the will of the people.

18. The people is the sovereign, the government is its work, the public functionaries are its clerks; the people may change its government and recall its representatives when it pleases.

19. No portion of the people may employ the power of the entire people; but the wish which it expresses must be respected as the wish

of a portion of the people, which is to concur in forming the general will. Each and every section of the assembled sovereign must enjoy the right to express its will with entire liberty; it is essentially independent of all constituted authorities and master of regulating its police and its deliberations.

20. The law must be equal for all.

21. All citizens are admissible to all public offices, without any distinction other than that of virtues and talents, without any title other than the confidence of the people.

22. All citizens have an equal right to concur in the nomination of the representatives of the people and in the formation of the law.

23. In order that these rights may not be illusory, and equality chimerical, society must pay the public functionaries and must arrange that citizens who live by their labor may be present at the public assemblies to which the law summons them without compromising their existence or that of their family.

24. Every citizen must obey religiously the magistrates and agents of the government when they are the spokesmen or the executors of the law.

25. But every act against the liberty, the security, or the property of a man, performed by anyone whomsoever, even in the name of the law, except in the cases determined and the forms prescribed thereby, is arbitrary and null; every respect for the law forbids submission thereto; and if it is executed by violence, it is permissible to repel it by force.

26. The right to present petitions to the depositaries of public authority appertains to every individual. Those to whom they are addressed ought to legislate on the matters which are the object thereof; but they may never forbid, restrain, or condemn the exercise of said right.

27. Resistance to oppression is the consequence of the other rights of man and citizen.

28. There is oppression against the social body when a single one of its members is oppressed. There is oppression against each and every member of the social body when the social body is oppressed.

29. When the government violates the rights of the people, insurrection is the most sacred of rights and the most indispensable of duties for the people and for each and every portion thereof.

30. When the social guarantee is lacking to a citizen, he returns to the natural right of defending all his rights himself.

31. In either case, to make resistance to oppression subject to legal forms is the last refinement of tyranny. In every free state the law must, above all, defend public and individual liberty against the abuse of the

authority of those who govern: every institution which does not assume that the people are good, and the magistrate corruptible, is vicious.

32. Public functions may not be considered as distinctions or rewards, but only as public duties.

33. Offenses of the mandataries of the people must be punished severely and promptly. No one has a right to claim himself more inviolable than other citizens. The people have a right to know what their mandataries are doing; these must render a faithful account of their activities and must submit to public judgment respectfully.

34. The men of all countries are brothers, and the different peoples must help one another, according to their power, as citizens of the same State.

35. Whoever oppresses a single nation declares himself the enemy of all.

36. Whoever make war on a people in order to check the progress of liberty and annihilate the rights of man must be prosecuted by all, not as ordinary enemies, but as rebels, brigands and assassins.

37. Kings, aristocrats, tyrants, whoever they be, are slaves rebelling against the sovereign of the earth, which is the human race, and against the legislator of the universe, which is nature.

6

On Revolutionary Government (December 25, 1793)[1]

Robespierre made this speech to the National Convention three weeks after the Revolutionary government was formally constituted by the Law of 14th Frimaire (December 4, 1793).

Citizen Representatives of the People,

Success blunts the energy of the weak, but it spurs the strong to further activity.

Let us leave Europe and posterity to acclaim the miracle of Toulon[2] while we prepare for further victories in the cause of freedom.

The defenders of the Republic must adopt Caesar's maxim, for they believe that *nothing has been done as long as anything remains to be done.* Enough dangers still face us to engage all our efforts.

It has not fully extended the valor of our Republican soldiers to conquer a few Englishmen and a few traitors. A task no less important, and one more difficult, now awaits us: to sustain an energy sufficient to defeat the constant intrigues of all the enemies of our freedom and to bring to a triumphant realization the principles that must be the cornerstone of the public welfare.

Such are the first duties that you have imposed on your Committee of Public Safety.

We shall first outline the principles and the needs underlying the creation of a revolutionary government; next we shall expound the cause that threatens to throttle it at birth.

The theory of revolutionary government is as new as the Revolution that created it. It is as pointless to seek its origins in the books of the political theorists, who failed to foresee this revolution, as in the laws of the tyrants, who are happy enough to abuse their exercise of authority without seeking out its legal justification. And so this phrase is for the

---

[1] *Rapport sur les principes du Gouvernement révolutionnaire fait au nom du Comité de Salut public par Maximilien Robespierre* (Paris, December 1793); trans. G. Rudé.

[2] Surrendered to the British on August 29 and recovered by the French on December 19, 1793.

aristocracy a mere subject of terror or a term of slander, for tyrants an outrage and for many an enigma. It behooves us to explain it to all in order that we may rally good citizens, at least, in support of the principles governing the public interest.

It is the function of government to guide the moral and physical energies of the nation toward the purposes for which it was established.

The object of constitutional government is to preserve the Republic; the object of revolutionary government is to establish it.

Revolution is the war waged by liberty against its enemies; a constitution is that which crowns the edifice of freedom once victory has been won and the nation is at peace.

The revolutionary government has to summon extraordinary activity to its aid precisely because it is at war. It is subjected to less binding and less uniform regulations, because the circumstances in which it finds itself are tempestuous and shifting, above all because it is compelled to deploy, swiftly and incessantly, new resources to meet new and pressing dangers.

The principal concern of constitutional government is civil liberty; that of revolutionary government, public liberty. Under a constitutional government little more is required than to protect the individual against abuses by the state, whereas revolutionary government is obliged to defend the state itself against the factions that assail it from every quarter.

To good citizens revolutionary government owes the full protection of the state; to the enemies of the people it owes only death.

These ideas are in themselves sufficient to explain the origin and the nature of the laws that we term revolutionary. Those who call them arbitrary or tyrannical are foolish or perverse sophists who seek to reconcile white with black and black with white: they prescribe the same system for peace and war, for health and sickness; or rather their only object is to resurrect tyranny and to destroy the fatherland. When they invoke the literal application of constitutional principles, it is only to violate them with impunity. They are cowardly assassins who, in order to strangle the Republic in its infancy without danger to themselves, try to throttle it with vague maxims which they have no intention of observing.

The ship of the constitution was certainly not built to remain on the ways forever; but should we launch it at the moment when the storm is at its height and the winds are driving most furiously against us? This was the demand of the tyrants and the slaves who, in the first place, resisted its construction; but the people of France has commanded you to wait till the calm returns. Its unanimious wish and its command, drowning the clamor of aristocrats and federalists,[3] is that you first deliver it from all its enemies.

The temples of the gods were not created to serve as a refuge for the sacrilegious to profane, nor was the constitution designed as a cover for the conspiracies of the tyrants who seek to destroy it.

Is a revolutionary government the less just and the less legitimate because it must be more vigorous in its actions and freer in its movements than an ordinary government? No! for it rests on the most sacred of all laws, the safety of the people, and on necessity, which is the most indisputable of all rights.

It also has its rules, all based on justice and on public order. It has nothing in common with anarchy or disorder; on the contrary, its purpose is to repress them and to establish and consolidate the rule of law. It has nothing in common with arbitrary rule; it is public interest that governs it and not the whims of private individuals.

It must adopt the general principles of ordinary government whenever these can be rigorously applied without endangering public liberty. But its force to repress must be commensurate with the audacity or treachery of those who conspire against it. The greater its terrors for the wicked, the greater must be its favors for the good. The more it is compelled by circumstance to act with necessary rigor, the more it must refrain from measures that needlessly interfere with freedom and offend private interests without any advantage to the public.

It must sail between the twin reefs of weakness and temerity, of moderatism and exaggeration: moderatism which is to moderation as impotence is to chastity, and exaggeration whose resemblance to energy is like that of dropsy to good health.

The tyrants have constantly tried to drive us back to servitude by the path of moderatism; but sometimes they have sought to throw us into the opposite extremity. The two extremes lead to the same point along the line. Whether one overshoots or undershoots the mark, the goal is missed. No one is as akin to the advocate of federalism as the *untimely* preacher of the one universal Republic. The friend of kings and the "attorney general of the human race" [4] have much in common, as have the religious fanatic and the fanatical preacher of atheism. Barons masquerading as democrats are the brothers of the marquesses of Co-

---

[3] Advocates of a decentralized, or federal, republic.
[4] A reference to the ex-Prussian Baron, "Anarcharsis" Cloots, usually styled "the orator of the human race."

blenz;[5] and red caps are sometimes closer to red heels[6] than one would imagine.

But it is here that the government needs to display the greatest circumspection, for every enemy of liberty is waiting for the opportunity to use against it not only its mistakes, but its wisest measures. If it strikes at what is called exaggeration, they try to revive moderatism and aristocracy. If it turns against these two monsters, they fling themselves into the other extreme, exaggeration. It is dangerous to allow them the means to lead good men astray, yet it is even more dangerous to discourage and persecute the good citizens they have misled. We have to avoid the two abuses, for by one the Republic would be threatened with death from internal dislocation, and by the other it would inevitably perish from a failure to adopt energetic measures . . .

If we have to choose between an excess of patriotic zeal and the empty shell of bad citizenship, or the morass of moderatism, we will not hesitate. A vigorous body suffering from an overabundance of sap is a richer source of strength than a corpse.

Let us above all be careful not to kill patriotism in our efforts to heal it.

Patriotism is by its very nature ardent. Who can love his country without warmth? Most patriots are simple men who are not easily capable of estimating, from its underlying motives, the political consequences of a public act. Where is the patriot, however enlightened, who has never been mistaken? And if we allow that there are well-intentioned moderates and cowards, why should there not be well-intentioned patriots whose laudable feelings sometimes carry them too far? If, then, we were to regard as criminal all those in the revolutionary movement who crossed the narrow line traced by prudence, we should envelop in a common proscription bad citizens with all the natural friends of freedom, your own friends and all the staunchest upholders of the Republic. And so the artful emissaries of tyranny, having first deceived them, would become their accusers and perhaps even their judges.

Who then shall unravel all these subtle combinations? Who shall trace the exact dividing line that marks off one form of extremism from its opposite? It can be done only by a love of country and a love of truth. Kings and knaves will always try to destroy this love, for they shun reason and truth like the plague.

In outlining the duties of a revolutionary government we have shown

---

[5] The center of Prince Louis de Conde's *émigré* army in Germany.
[6] Courtiers.

you the pitfalls that lie in its path. The greater its authority and the freer and swifter its means of action, the more it must be governed by good faith. The day that it falls into the hands of impure or treacherous men will see the end of liberty. Its name will become the pretext and the excuse for counterrevolution and the power of its appeal will be abused as a deadly poison.

It is the policy of the Convention, therefore, rather than the institution itself that has won the confidence of the people of France. In placing its full authority within your hands, it expects from you that your rule shall be as great a boon to patriots as it shall be a terror to the nation's enemies. It has imposed on you the duty to display all the courage and to devise all the measures required to crush them and, above all, to maintain among yourselves that unity without which your great destiny cannot be fulfilled.

The task of firmly establishing the French Republic is not a child's game. It cannot be the work of indifference or idle fancy, nor can it be the chance outcome of the impact of all the rival claims of individuals or of all the revolutionary interests and groups. It took wisdom as well as power to create the universe. By handing over to men drawn from your own ranks the formidable task of continuously watching over the destinies of France, you have assumed the obligation of lending them the full support of your confidence and strength. If the revolutionary government is not sustained by the energy, intelligence, patriotism and good will of all the people's representatives, how will it summon up the strength to meet and defeat that arrayed against it by Europe's invading armies and by all the enemies of liberty who are pressing in on every side?

Woe unto us if we open our minds to the treacherous insinuations of our enemies, whose only hope of victory lies in our division. Woe unto us if we break the bond of union instead of knitting it more closely and if we allow private interest or injured vanity to guide us rather than fatherland and truth!

Let us emulate the Republican virtues and the example of the men of ancient times. Themistocles was a greater genius than the Spartan general who commanded the Greek fleet; yet when the latter, in reply to a wise counsel that would later save the country, raised his stick to strike him, Themistocles merely replied, "Strike, but listen too." And Greece triumphed over the Asian tyrant. Among Roman generals there was none better than Scipio; yet, after conquering Hannibal and Carthage, he accounted it an honor to serve under his old enemy's command. O virtue of noble hearts! compared with you how mean do all these squabbles born of pride and the ambitions of petty men appear! O virtue! are you not needed as much to found a Republic as to govern it in times of peace? O fatherland, have you any less claim on the representatives of the people of France than Greece and Rome had on their generals? Indeed, I would say that if ever the task of revolutionary government becomes for us not a painful obligation, but an object of ambition, the Republic will be lost.

We must assure that the authority of the National Convention shall be respected by the whole of Europe, for today the tyrants are drawing on every political resource and squandering all their treasure to degrade its authority and stamp it out. Let the Convention adopt a firm resolution declaring its preference for its own government over that of the cabinet of London and the European courts; for if the Convention refuses to rule, the tyrants will govern in its place.

And let us not be blind to the advantages that the tyrants enjoy in the war of deceit and corruption that they are waging against the Republic! Every vice is enlisted in their service; the Republic has only virtue on its side. Virtue is simple, modest, humble, often ignorant and sometimes boorish; it is the natural lot of the poor, the patrimony of the people. Vice is surrounded by wealth, armed with every device to lure the voluptuary and ensnare the weak; it is attended by all the sinister talents that have been trained in the service of crime. With what subtle skill the tyrants use against us not only our passions and our weaknesses, but even our love of fatherland! How swiftly the seeds of division which they sow among us may grow unless we choke them from the start.

Thanks to five years of treason and tyranny, thanks to our credulity and lack of foresight and to the pusillanimity that followed too brief an exercise of vigor, Austria and England, Russia, Prussia and Italy have had time to set up in our country a secret government to challenge the authority of our own. They have also their committees, their treasury and their undercover agents. This government assumes whatever strength we deny to ours; it has the unity which ours has lacked, the policies that we have been too often willing to forego, the sense of continuity and concert whose need we have too often failed to appreciate.

Thus the courts of Europe have been able to spew over France all the artful rogues enlisted in their service. Their agents still infect our armies: even our victory at Toulon is the proof of it, for it took all the valor of our soldiers, the loyalty of our generals and the heroism of our people's representatives to triumph over treason. They deliberate within our organs of administration and within the meetings of our Sections; they enter our revolutionary clubs and have even held seats in the sanctuary of Parliament itself; and they direct, and will continue to direct, the counterrevolution by these and similar means.

They roam about us, they steal our secrets, they seek to inspire our very opinions, they turn our own resolutions against us. Be prudent, and they will accuse you of weakness; they call your courage folly and your justice cruelty. Humor them, and they will conspire in the open; threaten them, and they will conspire in secret, assuming the mask of patriotism. Yesterday they were assassinating the defenders of liberty; today they attend their funerals demanding that they be honored like gods, while awaiting the opportunity to cut the throats of others like them. To stoke up civil war they preach all the follies of religious superstition. But once, after the copious effusion of French blood, the civil war is about to end, they call on their priesthood and their gods to kindle its flames anew.

We have seen Englishmen and Prussians traveling through our towns and villages, spreading senseless doctrines in the name of the National Convention. We have seen unfrocked priests at the head of seditious demonstrations, in which religion served merely as a motive or a pretext. There have been patriots assassinated after being drawn into foolhardy ventures by their hatred of fanaticism; in several of our provinces blood has been spilled as the result of these wretched quarrels, as though we had blood enough to spare from our fight with the European tyrants. O shame! O weakness of the human intellect! A great nation has become the toy of the most contemptible slaves of tyranny.

For some time past, our public order has been dependent on the whim of foreigners. It was at their behest that money flowed or disappeared from circulation. It was when they wished it that the people found bread or were compelled to do without it; and crowds gathered at bakers' shops or dispersed at their beck and call. They surround us with their spies and hired assassins. We know it and see it happen; yet they continue to live in our midst, and the sword of justice eludes them. It is harder, even today, to punish a highly placed conspirator than to save a friend of liberty from slander.

Hardly had we denounced the excesses, committed in the name of revolution yet provoked by France's enemies; hardly had the term "ultra-revolutionary" been used by patriots in the Assembly to describe them; when the traitors of Lyons and all the satellites of tyranny hastened to apply it to the brave and zealous patriots who had taken arms to avenge the people and uphold the laws. On the one hand, they renew the old methods of persecuting the friends of the Republic; on the other, they demand indulgence for the rascals stained with the blood of their countrymen.

Meanwhile their crimes accumulate; their agents are recruiting their impious cohorts every day; France is flooded with them. They wait, and will go on waiting, for a moment favorable to their sinister designs. They entrench themselves, they settle in our midst; they raise new earthworks, new batteries of counterrevolution, while their paymasters, the tyrants, put new armies in the field.

Yes, these perfidious emissaries that speak to us and flatter us are the brothers and accomplices of the savage satellites who have taken over French ships and cities sold to their masters, who have massacred our brothers, our wives and children, and the nation's representatives. Yet the monsters who have committed these crimes are a thousand times less detestable than the wretches who secretly devour our entrails; and yet they still live and conspire against us with impunity.

All they need in order to rally is leaders, and they hope to find them within this Assembly. Their principal purpose is to set us at each other's throats. Such a disastrous struggle would raise the hopes of the aristocracy and revive the federalist conspiracy; it would revenge the Girondin faction for the law that punished their crimes; it would punish the Mountain for its exemplary devotion, for it is the Mountain—or rather it is the Convention—that is being attacked by dividing it and destroying its work.

As for us, we shall make war only on the English, the Prussians, the Austrians and their accomplices. It is only by exterminating them that we shall reply to their slanders. We hate no one but the enemies of our country. We shall strike terror, not in the hearts of patriots or of the weak and humble, but in the haunts of the foreign brigands, where they divide out the spoils and drink the blood of the people of France.

The Committee has observed that the law does not act swiftly enough to punish the principal culprits. Foreigners, known agents of the royal coalition, and generals stained with the blood of Frenchmen and old accomplices of Dumouriez, Custine and La Marlière,[7] have long been under arrest but have not yet been brought to justice. The conspirators can be numbered in thousands; they seem to multiply, and yet examples of such judgments are few and far between. The punishment of a hundred obscure and unimportant culprits is of less value to the cause of freedom than the execution of a single chief conspirator.

The members of the Revolutionary Tribunal, whose patriotism and sense of justice are generally beyond reproach, have themselves outlined

[7] Revolutionary generals convicted of treason in the spring and summer of 1793.

to the Committee of Public Safety the causes that impede its conduct without making justice the more sure; and they have asked us to reform a law that bears the stamp of the unhappy days in which it was enacted. So we propose to you to authorize the Committee to lay before you certain changes to the law that will have the effect of making the course of justice more merciful to the innocent while making it more inexorable to conspirators and criminals. You have, in fact, already referred this matter to us by an earlier decree.

Even now, we propose that you should speed the judgment of foreigners and of generals who have been charged with conspiring with the tyrants that make war on us.

But it is not sufficient to affright the enemies of France; we must succor her defenders. We shall therefore beg of you that in your justice you will show some favors to the soldiers who fight and suffer for our freedom.

The French army is not only an object of terror to the tyrants; it is also the glory of our country and of humanity at large. As they march to victory or as they fall before the bullets of the enemy, our noble warriors cry, "Long live the Republic!" Their last words are hymns to liberty, their last prayers are for their country's safety. If all the generals had been worthy of their soldiers, Europe's armies would long since have been defeated. Any charitable act towards the army will be an act of national gratitude.

We have long thought the benefits given to the soldiers and their families too modest. We believe that there should be no objection to their being raised by one third. The immense financial resources of the Republic permit this measure; the country demands it.

We believe, too, that disabled soldiers and the widows and children of those who have died for France have met with obstacles—either in the formalities that the law demands, or from the multiplicity of applications, or in the coldness or ill will displayed by junior officials—that have delayed their enjoyment of the benefits to which they are entitled by law. We thought that the best way to remedy this abuse would be to provide them with official counsel, appointed by law, in order to make it easier for them to assert their rights.

With these aims in view, we propose the following decree:

The National Convention decrees:

Article I. The public prosecutor of the Revolutionary Tribunal shall immediately bring to trial Dietrich, Custine [the son of the general already sentenced], Desbrullis, Biron, Barthélemy, and all the generals and officers charged with complicity in the affairs of Dumouriez, Custine,

La Marlière and Houchard.[8] . . . He shall also bring to trial the foreigners, bankers and other persons charged with treason and connivance with the kings who have combined against the Republic.

Article II. The Committee of Public Safety shall, without delay, present its report on the means proposed to improve the organization of the Revolutionary Tribunal.

Article III. The benefits and rewards granted by earlier decrees to the defenders of the country wounded in its defense, or to their widows or children, are increased by one third.

Article IV. There shall be established a commission with the task of assuring to them the enjoyment of the rights provided by the law.

Article V. The members of the commission shall be proposed by the Committee of Public Safety and appointed by the National Convention.

Note. The proposed decree has been adopted by the National Convention.

[8] Revolutionary generals and officers charged with or suspected of treason in 1792-3.

7

On the Cult of the Supreme Being (May 7, 1794)[1]

The early months of Jacobin rule had been attended by attacks on priests, the wholesale closure of churches, and the enthronement of the Goddess of Reason in the Cathedral of Notre Dame. This "de-christianization" movement had been largely inspired and directed by Hébert and his associates in Paris and the generals of the armées révolutionnaires[2] in the Departments. Its excesses alarmed Robespierre, both because he abhorred "atheism" and believed in the "immortality of the soul" and because he feared that it would cost the Revolution support among the peasants. He condemned the movement in a speech made to the Jacobins on November 21, 1793, and on December 8 the Assembly reaffirmed the principle of freedom of worship.[3] Early the following year, it went on to debate Robespierre's proposal for a new civic religion, based on Rousseau's teaching—the Cult of the Supreme Being—that was intended to appeal to all religious-minded revolutionaries, whether professedly Christian or not.

In this speech, Robespierre outlines his views on the new cult. The Convention adopted his plan, and on June 8 Robespierre, as President of the Convention, headed the procession at the inaugural ceremony that introduced it. His demeanor on this occasion won him many enemies, particularly among "de-christianizers" and Voltairian deists, and the incident added to the number of his enemies in Thermidor.

---

[1] *Speech* from A. Mathiez, *The Fall of Robespierre and Other Essays* (London: Williams and Norgate, 1927), pp. 96-105; reprinted by permission of Ernest Benn Ltd., London. *Decree* from J. M. Thompson, *Robespierre* (Oxford: Basil Blackwell, 1939), pp. 494-6; reprinted by permission of Basil Blackwell, Oxford.

See also, Albert Mathiez on Robespierre and religion on page 141.

[2] Citizen armies recruited in Paris and other cities mainly for the purpose of ensuring an adequate supply of grain to the armies and urban population, but also active in "de-christianizing" the countryside.

[3] Limited to attendance at services conducted by the "constitutional" clergy, i.e., those who had, since November 1790, publicly sworn support for the Civil Constitution of the Clergy of that year.

The world has changed, and is bound to change again. What is there in common between that which is and that which was? Civilized nations have taken the place of savages wandering in the desert; fruitful crops have taken the place of the ancient forests that covered the globe. A world has appeared beyond the limits of the world; the inhabitants of the earth have added the seas to their immeasurable domain; man has conquered the lightning and averted the thunderbolts of heaven. Compare the imperfect language of hieroglyphics with the miracles of printing; set the voyage of the Argonauts beside that of La Pérouse; measure the distance between the astronomical observations of the wise men of Asia and the discoveries of Newton, or between the sketch drawn by the hand of Dibutade and the pictures of David. . . .

All has changed in the physical order; all must change in the moral and political order. One half of the world revolution is already achieved, the other half has yet to be accomplished. . . .

The French people appear to have outstripped the rest of the human race by two thousand years; one might even be tempted to regard them as a distinct species among the rest. Europe is kneeling to the shadows of the tyrants whom we are punishing.

In Europe a ploughman or an artisan is an animal trained to do the pleasure of a noble; in France the nobles seek to transform themselves into ploughmen and artisans, and cannot even obtain this honour.

Europe cannot conceive of life without kings and nobles; and we cannot conceive of it with them.

Europe is lavishing her blood to rivet the fetters on humanity; and we to break them.

Our sublime neighbours discourse gravely to the universe of the King's health, amusements and travels; they insist upon informing posterity of the time at which he dined, the moment at which he returned from hunting, the happy soil which had the honour of being trodden by his august feet at each hour of the day, the names of the privileged slaves who appeared in his presence at the rising and the setting sun.

As for us, we shall make known to it the names and virtues of the heroes who died in the fight for liberty; we shall make known to it on what soil the last satellites of tyrants hit the dust; we shall make known to it the hour which sounded the death-knell of the oppressors of the world.

Yes, this delightful land which we inhabit, which Nature favours with her caresses, is made to be the domain of liberty and happiness; this proud and sensitive people is truly born for glory and virtue. O my country, had fate caused me to be born in a foreign and distant land, I should have addressed to heaven my constant prayers for thy prosperity; I should have shed tears of emotion at the story of thy combats and thy virtues; my eager soul would have followed with ardent anxiety every movement of thy glorious Revolution; I should have envied the lot of thy citizens, I should have envied that of thy representatives. . . . O sublime nation! Receive the sacrifice of all my being; happy is he who is born in thy midst! Still happier he who can die for thy happiness! . . .

The sole foundation of civil society is morality! . . . Immorality is the basis of despotism, as virtue is the essence of the Republic. . . .

Study the good of the country and the interests of humanity alone. Every institution, every doctrine which consoles and elevates men's souls ought to be welcomed; reject all those which tend to degrade and corrupt them. Encourage and exalt all generous sentiments and great moral ideas which men have attempted to extinguish; draw together by the charm of friendship and the bonds of virtue those men whom there have been attempts to divide. . . .

You who lament a virtuous friend, you love to think that what is finest in him has escaped death! You who weep over the bier of a son or a wife, are you consoled by him who tells you that all that remains of them is base dust? Wretch expiring beneath the assassin's blow, your last sigh is an appeal to eternal justice! Innocence on the scaffold makes the tyrant turn pale upon his triumphal chariot: would it have this power if the tomb levelled the oppressor with the oppressed? Wretched sophist! By what right dost thou come and wrest the sceptre of reason from innocence to place it in the hands of crime, to encourage vice, to sadden virtue and to degrade humanity? The more richly a man is endowed with sensibility and genius, the more attached he is to the ideas which expand his being and elevate his heart; and the doctrine of men of that stamp becomes that of the universe. Ah! Can such ideas be other than truths? At any rate I cannot conceive how nature can have suggested to men fictions more beneficial than all realities; and if the existence of God, if the immortality of the soul were but dreams, they would still be the finest of all the conceptions of human intelligence.

I need hardly say that there is no question here of arraigning any particular philosophical opinions, or of denying that this or that philosopher may be virtuous, whatever his opinions may be, and even in spite of them, by virtue of a fortunate disposition or a superior intelligence. The point is to consider nothing but Atheism, in so far as it is national in character and bound up with a system of conspiracy against the Republic.

Ah! What does it matter to you, legislators, by what varied hypotheses certain philosophers explain the phenomena of nature? You may hand over all these subjects to their everlasting discussions: it is neither as metaphysicians nor as theologians that you have to consider them. In the eyes of the legislator, truth is all that is useful and of practical good to the world. . . .

Fanatics, hope for nothing from us. To recall men to the pure cult of the Supreme Being is to strike a death-blow at fanaticism. All fictions disappear before the truth, and all follies collapse before Reason. Without compulsion, without persecution, all sects must mingle spontaneously in the universal religion of Nature. We shall counsel you, then, to maintain the principles which you have hitherto displayed. May the liberty of worship be respected, that reason may triumph indeed, but let it not disturb public order or become a means of conspiracy. If counter-revolutionary malignity is shielding itself beneath this pretext, repress it, and, for the rest, rely upon the might of principle and the innate force of things. . . .

Ambitious priests, do not wait for us to work for the restoration of your dominance; such an enterprise would indeed be beyond our power. It is you who have killed yourselves, and one can no more return to moral life than to physical existence. Besides, what is there in common between the priests and God? Priests are to morality what charlatans are to medicine. How different is the God of nature from the God of the priests! The God of nature knows nothing which resembles Atheism so much as priest-made religions. By dint of distorting the Supreme Being, they have destroyed Him, as much as in them lay; they have made of Him sometimes a ball of fire, sometimes an ox, sometimes a tree, sometimes a man, sometimes a king. The priests have created God in their own image; they have made Him jealous, capricious, greedy, cruel and implacable. They have treated Him as the Mayors of the Palace in olden days treated the descendant of Clovis, in order to reign in his name and put themselves in his place. They have relegated Him to heaven as to a palace, and have only brought Him down to earth in order to demand tithes, riches, honours, pleasure and power for their own profit. The real priest of the Supreme Being is Nature; His temple, the universe; His worship, virtue; His festivals, the joy of a great people gathered together beneath His eyes in order to draw close the sweet bonds of universal brotherhood and offer Him the homage of pure and feeling hearts. . . .

May they all tend to arouse those generous sentiments which are the charm and adornment of human life: enthusiasm for liberty, love of country and respect for law. May the memory of tyrants and traitors be held up to execration at them; may that of heroes of liberty and benefactors of humanity receive the just tribute of public gratitude; may they draw their interest, and their very names, from the immortal events of our Revolution, and even from the things dearest and most sacred to the heart of man; may they be beautified and distinguished by emblems suggesting their special objects. Let us invite nature and all the virtues to our festivals; let them all be celebrated under the auspices of the Supreme Being; let them be consecrated to Him, and let them open and close with a tribute to His power and goodness. . . . [He went on to propose the following decree:]

Article I. The French people recognizes the existence of the Supreme Being, and the immortality of the soul.

Article II. It recognizes that the best way of worshipping the Supreme Being is to do one's duties as a man.

Article III. It considers that the most important of these duties are: to detest bad faith and despotism, to punish tyrants and traitors, to assist the unfortunate, to respect the weak, to defend the oppressed, to do all the good one can to one's neighbour, and to behave with justice towards all men.

Article IV. Festivals shall be instituted to remind men of the Deity, and of the dignity of their state.

Article V. These festivals shall be named after the glorious events of our Revolution, the virtues which are most dear to men, and most useful, and the chief blessings of nature.

Article VI. The French Republic shall celebrate every year the anniversaries of July 14, 1789, August 10, 1792, January 21, 1793, and May 31, 1793.[4]

Article VII. It shall celebrate, on successive *décadis,* the following festivals: the Supreme Being, and Nature; the human race; the French people; the benefactors of mankind; the martyrs of freedom; liberty and equality; the Republic; the liberty of the world; patriotism; hatred of tyrants and traitors; truth; justice; modesty; glory and immortality; friendship; temperance; courage; good faith; heroism; impartiality; Stoicism; love; conjugal fidelity; fatherly affection; mother-love; filial piety; childhood; youth; manhood; old age; misfortune; agriculture; industry; our ancestors; posterity; happiness.

Article VIII. The Committees of Public Safety and of Education are instructed to present a scheme for the organization of these festivals.

Article IX. The National Convention invites all those whose talents

---

[4] These dates commemorate respectively the fall of the Bastille, the fall of the Monarchy, the execution of Louis XVI, and the expulsion of the Girondin deputies.

are worthy of serving the cause of mankind to the honour of assisting in the establishment of these festivals by submitting hymns or civic songs, or anything else likely to contribute to their beauty or utility.

Article X. The Committee of Public Safety shall award distinction to such works as appear to it calculated to achieve these objects, and shall reward their authors.

Article XI. Freedom of worship is confirmed, in the terms of the decree of 18th Frimaire.[5]

Article XII. Any meeting of aristocrats, or any that contravenes public order, shall be suppressed.

Article XIII. In the event of troubles caused by or arising out of any form of public worship, all those who excited them by fanatical preaching or counter-revolutionary suggestions, and all those who provoked them by unjust or uncalled-for acts of violence, shall be equally punished, with all the rigour of the law.

Article XIV. A separate report shall be prepared, dealing with the detailed arrangements consequential upon the present decree.

Article XV. There shall be celebrated, upon the 20th Prairial next,[6] a national festival in honour of the Supreme Being.

[5] December 8, 1793.
[6] June 8, 1794.

8
Last Speech to the Convention (July 26, 1794)[1]

Robespierre made this speech to the Convention on 8th Thermidor (July 26, 1794) in a final attempt to justify his own conduct and to rally support against his opponents within the Committees of Public Safety and General Security. But the threats that he made against persons unnamed alarmed many of his listeners, and he was heard in silence. The same speech, read in the Jacobins that night, received an ovation. But he had lost his hold on the Convention; the next day he was refused a hearing and placed under arrest. He was sent to the guillotine the following morning.

Citizens, let others draw flattering pictures for you; I am here to tell you wholesome truths. I have not come to play on ridiculous fears, spread by treachery. I want to put out, if I can, the truth of discord by the force of truth alone. . . .

Here I need to open my heart, and you need to hear the truth. . . . I have come here to dispel, if I can, cruel errors. I have come here to stifle the horrible oaths of discord with which certain men want to fill this temple of liberty and the entire Republic. I am here to unmask the abuses which are bringing about the ruin of the *patrie* and which your incorruptibility alone can restrain. . . .

What is the foundation of this odious system of terror and slander? To whom must we show ourselves terrible, the enemies or the friends of the Republic? Is it tyrants and rascals who have to fear us, or men of good will and patriots? Do we strike terror into patriots—we who have rescued them from the clutches of all the factions arrayed against them? . . . Do we strike terror into the National Convention? And what are we, without the Convention? Who have defended the Convention at the peril of their lives? Who have devoted themselves to its preservation while detestable factions plot its ruin for all France to see? . . . For whom were the first blows of the conspirators' daggers intended? . . .

[1] From H. Morse Stephens, *op. cit.*, II, 143-63; trans. W. J. Gardner, to whom the Editor's thanks are due.

It is we whom they seek to assassinate; it is we whom they call the scourge of France. And what are the terrible acts of cruelty with which they reproach us? Who have been the victims? Hébert, Ronsin, Chabot, Danton, Lacroix, Fabre d'Eglantine,[2] and some of their accomplices. Are we reproached for their punishment? No one would have to defend them. But if all we have done is to denounce monsters whose death has saved the National Convention and the Republic, who can fear our principles? Who can arouse us in advance of injustice and tyranny except those who resemble these men? No, we have not been too severe. . . . They speak of our severity, yet France reproaches us with weakness.

You know the methods of your enemies. They attacked the Convention itself. That plan failed. Some time ago they declared war on certain members of the Committee of Public Safety. Finally, they seemed to aim only at destroying one man. . . .

It is true that certain men have hawked round lists containing the names of a number of intended victims in the Convention, lists which it was claimed were the work of the Committee of Public Safety, and indeed of myself alone. . . . What are the authors of these intrigues after? . . . If they accuse us of having denounced traitors, then let them accuse also the Convention that accused the traitors. . . . And what have I done to deserve their persecutions if they were not part of their general plan of conspiracy against the National Convention? . . . And when they attempt to give to one feeble individual a gigantic and ridiculous importance, what can their aim be but to divide you, to swallow you up, even while denying your existence, like the infidel who denies the existence of the God whom he fears?

Such, then, is the basis of these schemes of dictatorship and of the plots against the National Convention, which are in the first instance imputed to the Committee of Public Safety in general. By what fatal chance has this terrible charge been suddenly directed at one alone of its members? What a ghastly scheme for a man to conceive: to drive the members of the National Convention to cut their own throats in order to pave his road to absolute power! Others may see the ridiculous side of these charges. I can only find them horrifying. . . .

As for the National Convention, my first duty, as it is my first desire, is to pay them unbounded respect. . . . I say that every representative of the people, whose heart is pure, must take up again the confidence and the dignity which rightly belongs to him. I know only two parties, the party of good citizens and the party of the bad. Patriotism is not an affair of party, but an affair of the heart. . . . I see a world peopled

[2] Executed in March and April 1794.

with dupes and impostors, but the number of the impostors is the smaller. It is they who must be punished for the wrongs and the ills of the world.

I do not impute the crimes of Brissot and the Gironde to the men of good faith whom they sometimes deceived, nor to those who believed Danton the crimes of this conspirator; nor do I impute those of Hébert to those citizens whose sincere patriotism was sometimes enticed over the strict limits of reason . . . there are certain signs by which dupes can be distinguished from criminals, and errors from crimes. What is it that can make this distinction? Good sense and justice! . . .

. . . *Virtue?* It is a natural passion, without doubt . . . but it exists, this tender, imperious, irresistible passion, the torment and the delight of magnanimous souls; this profound horror of tyranny, this compassionate zeal for the oppressed. It exists, this generous ambition to found on earth the first Republic of the world; this self-assertion of free men who find a pure pleasure in the calm of a clear conscience and in the delectable vision of public happiness. You feel it now burning in your souls, just as I feel it in mine. . . .

They call me a tyrant . . . One arrives at a tyrant's throne by the help of scoundrels . . . What faction do I belong to? You yourselves. What is that faction which, since the Revolution began, has crushed the factions and swept away hireling traitors? It is you, it is the people, it is the principles of the Revolution. . . .

It is now that I must sound forth the truth and lay bare the real wounds of the Republic. Public affairs are again taking a treacherous and alarming turn. The combined system of the Héberts and the Fabres d'Eglantine is pursued again with an unheard of audacity. The counter-revolutionaries are protected. Those who dishonour the Revolution with the rites of Hébertism do it openly, the others with more reserve. . . . I shall not investigate the causes of these abuses, but I will show you just one . . . it exists in the excessive perversity of subordinate officials of a respected authority drawn from your midst. There are in the Committee men whose civic virtues it is impossible not to love and respect. That is all the more reason to destroy an abuse which is going on behind their backs and which they will be the first to fight. . . . The arms of liberty must not be touched except by pure hands. Let us purify the national system of surveillance [vigilance], instead of covering up vice. . . .

When the victims of the perversity of [these men] complain to them, they say: "It is Robespierre who wants it, and we can't get rid of him. . . ." They were particularly anxious to prove that the Revolutionary

Tribunal was a *tribunal of blood,* created by me alone and which I dominate absolutely for the purpose of beheading all men of good will. . . . This was not all. Recently, certain financial proposals were made which appeared to me calculated to impoverish citizens of small means and to multiply the discontented. I have often called the attention of the Committee of Public Safety to this matter, but in vain. . . .

What then? Ah! I dare not name [these men] here and now. I cannot bring myself to tear away entirely the veil which covers this profound mystery of crimes. This I do affirm positively: that among the authors of this plot are the agents of that system of corruption and extravagance [Pitt's alleged spy system], the most powerful of all the means invented by foreigners to destroy the Republic, and also the impure apostles of atheism and immortality. . . .

They are giving the revolutionary government a hateful name in order to destroy it. . . . If we succeeded, say the conspirators, it would be necessary to have recourse to extreme indulgence in order to make a complete break with the present state of affairs. That word "indulgence" sums up the whole of the conspiracy. What were the crimes imputed to Danton, to Fabre, and to Desmoulins? To preach mercy for the enemies of France and to conspire to gain for them an amnesty which would have been fatal to liberty. . . .

How atrocious is their end! How contemptible are their means! Judge them by a single instance. I was temporarily in charge, in the absence of one of my colleagues, of a bureau of general police recently and feebly organized by the Committee of Public Safety. My short administration was limited to authorizing about 30 arrests . . . Would you believe it, those two words *general police* were used as a pretext to heap on my head the responsibility for all the activities of the Committee of General Security, all the mistakes of constituted authorities, and all the crimes of my enemies! There was hardly an individual arrested, not a citizen with a grievance to whom they did not say: "There is the cause of all your troubles. You should be happy and free if he did not exist."

. . . On the very day before the Feast of the Supreme Being, they wanted to put it off, on a foolish pretext. Since then, they have not ceased to throw ridicule on all those who hold these ideas. . . . If I must keep silent on these truths, then bring me the hemlock. My reason, not my heart, is on the point of doubting that Republic of virtue whose outlines I have traced for myself. . . . What friend of the *patrie* would wish to survive the moment when it is no longer permitted to serve France and defend oppressed innocence? Why live in a society where intrigue always triumphs over truth, where justice is a lie . . . ?

. . . Counterrevolution is in the administration of finance . . . Counterrevolution is in all parts of the economic system. . . .

They will provoke violent debates in the National Convention. The traitors, hidden even here under false exteriors, will throw off the mask. The conspirators will accuse their accusers and multiply all the stratagems formerly used by Brissot to stifle the voice of truth. . . .

Such is part of the plan of conspiracy. To whom must we impute these evils? To ourselves, to our cowardly weakness in the face of crime. Let us not be deceived. To found a great Republic on the rock of reason and equality is not an enterprise lightly brought to a successful conclusion. It is the masterpiece of virtue and human reason. All factions thrive in the bosom of a great revolution. How can they be crushed unless you constantly submit all passions to justice? . . .

Shall we say that all goes well? . . . Shall we reveal hidden abuses? Shall we denounce the traitors? They will say that we are overthrowing constituted authorities, that we want to acquire personal power at their expense. What shall we do then? Our duty. How can one reproach that man who wishes to tell the truth and who is willing to die for it? Let us say that a conspiracy against public liberty exists; that it owes its strength to a criminal coalition intriguing within the very walls of the Convention; that this coalition has accomplices in the Committee of General Security and in the *bureaux* of that Committee, which it dominates; that certain members of the Committee of Public Safety have taken part in this plot. . . . What is the remedy of this evil? To punish the traitors, make a clean sweep of the *bureaux* of the Committee of General Security, purge the Committee itself and subordinate it to the Committee of Public Safety; purge the Committee of Public Safety itself, constitute a unified government under the authority of the National Convention, which is the heart and the judge of all, and thus to crush all the factions with the weight of the national authority, to raise on their ruins the power of justice and liberty: such are the principles we must follow. If it is impossible to insist on them without being branded as ambitious, I will conclude that principles are proscribed, that tyranny reigns among us, but not that I must keep silence. How can one reproach a man who has truth on his side and who knows how to die for his country?

I was made to combat crime, not to control it. The time has not yet come when men of good will can serve their country unmolested. The defenders of liberty will be so many names for the proscription lists as long as the horde of rascals is in control.

THE WORLD LOOKS AT ROBESPIERRE

9

Robespierre at Home

The following three extracts illustrate some of the more personal and intimate aspects of Robespierre's life, showing how he appeared to some of his contemporaries who visited him at Maurice Duplay's, no. 366 (not 396, as the first of these accounts wrongly has it) Rue St. Honoré. All three sketches describe visits paid to him in the year 1794: the first by a young English boy, John Millingen, who was taken to see the "Incorruptible" by a French friend of his family; the second by a German traveler; and the third by Pierre-Jean Barras and Louis-Marie Fréron, two former associates with whom Robespierre's relations had recently become strained.

A YOUNG ENGLISH VISITOR (EARLY 1794) [1]

He lived in an obscure house, No. 396, in the Rue St. Honoré, at a carpenter's, of the name of Duplay, with whose family he boarded. Strange to say, I observed, over the street entrance, a wooden eagle, that looked like a figurehead of a ship. A singular coincidence in the dwelling of a man who, beyond a doubt, aimed at dictatorship. I was ushered into a large room in the *rez-de-chaussée*, at the bottom of a timber-yard, and was most kindly received by an intelligent young man with a wooden leg, whom I thought was his brother, but found to be a nephew of the landlord, and Robespierre's secretary: I read to him my memorial, but when he saw that it was in favour of an Englishman, he shook his head, and frankly told me, that I had but little prospect of succeeding in my application. He himself ushered me into Robespierre's *cabinet*. He was reading at the time, and wore a pair of green preservers [specta-

---

[1] From J. M. Thompson, *English Witnesses of the French Revolution* (Oxford: Basil Blackwell, 1938), pp. 253-5. Reprinted by permission of the publisher.

Compare the description of Robespierre, reconstructed by Thompson himself, beginning on page 164.

cles]; he raised his head, and turning up his spectacles on his forehead, received me most graciously. My introducer having stated that I was *un petit ami de Dorival Albitte—un petit Anglais, Que veux-tu? que demandes-tu?* was his brief and abrupt question. I referred him to the contents of my memorial, on which he cast a mere glance, and then said, 'If it were in my power to liberate an Englishman, until England sues for peace, I would not do it—but why come to me? Why not apply to the Comité? Every one applies to me, as if I had an omnipotent power.' Here a strange twitching convulsed the muscles of his face. At this present moment I recollect the agitation of his countenance. He then added, 'Your brother is much safer where he is. I could not answer for the life of any Englishman were he free. All our miseries are the work of Pitt and his associates; and if blood is shed, at his door will it lie. Do you know, *enfant,* that the English here set a price on my head, and on the heads of every one of my colleagues? That assassins have been bribed with English gold—and by the Duke of York—to destroy me? The innocent ought not to suffer for the guilty, otherwise every Englishman in France should be sacrificed to public vengeance.'

I was astonished. After a short pause he added, 'Do you know that the English expected that this Duke of York would have succeeded the Capets? Do you know Thomas Paine and David Williams?' he continued, looking at me with an eagle eye; 'they are both traitors and hypocrites.'

He now rose, and paced up and down his room, absorbed in thought; he then suddenly stopped, and, taking me by the hand, said *'Adieu, mon petit, ne crains rien pour ton frère.'* He then turned off abruptly, and my guide led me out.

There was something singularly strange and fantastic in this extraordinary man, at least, so it appeared to me. He smiled with an affected look of kindness; but there was something sardonic and demoniac in his countenance, and deep marks of the small-pox added to the repulsive character of his physiognomy. He appeared to me like a bird of prey— a vulture; his forehead and temples were low and flattened; his eyes were of a fawn colour, and most disagreeable to look at; his dress was careful, and I recollect that he wore a frill and ruffles, that seemed to me of valuable lace. There were flowers in various parts of the room, and several cages, with singing-birds, were hanging on the walls and near the window, opening on a small garden. There was much of the *petit-maître* in his manner and appearance, strangely contrasting with the plebeian taste of the times.

On taking my leave, his secretary told me that he was certain

Robespierre would be glad to see me, if ever I needed his assistance. I availed myself of this permission, and called upon him several times, although I only saw him once after my first introduction; indeed, it was very difficult to obtain access to his presence. On these occasions I never observed about the house those bands of ruffians by whom he was said to be guarded, although his door was crowded with wretched postulants who claimed his protection and influence.

A GERMAN VISITOR TO PARIS (MAY 1794) [2]

Today, Robespierre is a man of about forty years of age.[3] Although he is tall and slim, he does not give the appearance of having a weak physique: on the contrary, one has the impression that he is powerfully built. He has good muscles, though without much flesh to cover them. His arms and legs are straight and well rounded; he is over six feet tall and bears himself well. His face is not lined from a lack of sleep or mental fatigue. His chest is broad, and his breathing is deep and strong. As for his belly, it is not disfiguring by being either too large or too sunken. So we may say that Robespierre's physique entitles him to be considered a handsome man; nor do his face and features in any way offset this judgment.

He has a broad brow unfurrowed by any wrinkle, and beneath the dark arches of his eyebrows are eyes of a deep blue that are at once flashing, solemn and reflective and in which the flame of fanatacism is blended with an indescribably gentle expression. Between his eyebrows curves a nose of the most agreeable shape, which neither juts nor droops. His cheeks, which are not too full, have the healthy glow that becomes a man in the prime of life, and his mouth has a grace which disappears only when his lips are set in an expression of righteous indignation. Dark hair, which is generally allowed to fall freely in light curls, frames a face whose beauty and agreeable hue are enhanced by the shadow of his beard.

Robespierre dresses with scrupulous care and with a complete absence of caprice. His usual attire is a green coat, a colored jacket, dark breeches and half-boots. In summer he wears no cravat, and whenever he wears one that constrains his speech, he removes it abruptly. He always wears a round hat; lately, he has entirely abandoned the use of the red

[2] From L. Jacob, ed., *Robespierre vu par ses contemporains* (Paris: Armand Colin, 1938), pp. 145-9; trans. G. Rudé. Reproduced in English translation by permission of the Librairie Armand Colin, Paris.
[3] At this time, Robespierre was just 36.

Phrygian cap. It is only on official occasions that he dons the deputy's uniform. To conduct his business, he now always goes on foot. Formerly, he went by carriage; but one day, as is known, after he had promoted an important decree (whose nature I have forgotten), the people unharnessed the Incorruptible's horses and wished to draw his carriage to his lodging. Robespierre, however, jumped from the coach, severely scolded the citizens for their unrepublican conduct and, despite the heavy rain that was falling, finished his journey on foot. I have never seen him ride a horse, and I presume that he is afraid to do so.

His household is one of extreme simplicity; he has about him only the family of the carpenter in whose house he has lodged since his arrival in Paris.[4] On the same floor as he, and directly opposite his room, dwells a young girl. It is believed that she has intimate relations with the Incorruptible. This appears to be highly probable to persons who indulge in idle speculations on their account. Robespierre has never spoken of her, but in truth one should not attach too great an importance to this silence.

In the carpenter's family he is like the son of the house. The wife is like a mother to him and provides for all his needs. He rises at a very early hour and the first task he performs—one he adopted some years ago—is to go into his host's workshop and wish him good day. He then works for several hours without other refreshment than a glass of water; during this time no one may disturb him. Then he has his hair dressed, an operation which generally takes place in the courtyard on an open gallery leading to his bedroom. Immediately after, people throng to see him; this has been the case since he became so popular.

As for him, he pays no heed to this eagerness to see him. He reads, meanwhile, the gazette and the pamphlets of the day and takes a breakfast composed of a little wine, some bread and some fruit. If he does not read, he looks ahead of him with his eyes fixed on the ground, often resting his head on his hand and appearing to meditate on affairs of the greatest importance. After breakfast he returns to his work until his public duties call him away; he never receives visits in the morning unless his visitor takes advantage of the brief moment when his hair is being dressed. He dines at his host's table, and it is always he who recites the prayer before the meal. When once the lady of the house suggested that her fare might no longer be good enough for him, Robespierre took it very ill. He pays no more today than he did when he first came there, in order that his hosts should not take on bad

---

[4] Robespierre did not go to live at Duplay's until July 1791. Before then, he lived in the Rue Saintonge on the other side of Paris.

habits; and even during the food shortage he gave them no more, so that they might be compelled to treat him exactly as before. If he is invited out to dine, he never gives notice of his absence to his hosts, as he supposes that no particular dish is being prepared for him. Desiring, however, that the good people who shared his earlier straits should reap some advantage from his new situation, he has done much good for their children. The son, who is also a carpenter, he has set up in business, or rather he has helped him to acquire his own shop. As for their daughter, he has promised her a wedding gift provided that she marry a citizen who has fought for his country. At meals, he eats the same fare as his hosts and shares with them an inferior wine. When dinner is over, he drinks coffee, then stays in the house for an hour to receive visitors, after which he commonly goes out. Since becoming a member of the National Convention, he has taken a secretary; before, he employed an orphan child, brought up by his hosts, to do his errands.

He returns home at a remarkably late hour. He often works past midnight at the Committee of Public Safety; but even when not attending the Committee, he never returns before midnight. Where he is, at such times, no one knows. Whoever seeks him in the evening must wait until the morrow to see him. . . . Robespierre rarely misses a meeting of the Convention. Equally important to him are the Jacobin Club and the business of the Committee of Public Safety, for his influence and authority derive entirely from the Club and the Committee. The Convention, the Committee and the Club: he is now the leader of all three of these assemblies and therefore the leader of the whole of France. In Paris, where everyone delights in hearing him speak, the matter of his speeches is well known; also in the departments since most of his speeches appear in print. I must say a few words regarding his bearing as an orator. When he mounts the rostrum, it is not with a studied indifference or exaggerated gravity, nor does he rush upon it like Marat; but he is calm, as though he wished to show from the outset that this is the place which, without challenge, is his by right. As soon as he appears before his audience, one can tell whether he will speak for long or whether he intends merely to utter an opinion in two words, or simply to impose his *veto*. In the first case, he remains silent for a few moments, as if he wished to collect his ideas or to await the silence that his words deserve; then, placing his hand upon his chest, he undoes a few buttons on his jacket, unties his cravat, looks around him, and begins slowly, but with emotion and on a pitch that rises little by little as his speech proceeds. On the other hand, when he intends to be brief, he explodes all at once, violently and without delay; his voice is strained, inspiring awe and compelling an absolute silence.

He uses few gestures as he speaks; he does not wave his arms about him, nor does he keep them closely stuck to his body; but he holds them, lightly poised, against his chest. At that moment, it is his eyes that are the most lively part of him; they search the faces of his hearers and appear almost to read the opinion of each one of them in the expression on his countenance. It is certainly this optical power that is the cause of the spell that he casts over many of his audiences. His facial expression serves as a marvelous accompaniment to his words and is a living interpreter of his hidden thoughts. Such matter as the unsuspecting listener might take to be spoken in earnest is suddenly transformed into the most bitter irony by a single line of scorn that plays around the speaker's mouth. Such was always his manner, even when he was still a provincial lawyer. In general, his guiding rule is to remain firmly attached to principle. Once a decision has been taken, he has never wavered. The Republic has always been his goal, and he has always fought atheism, which the nation seemed bound to adopt one day.

This firmness of principle, however, need not surprise us—as long as Robespierre obeys the laws and fears to disobey them as much as any one of his own subjects.

A VISIT BY FRÉRON AND BARRAS (EARLY 1794) [5]

We arrived at Robespierre's lodging. It was a small house situated in the Rue Saint-Honoré, almost opposite the Rue Saint-Florentin. I believe it has disappeared today, since the Rue Duphot was cut through in this place. . . .

To reach our eminent host, who deigned to live in this modest and ramshackle dwelling, we had to pass through a long passage stacked with carpenter's planks. This passage ended in a small courtyard about

[5] From Barras' *Mémoires,* published in the 1820's; reproduced by Jacob, *op. cit.,* pp. 157-60; trans. G. Rudé (by permission of the Librairie Armand Colin).

L. M. *Fréron* (1754-1802), one-time editor of the radical *Orateur du Peuple,* was a deputy to the National Convention, a bitter opponent of Robespierre in Thermidor, and, in the reaction that followed, was the organizer of the anti-Jacobin middle-class youth, or *jeunesse dorée.* P. J. *Barras* (1755-1829) was the commander of the militia sent to arrest Robespierre and his companions at the Hôtel de Ville in the night of 9th-10th Thermidor; later he became a Director and the patron of the young Napoleon Bonaparte. Alexandre Dumas relates in his *Mémoires* that, late in life, Barras told him he had but two regrets: "to have overthrown Robespierre and to have promoted Bonaparte by means of the 13th Vendémiaire" [Paris royalist rising of October 5-6, 1795, crushed by Barras and Bonaparte] (Jacob, *op. cit.,* pp. 157-8).

seven or eight feet square, which was similarly festooned with timber. A little wooden staircase led up to a room on the first floor. Before mounting the stairs, we saw in the courtyard the daughter of the carpenter Duplay, the owner of the house. This girl was devoted to Robespierre and allowed none other to tend to his needs. As women of her class at that time held political opinions and she held most decided ones, Danton had named her Cornelia Copeau after the mother of the Gracchi. Cornelia appeared to have been hanging up linen to dry in the courtyard; she held in her hand a pair of striped cotton stockings of the kind that we were accustomed to see Robespierre wear each day that he attended the Convention. On the other side of the yard, Madame Duplay sat cleaning pot-herbs between a bucket and a salad-bowl. Two men in military uniform sat respectfully at her side; they appeared to form an intimate part of the household and, in order to speak more freely as members of the family circle, were also engaged in cleaning herbs. Of these two soldiers, later to become famous by different means, one was General Danican, who was to declare himself a royalist on the 13th Vendémiaire (and may still believe himself to be so, seeing his passion for the English), and the other was General (later Marshal) Brune.

Fréron and I told Cornelia Copeau that we had come to visit Robespierre. At first she replied that he was away, but then she asked if he was expecting us. Fréron, who knew the place, continued to advance towards the stairs. Mother Duplay made signs to her daughter to deny us entry. The two generals, smiling at the women and entering into their thoughts, looked alternately at them and at us, saying to them that he was not there and to us that he was. Cornelia Copeau seeing that Fréron, who had already mounted two steps, was insistent, placed herself in front of him and cried, "Very well, I will announce you." Walking quickly, she cried again from the bottom of the stairs: "It is Fréron and a friend whose name I do not know." Fréron said: "It is Barras and Fréron," as though to announce himself, and passed through the door of Robespierre's room, which Cornelia Copeau had just opened, with me in close pursuit.

Robespierre stood wrapped in a kind of short dressing gown. His hair, which had just been dressed, was freshly set and powdered white. He was not wearing his usual spectacles, and through the powder covering his face, already white owing to the pallor of his complexion, we saw two clouded eyes which we had never seen before without the protective covering of his lenses. These eyes fixed themselves on us with an air of astonishment at our unexpected appearance. We greeted him in our fashion, without restraint and with the simplicity of manner of the times. He did not reply to our greeting, but turned first toward his toilet mirror, which hung at his window overlooking the courtyard, and then towards a little mirror, intended no doubt to decorate his mantlepiece but which, in fact, served no such purpose. He took his toilet knife and scraped off the powder covering his face while being careful not to disturb the contours of his hair; he then removed his dressing gown, which he placed on a chair that stood near us in such a manner as to soil our garments yet without offering any excuse and without appearing to pay any attention to our presence. He washed himself in a kind of bowl that he held in his hand, cleaned his teeth, and spat several times on the ground onto our feet without giving us any mark of attention and almost with the directness of Prince Potemkin, who, as is known, never bothered to turn his head and, without care or warning, would spit in the faces of those who stood before him. Even once this ceremony was completed, Robespierre refrained from saying a word to us. Fréron, thinking he might begin the conversation, presented me to him, saying: "This is my colleague Barras who played a more decisive part than I did, and more so than any soldier, at the capture of Toulon; we have done our duty at the peril of our lives on the battlefield, as we shall do in the Convention. It is very painful for two men who have shown such zeal as we have to find themselves not only denied justice, but the object of the most vile accusations and the most monstrous calumnies.[6] We are confident that those who know us, at least, such as you, Robespierre, will do us justice and see that it be done to us by others."

Robespierre kept silent, but Fréron thought he observed, from a slight movement of his otherwise impassive features, that the familiar mode of address, based on the old revolutionary tradition, displeased him; so, in the course of his speech, he found a means of substituting the formal "vous" for the familiar "tu" in order to placate this haughty and susceptible individual. Robespierre did not betray the slightest sign of satisfaction at this mark of deference. He remained standing as he was and did not invite us to be seated. I told him politely that our approach to him had been dictated by the esteem in which we held his political principles. He answered not a word, and I was unable to distinguish the sign of any feeling whatsoever on his face. I never saw anything so impassive, either in the icy marble of statues or in the faces of the buried dead.

[6] Barras and Fréron were among the Terrorists who, in the fall of 1793, were recalled at Robespierre's instigation to account for their excesses in stamping out counterrevolution at Lyons, Bordeaux, Toulon and elsewhere.

10
The Politician: In the Constituent Assembly

The three extracts that follow give varying impressions of Robespierre as a politician during his first two years in Paris, at the time of the Constituent Assembly. The first is a remarkably shrewd portrait by William Augustus Miles, an English liberal who spent several years in Paris during the Revolution; it comes from a letter sent to London in March 1791. The second, which gives a picture of Robespierre's role during the two years of the Constituent Assembly, appeared in a pamphlet published in 1792 by Dubois de Crancé (1747-1814), the Jacobin military expert, an active opponent of Robespierre in Thermidor and a later War Minister under the Directory. The third is a letter written to Robespierre in September 1791 by the famous Madame Roland, whose husband became Girondin Minister of the Interior in 1792 and who was herself to be guillotined by the Jacobins as a leading Girondin in October 1793. One can see what a high regard she earlier had for Robespierre, whom she considered to be one of the few men of principle in the Assembly.

AN ENGLISH OBSERVER (MARCH 1791)[1]

The man held of the least account in the National Assembly by Mirabeau, by Lafayette, and even by the Lameths and all the Orleans faction, will soon be of the first consideration. He is cool, measured, and resolved. He is *in his heart* Republican, honestly so, not to pay court to the multitude, but from an opinion that it is the very best, if not the only, form of government which men ought to admit. Upon this principle he acts, and the public voice is decidedly in favour of this system. He is a stern man, rigid in his principles, plain, unaffected in his manners, no foppery in his dress, certainly above corruption, despising wealth, and with nothing of the volatility of a Frenchman in his character. I do not enter into the question of the forms of government, but I say that Robespierre is *bona fide* a Republican, and that nothing which

[1] From *The Correspondence of William Augustus Miles 1789-1817* (London, 1890), I, 245.

the King could bestow on him, were his Majesty in a situation to bestow anything, could warp this man from his purpose. In this sense of the word, that is, *in his heart meaning well,* as to the destruction of the monarchy, he is an honest man. I watch him very closely every night. I read his countenance with eyes steadily fixed on him. He is really a character to be contemplated; he is growing every hour into consequence, and, strange to relate, the whole National Assembly hold him cheap, consider him as insignificant, and, when I mentioned to some of them my suspicions and said he would be the man of sway in a short time, and govern the million, I was laughed at.

An infatuation marks the Court. The Queen looks to Sardinia and Austria. So strong is the delusion of the royal family, that the wench or valet who sweeps their apartments is listened to with affection when they talk of counterrevolution, and are caressed if they say it will infallibly take place. The National Assembly is also cursed by an infatuation of a different kind. The two great factions in it work for their own purposes. The welfare of the country is out of the question. The Tuileries is said to have purchased Mirabeau. I would rather buy Robespierre, if Robespierre could be bought, or even that vile incendiary, Marat. Mirabeau has no longer any credit with the people; with the nobility and clergy he never had any. The Bishop of Autun[2] and he cling together. Clubs abound in every street, and almost in every hovel in Paris. The women assemble and discuss political questions. All is uproar and confusion; and, during the illusory pursuits of the red-hot Royalists, and the interested cabals of the Limited Monarchy party, the Republicans, under the cautions and wily guidance of Robespierre, are silently and rapidly marching to the great object they have in view.

DUBOIS DE CRANCÉ [3]

As the acknowledged leader of the *sans-culottes,* the enemy of every kind of domination and the defender of the rights of the people, Robespierre had great attributes: he merely lacked an imposing stature, the oratorical power of a Danton, and a certain capacity to be less stubborn and self-opinionated. These minor blemishes often injured the cause that he defended. He was proud and jealous of his reputation, yet just and virtuous; even his severest critics have never been able to reproach him with a moment's lack of constancy. He was firmly attached to the most

---

[2] Talleyrand.
[3] From Jacob, *op. cit.,* pp. 82-4; trans. G. Rudé (by permission of the Librairie Armand Colin).

austere of principles, and from these he never alllowed himself to deviate. As he was when the Assembly first met, so he was when it ended: there are remarkably few men to whom such a tribute may be paid.

In the Constituent Assembly Robespierre never was president or secretary, and he never belonged to a committee. Even the "patriots," while holding him in great respect, had no love for him. The reason was quite simple: this man, who was steeped in Rousseau's moral teaching, had the strength to emulate his master; he shared the austerity of his principles, his manner of life, his unsociability, unwillingness to compromise, proud simplicity, and even the moroseness of his disposition; and although he lacked Rousseau's talents, Robespierre was no ordinary mortal. Taking no counsel but that prompted by his heart, his opinions were often unpopular and generally considered to be extreme; for Robespierre, who was always an enemy of monarchy and for whom liberty was nothing if not consorted with equality, argued ever from first principles; and when our Constitution was finally accepted, he spoke of it as though it had undergone no changes or amendments.

He was discerning enough always to despise Barnave and the Lameths,[4] and others among the minority of nobles who had betrayed their own order merely to raise themselves above its ruins. He was never discomfited by slander or hostile interruption; I have seen him resist the whole Assembly and demand with calm dignity that the President call it to order.

It was in the Jacobin Club, and not in the Assembly, that Robespierre won his fame. In the Jacobins he had friends who listened to him and encouraged him, and there he often presented excellent opinions; he rarely had this advantage in the Assembly. When it first met, he made very little impression, and unless decisions were entirely to his liking, he displayed a deplorable indifference to the outcome: at such moments he would as soon have voted for slavery as for a restricted freedom. He refused to support the *suspensive veto* because he wanted none. In this he was right, but once his cause was lost, was it better to allow the Court party the chance of winning an *absolute veto*?[5]

After Mirabeau's death, the defection of the "patriot" party and the Lameth brothers' treachery, Robespierre displayed great moral courage, and in spite of the great disfavor in which his views were held, he compelled his enemies to respect him. Indeed, he triumphed over them on

---

[4] Constitutional monarchists and leaders of the majority in the Constituent Assembly.

[5] A reference to the debate in August 1789 on the King's powers to "veto" the legislation proposed by the Assembly. The outcome was the compromise of a "suspensive veto," valid for two consecutive parliaments, or four years.

a number of difficult occasions; in particular, he denied them the opportunity to continue their intrigues in the subsequent Assembly.[6]

I do not know whether Robespierre had a clear understanding of parliamentary tactics. I think it improbable, for if he had, he would have sacrificed his enthusiasm or *amour-propre* more readily to the public weal. He would not so frequently and so deliberately have placed himself by the President's desk in order to take the floor and to hold it with such obstinacy against every challenge. He would have known that the intriguers who led the Assembly called him their *Maury*[7] and were glad to leave him a clear field (for the President at that time obeyed their instructions), in order to provoke the moderates, win them to their side and assure themselves of a majority. He would have seen that by winning the applause of the press and the public gallery he was prejudicing the public interest within the Assembly itself. And, finally, he would have left the floor to men as principled as himself but who in less exaggerated terms would have reminded the Assembly of its duty and of the principles of the Constitution.

But let us do justice to virtue, honor and probity where it is due. Robespierre never belonged to a fractious group. He always stood alone with his conscience, and with great courage he weathered the most violent storms.

If there had been none but Robespierre in the Assembly, France would today perhaps be nothing but a heap of ruins. But in the midst of so much intrigue, baseness, vice and corruption and in the clash of so many opposing interests and conflicting views, in the middle of the tumults, slanders, fears and even murders, Robespierre stood as an impregnable rock. In a word, he has done his duty, he has deserved well of his country, and his example will serve as a precious model for those who came after us.

[6] This refers to the "self-denying ordinance" of May 1791, proposed by Robespierre, which made deputies to the outgoing (Constituent) Assembly ineligible for election to the Legislative Assembly that followed.

[7] The Abbé Maury: a deputy of the Right, whose views were so extreme that his active support for a measure was considered a sure guarantee of its defeat.

MADAME ROLAND [8]

To Robespierre in Paris.
September 27, 1791. From Le Clos Laplatière, parish of Thésée.

It may be of some interest to you, Sir, to receive in the heart of the capital, the center of so many passions where your patriotism shines like a lighted beacon, a letter dispatched from deep in the desert, written by the hand of one not committed to any faction and who is prompted to write to you by that sentiment of pleasure and esteem that men and women of honor experience in communicating with one another. Even if I had only followed the course of the Revolution and the work of the Legislature in the public press, I should have been able to distinguish the small number of courageous men who have remained faithful to their principles, and among these the man whose energy has never flagged in his unremitting opposition to the pretensions and maneuvers of the despots and intriguers; and to these representatives my attachment and my gratitude would have been due as would those of every lover of humanity to its generous defenders. But these sentiments acquire an even greater force when one has seen close-to the depths of the intrigues and the full horror of the corruption to which despotism resorts in order to enslave and degrade the human race, to maintain or to increase the ignorance of the peoples, to mislead opinion, seduce the weak, and to drive terror into the hearts of the unthinking mob while bringing honest citizens to their ruin. History has traced for us only in broad outline the activities and consequences of tyranny, and this dreadful picture is more than enough to inspire in us a violent hatred of all arbitrary power; but I can conceive of nothing as base and revolting as the hundred different guises its efforts, tricks and atrocities have assumed in order to maintain it in our Revolution. No one born with a soul that has remained free from taint cannot have seen Paris in these last months without groaning in spirit over the blindness of nations corrupted and the abysmal evils that threaten to engulf them.

I have made a methodical observation of that city, and its unhappy results are similar to those that one almost always draws from a study of mankind. They are that men in their majority are infinitely contemptible and that they are made so by our social institutions; that if one wishes to work for the good of humanity, one must, like the gods, do so from a love of good works, from the pleasure of being oneself,

[8] From Jacob, *op. cit.*, pp. 64-8; trans. G. Rudé (by permission of the Librairie Armand Colin).

from fulfilling one's destiny and enjoying one's own esteem, but without expecting either gratitude or justice at the hands of one's fellow mortals; and, furthermore, that the small number of superior beings who might be capable of achieving great results, being scattered over the surface of the earth and often the prisoners of circumstance, are rarely able to come together in order to concert their efforts.

On my way here, as in Paris, I found the people deceived by its own ignorance or by the machinations of its enemies, judging ill or knowing little of the state of affairs. Everywhere the masses are good; their inclinations are just because their interest is that of all, but they have been blinded or suborned. Nowhere did I find people with whom I could speak openly or usefully of our political situation. I merely left, in all the places through which I passed, copies of your Address; these will have been found after my departure and will have provided some persons with an excellent text for their meditations.

I stopped for a few days at Villefranche, a little town in which I have a dwelling. It has only patriots made to measure, who love the Revolution because it has destroyed what is above them but who understand nothing of the theory of a free government and are complete strangers to that sublime and delicious sentiment which makes us see all those of our kind as brothers and which combines a love of mankind with an ardent love of that liberty which alone can assure the happiness of all. Such men therefore bristle at the very mention of a Republic, and a king seems to them essential to their own well being.

I embraced my child with rapture; I swore, as I wept tears of joy, that I would forget politics, and I hastened to reach the country.

An exceptional drought had added immeasurably to the natural aridity of a stony and unyielding soil and to the mournful aspect of a rustic estate, which had been abandoned for six months and which only its master's presence could bring to life. The harvest, besides, demanded my attention and added further to my concern; yet rural pursuits bring with them peace and joy, and I should have wholeheartedly relished them had I not discovered that slander, propagated at Lyons to keep my husband away from the Assembly, had found its way to my retreat and that men who have had every reason to be aware of our devotion to the public welfare and to their own in particular were attributing our absence to the supposed arrest of M. Roland as a counterrevolutionary; and, to add to it all, I heard the cry of *les aristocrates à la lanterne* ["Hang the aristocrats"] as I passed.

I have no fear of the consequences of these absurd notions, which have affected but a minority; besides, our mere presence and our return

to that simple, healthy life to which we are accustomed will soon dispel
the slightest trace of them; but how easy it is to mislead the people and
turn them against their own defenders!

As for Lyons, it is a town that remains devoted to the Aristocracy;
the elections have had the most unfortunate results; the deputies are
nothing but enemies of liberty, speculators and persons of ill repute or
of none at all; there is not a man of even mediocre talent among them;
those elected to the department are of much the same complexion as
their representation in the National Assembly. A few patriots, it is true,
have found seats in the district; but they are too few to do much good
or to prevent evil from being done.

If we are to judge the merits of a representative system of government
by the little experience we have already had of it, we must not deem
ourselves too fortunate.

The mass of the people cannot be grossly deceived for long; but first
the electors, then the administrators are bought, and finally the representatives, who in turn sell the people. Could we but feel with increasing conviction, while mindful of the vices that prejudice and ambition
have had inserted in our Constitution, that every step we take away from
perfect equality and perfect liberty must necessarily tend to degrade
mankind, must corrupt it and destroy the possibility of its happiness!

You, Sir, have done much to demonstrate and propagate these principles. It is a noble and comforting thought that one may feel so persuaded in an age in which so many others are as yet uncertain where
their future lies. You have a great task to fulfill in order that every party
may embark on this course, and you stand in an arena in which your
courage will have ample means to express itself.

From the depths of my retreat I shall joyfully await the news of what
your present successes may bring in their train. I give this name to the
steps you have taken for the triumph of justice, for the publication of
truths that concern the public weal must be counted a success for the
cause that we all hold dear.

If the purpose of my letter had been only to send you such news as I
have myself to offer, I should not have written; but although I have
nothing of this sort to send you, I was confident that you would be glad
to receive word from two persons whose sentiments are similar to your
own and who are happy to express for you an esteem that they feel for
few others and an attachment that they have pledged only to those whose
greatest glory is to have a reputation for justice and the happiness of
being men of sensibility.

M. Roland has just come to join me. He is weary and saddened by the inconsequence and frivolity of Parisians; and we shall engage together in rural pursuits, interspersed with hours of writing and reflection, and seek in the exercise of private virtues a consolation for the public misfortunes which it may be our lot to witness at the hands of a treacherous court and a set of ambitious scoundrels.

We beg you to accept our wishes and our sentiments in the spirit in which they are offered to you.

ROLAND, *née* PHLIPON.

11

In the Jacobin Club: as Seen by Marat (1792)[1]

Jean-Paul Marat (1743-93), former doctor and revolutionary journalist, termed "the people's friend," was, after Robespierre and Danton, probably the best known, and in Paris the most popular, of all the leaders of the French Revolution. After his assassination by Charlotte Corday in July 1793, he was venerated as a "martyr," a cult was dedicated to his memory, and, in 1794-5, his remains were temporarily lodged in the Panthéon.

Here Marat, whose ebullient and somewhat reckless personality stood in marked contrast with Robespierre's and whose relations with him were not always of the most cordial, is defending Maximilien against the attacks made on him by Brissot, Guadet and other Girondins. The extract is from Marat's daily newspaper, L'Ami du Peuple, of May 3, 1792.

The discussions agitating the Jacobin Society and the scission with which it is menaced are the talk of the town. Here is the gist of the discussion, which redounds little to the credit of the Jacobin leaders and their cowardly followers.

The nation has learned from cruel experience that its deputies to the Estates General were only too ready to bargain away, in favor of the monarch, certain of its fundamental interests and imprescriptible rights and that only seven or eight men among them consistently refused the temptation, so frequently offered them, to abandon their duty. Let us here recall names dear to every patriotic citizen: the names of Buzot, Grégoire, Antoine, Pétion and, above all of them, that of Robespierre. On laying aside his duties as a member of the legislative body, he was prompted by a concern for his reputation to serve his country while out of office, a course that would also have surely been prescribed to him by deep understanding of his fellow men. He merely followed the dic-

[1] From Jacob, *op. cit.*, pp. 99-106; trans. G. Rudé (by permission of Librairie Armand Colin).

tates of his heart in establishing himself among the Jacobins, in that whirlpool of intriguers whom he was charitable enough to regard as true friends of liberty. Men of little account are not readily given to sing the praises of their fellows, men of dubious virtue are offended by the high principles of others, and the public itself is inconstant in its affection for its heroes. These sentiments are too deeply ingrained in the hearts of men for it to be possible to flout them with impunity. It is for having taken no account of them that Robespierre finds himself today the target of accumulated envy. The glory brought him by his constant defense of the cause of the people and the popular favor that was the just reward of his civic virtues soon outraged those of his colleagues who had failed in the service of their country, as well as the new deputies, would-be patriots who were jealous of the public's applause, of which they claimed their full share without having done anything to deserve it.

So they began, all of them, to seek faults in him; but the gravest reproach they can make of him is to speak of him continuously, both of the services he has already rendered to the public and of those that he has yet to render, as though a citizen who is the perpetual butt of enemies of the Revolution masquerading as patriots were not already constantly reduced to the sad necessity of justifying his conduct. And those who resort to these petty devices are deputies of the people, who have the solemn duty to discharge its debts to all who have served their country well; and yet they treat with the basest ingratitude a man who has served her so long, with such zeal, and at the peril of his life.

If only, at least, he were not exposed to the cowardly intrigues and attacks of the rogues and traitors! But who is not aware of what Robespierre has suffered, and has yet to suffer, from the treachery of the Guadet and Brissot faction for having dared to oppose the war plans that these false patriots put before the public at the instigation of Master Mottié.[2]

In the speech that he made to the Jacobins on the 25th of last month, Master Brissot forgets to answer the most serious charges—such as that of having been a paid spy of Le Noir;[3] of having served the ministerial party in the City Hall for fear that Bailly[4] would reveal that his name is inscribed on the registers of the police; of having served the cause of despotism in his plan to reorganize the City administration; of having invented a hundred fairy tales to cover up the malversations of the royal

[2] Derogatory nickname for Lafayette.
[3] Former chief of police in Paris.
[4] Mayor of Paris, 1789-91.

food hoarders on the *comité des subsistances;* of having been the base apologist for Mottié's attacks on public liberty; and of having been criminally associated with him in the homes of Master Lamarque and Mistress Lanxade; but if he forgets to answer these charges, it is to boast of his so-called patriotism, to build up his accomplice Condorcet[5] as a great man, to rebut the charge of having brought the new ministers to office, and to slander Robespierre by accusing him of being a faction leader and of directing the activities of the public gallery through his lieutenants. Robespierre a faction leader! He would have a faction without a doubt if he had been willing to debase himself by intriguing, like his slanderer; but he has not, and never has had, any followers other than such citizens as remember with gratitude all he has done for the freedom that they cherish. How is it that Brissot does not see that by contrasting the actions of the majority in the Jacobin Club with those of the public gallery, which neither has been nor can be bought for money, and, above all, with that of a man who stands almost on his own among the Jacobins, having an income of barely six hundred livres and not drawing a cent from the civil list, he is turning the accusation against the Society itself which he thereby presents as a junta of intriguers?

But what is worthy of notice is that by placing Robespierre at the head of a faction, he is accusing him of sowing discord and division in the Society in such a way as to compel the withdrawal from it of men, such as himself, who profess the highest degree of independence and have fought with the greatest energy against the misuse of the civil list, and against the recent Triumvirate and the Feuillants.[6] What is the object of this faction? he goes on to ask. Not knowing how to reply, he merely insinuates that those who control the civil list have the same opinions as Robespierre's party, that like him they slander the ministers, seek like him to discredit the National Assembly, and like him vent their fury against the same patriotic citizens. And he invites the sincere friends of liberty to reflect on these insinuations. I have said it a hundred times and I will repeat it once more: by such vague imputations a sincere friend of the Revolution and a declared enemy of the nation can be made to look as one, for both voice grave accusations against the present ministers, the National Assembly and the pretended patriots of the day. But it is only by examining the details that one may, from the differ-

---

[5] Distinguished philosopher and a leader of the *Brissotin* (or *Girondin*) group in the Legislative Assembly and the later Convention.

[6] *Triumvirate:* name given to the three "moderate" leaders of the Constituent Assembly, Barnave, Duport and Alexandre Lameth. *Feuillants:* Constitutional monarchists who broke with the Jacobins and formed their own club in June 1791.

ence in the nature of the accusation, tell the difference in principles and motives. The King reproaches the Assembly, his present ministers and the pretended patriots of the day for not submitting to his every wish; whereas Robespierre reproaches them for betraying the interests of the people under a mask of patriotism and for endangering the public safety by embarking on a senseless war.

What would Master Brissot say if, in order to direct opinion, Robespierre were merely to reproach him with using in respect to himself the language of the Gauthiers, the Royous and the Malets du Pans,[7] that is to say of the vilest scribblers and the most detestable enemies of freedom? And, moreover, if he were to confine himself to inviting all patriots to reflect on the similarity? But no, he will not stoop to such vague and treacherous insinuations: when he wishes to paint a horrifying portrait of that sycophant, he will not hesitate to paint him in his true, and ugly, colors.

While Brissot slanders Robespierre and commands another hundred venal hacks to slander him, Master Guadet, as a worthy acolyte among the new Tartufes[8] who have sold themselves to Mottié, rises on his spurs to administer a few strokes of his own. Who would believe that this little backstage intriguer has had the folly to number among the charges that he proffers against Robespierre "that he has become, either by ambition or misfortune, the idol of the people, a role he seeks to perpetuate every day; that he has deserted the post to which public confidence and the public interest had called him,[9] and yet without imposing on himself the duty to be silent"; as if a simple citizen without either fortune or party had any other means to woo the people whose rights and interests he champions than by the mere exercise of his civic virtues! As if he could serve the public cause on a public tribunal on which there are not to be found two honest men! As if he could stay at his post and impose a rule of silence on himself at the same time! As if a man whose only power lies in his feeble voice, surrounded by intriguers, hypocrites and rogues, ever attentive to condemn him to silence and ever ready to kill him when he prepares to unmask them, could become an object of terror! As if a man whose only dominion over an ignorant, loose, frivolous and inconstant people is that of reason could ever endanger the public liberty by the high esteem in which he is held and be called upon to leave his country in order to safeguard it!

[7] Royalist journalists.

[8] Tartufe: an arch-hypocrite (from Moliere's play, *Tartuffe*).

[9] Robespierre had recently resigned his post as Public Prosecutor for the Paris Commune.

Such follies merely lay bare the motives of those who have put them forward. Who does not see that the very sight of an honest patriot hurts the gaze of scoundrels whose hope is to squander the interest of the *patrie* without fear of detection? Who does not see that an incorruptible critic is an importunate witness whose removal is imperative? Who does not see that the sole purpose of their denigration is to present him as an object of suspicion to the people, whose confidence he enjoys? Yes, the Guadet-Brissot faction is far from being the dupe of the calumnies that its leaders peddle about concerning Robespierre. Who better than they know all their falsity? Let him but consent to leave them the stage, and they will be ready to disavow their abuse and sing his praises; yes, and demand that others sing them as well.

You see the cunning of it. Having abused Robespierre for opposing the war and foreseeing that it would bring the greatest misfortunes in its train by assuring the triumph of our enemies, Guadet accuses him of seeking to realize these misfortunes by dividing the patriots and by sowing mistrust and suspicion among them. But who, I beg you, are the patriots that he seeks to divide? The intriguers among the Jacobins? And who are the patriots against whom he sows mistrust and suspicion? The deputies of Paris and the Gironde, the new leaders in the Assembly. These are the rogues that he has unmasked, the intelligent reader will say! But whom will they persuade that patriots are the real objects of his censure?

And, to crown his folly, Guadet accuses Robespierre of "inspiring a statement in the journal *L'Ami du Peuple,* which he controls, that the moment has come to give France a dictator; and this at a moment when he is seeking to undermine, by means of the most ridiculous accusations, the confidence of the people in the majority of its representatives." This dictator is doubtless Robespierre himself, as an associate of Guadet stupidly accuses the *Ami du Peuple* of having suggested in a recent number.

This accusation concerns me personally; so I owe a clear and categorical reply to those citizens who are simple enough not to realize its absurdity. I solemnly declare then that not only is my pen not at Robespierre's personal disposal, although it has often served to do him justice, but I protest that I have never received any note from him, that I have never directly or indirectly had any dealings with him, and that I have only seen him once in my life; and, on that occasion, our conversation gave rise to an expression of ideas and a display of sentiments that are diametrically opposed to those that Guadet and his clique ascribe to me.

The first words that Robespierre addressed to me were in the form of a reproach: namely, that I had myself in part destroyed the prodigious influence that my paper had had on the Revolution, by dipping my pen in the blood of the enemies of liberty and by talking of ropes and daggers, no doubt against my own better judgment, as he preferred to believe that these were mere idle words dictated by circumstance. You must understand, I promptly replied, that the influence my newspaper has had on the Revolution did not derive, as you imagine, from the closely reasoned arguments in which I methodically presented the evils of the disastrous decrees drafted by the committees of the Constituent Assembly, but from the horror that it aroused among its readers when I boldly tore aside the veil covering the perpetual plots being hatched against our public liberties by the enemies of our country, in league with the King, the Assembly and the principal executive officers; from the audacity with which I crushed every slanderous critic underfoot; from the effusions of my spirit and the outbursts of my heart; from my violent denunciations of oppression; from my impetuous tirades against the oppressors; from my doleful accents and the cries of fury, indignation and despair that I raised against the scoundrels who abused the confidence and authority of the people in order to deceive it, despoil it, enslave it and plunge it into the abyss. Learn then that there never issued from the Assembly a decree threatening liberty and that no public servant ever dared to attack the weak and unfortunate without my sounding an immediate alarm and rousing the people against such unworthy perpetrators of injustice. The cries of alarm and fury that you take for idle words were the natural expression of a passionate spirit. Learn, too, that had I been able to count on the people of the capital after the terrible decree against the Nancy garrison,[10] I would have decimated the barbarians who passed it. Learn, moreover, that after the Châtelet inquiry into the events of the 5th and 6th October,[11] I would gladly have sent the iniquitous judges who composed that tribunal to the stake! And that if, after the massacre of the Champ de Mars, I could have found 2,000 men filled with the anger that tore my heart, I would have placed myself at their head, stabbed the general to death in the middle of his battalions of brigands, burned the despot within his palace, and impaled our odious representatives on their benches, as I told them at the time. Robespierre listened to me in horror, paled and for a while remained silent. This interview confirmed the opinion that I

[10] A mutiny of the Nancy garrison was brutally suppressed, with the Assembly's approval, in August 1790.

[11] The "days" of October 5-6, 1789, when Louis XVI was brought back to Paris from Versailles.

had always held of him: that he combined the intelligence of the wise legislator with the integrity of the man of honor and the zeal of the true patriot; but that he lacked both the vision and the audacity of the statesman.

12

On the Eve of Thermidor

Following are a number of sharply contrasting opinions of Robespierre as he appeared at the height of his power and on the eve of and during his fall. They are respectively by a sympathetic neutral, by three of his enemies, and by three of his friends or admirers.

The first portrait is by the Englishman, William Augustus Miles, who though clearly a liberal, had no particular axe to grind. His testimony has all the more value because it is a strictly contemporary document, undistorted by hindsight; it was sent to London in the form of a letter on June 22, 1794. It also contains a remarkably accurate prophecy of the nature of Robespierre's ultimate fate.

The other portraits are, of course, more strictly "slanted." With one exception (Saint-Just's), they were written after the dramatic events of Thermidor had divided former colleagues (they were all Jacobins) into two bitterly hostile camps. Therefore (again excepting Saint-Just), accusers and defenders alike are not so much recording what they saw at the time as how the picture appeared to them in restrospect after the events of Thermidor and in the light of the part they had themselves played in them, as well as in the light of the attitude they had by then developed towards Robespierre. So we must expect some of these sketches (particularly, perhaps, that of Fouché) to tell us as much (or even more) about the writer himself as about his subject.

"THE INCORRUPTIBLE": SEEN BY AN ENGLISH OBSERVER (JUNE 1794) [1]

In my vindication of Robespierre I used the word *incorruptible* in a very limited sense; it goes no further than to say that he cannot be diverted from his present object by any pecuniary consideration; and I repeat that, if it were possible to present him with Mexico and Peru on condition that he would abandon his design or consent to restore royalty to France, I firmly believe he would spurn the offer. There are, however, other modes of corrupting the mind than by the temptation of money,

[1] From *The Correspondence of William Augustus Miles,* pp. 175-8 (letter of June 22, 1794).

and when Sir Robert Walpole said that every man had his price, I am certain he did not confine himself between the extremes of a million and half a crown. Ambition, love, hatred, vengeance—in a word, all the variety of springs by which the machine is put in motion, may be considered as so many different instruments of corruption. I have known instances where a pretty woman has triumphed over gold at Wetzlar and obtained a decree of the Empire which no bribe could at that moment procure. Those who suspect that Robespierre is to be bought by money know him not; but if his views in the very dawn or infancy of the Revolution had been attended to—that is, before circumstances authorised him to entertain any hopes of success to a project deemed extravagant in 1789 and which is as good as accomplished in 1794—his foible might have been discovered, and himself diverted from the vast design which even then he began to conceive. The misfortune is that whenever a great popular commotion takes place in a nation, the men at the head of affairs generally *perdent la tête* and are the least capable of allaying the ferment. The blockheads have recourse to rigour and violence. We lost America by attempting to dragoon only one town on that immense continent; the French Minister lost monarchy by surrounding Paris with troops when his authority was in fact superseded. It is a perilous enterprise to war against opinion; the bayonet on such occasions may extirpate, but it can neither convince nor convert; and this is a truth which even the legislators of our own century have yet to learn. Believe me when I tell you that a general prejudice prevails throughout France against the *ancient* monarchy; nor do the fraudulent and swindling manoeuvres of that unprincipled man the King of Prussia tend to make it respectable anywhere else on the Continent.

But what wealth could seduce Robespierre from his enterprise? This judgment of him is formed not only from the magnitude of his ambition as compared with the poverty of even the greatest pecuniary bribe, but from the knowledge I obtained of his character and habits of life when I was a member of the same club with him in Paris; and I tell you again, he is beyond the reach of gold. I do not think he could have been bought at any period of the Revolution, because his penetrating mind foresaw in 1790 that power would soon be wrested from the feeble grasp of the aristocracy, who, instead of taking precautionary measures against the tempest brewing in every direction through the indefatigable exertions of the Jacobins, were caballing and endeavouring to cut the grass from under each other's feet in order to get into authority. Robespierre foresaw the issue of all this imbecility as manifested in the National Assembly. Ardent in his pursuits, although cold in his manner—conscious of his power whilst looking for support, not to the nobility, but to the people to whom he belonged, knowing that the *people* would soon be everything and *nobility* nothing—he waited patiently [through] the course of events, and with a progress evidently and constantly in his favour he looked forward with certainty to the eminence he has now attained. What bribe of money could have diverted him from his object? *Ce n'est pas par l'argent qu'il faut espérer séduire un ambitieux, sûr de son fait, de ses projets.* I do not mean to insult Horne Tooke[2] by comparing him with Robespierre, but on my soul I do not believe it is in the power of gold to purchase either of these men. I will even go further and assert that so convinced are his countrymen of the incorruptibility of Robespierre that you will never hear—whatever convulsions may hereafter happen in France—of his being publicly arraigned and tried for a delinquency of this description, nor for leaguing with the enemies or even with the pretended friends of his country for the restoration of monarchy. He may be assassinated or summarily condemned, but he will never be destroyed by a regular process, as were his companions Brissot and others. I hope that this explanation will convince you that what I have elsewhere said on the subject of this extraordinary man, whom I personally knew, was more from my respect for truth than from any affection for the individual.

THE "TYRANT": SEEN BY HIS ENEMIES

(1) Dubois de Crancé[3]

Robespierre had planned the total destruction of the Convention and the organization of a new authority even more subjected to his will. To him France's population was too widely dispersed; this mass weighed too heavily in the scales of his would-be supreme dictatorship. To achieve his purpose, the Convention would no longer serve: decimated by him and grown old with him, it threatened to engulf him in its own loss of popular esteem. He needed a higher title and new instruments of power to rouse the enthusiasm of his votaries and cast France in a new mould of his own fashioning. That is why Robespierre had for the past month abandoned the Committees[4] and had been daily parading the names of its members before his Jacobins as men no longer deserving of their confidence. That is why emissaries, sent out into every department,

---

[2] English radical reformer of the 1760s-90s and supporter of Revolutionary France.

[3] From Jacob, *op. cit.*, pp. 163-5; trans. G. Rudé (by permission of the Librairie Armand Colin).

[4] The Committees of Public Safety and Public Security.

had the mission of deploring the fate of those who had been thrown into prison. They said that the Convention was unwilling to modify its revolutionary system, that Robespierre was heartbroken by so much cruelty, but that he could do nothing in the face of the Committees' opposition, and that it was only by investing him with great authority that order and peace would be reestablished in France. That is why the (Paris) city council was preparing several new prisons, in particular the vast Mazarin college, in which three hundred beds were installed which, it was said, would only be used twice in twenty-four hours. And that is also why Couthon said on 2nd Thermidor [July 20, 1794] that there were still a few rotten members to root out of the Convention.

I was one of those proscribed and denounced. Denounced for the second time in eighteen months, this time by Robespierre himself in the Jacobins, and once more as having been overly tender to the Lyons rebels, I was immediately recalled by the Committee of Public Safety. I left St. Malo, where I had been sent to help in the brigading of an army, and, without even stopping for a night's rest, I arrived in Paris on 6th Thermidor and went straight to the Committee without calling at my house. I was made to wait in the antechamber before eventually being summoned to its presence. Collot said to me: "The custom is to note the date of arrival of deputies returning from their mission; we will enter your name." I asked to be told the reason for my recall. Billaud replied: "If the Committee requires further information, we will write to you; you may go!" I looked at him with contemptuous indignation, but I held my peace. Being accused, I had to justify my conduct, and I went directly to present myself at the Assembly. As I mounted the steps, one of my colleagues, Citizen Gaston, grasped my hand and said: "You must speak today or you are a dead man." Then he looked to see if anyone was watching him and turned his back on me. I confess that I was somewhat disconcerted by this air of mystery. I had been absent from the Assembly for some time and, having been occupied on my missions, I did not expect its stupor to be so great. Still smarting from the insolence with which I had been received by the Committee, I was determined at all costs to forestall my assassins. A deputation of Jacobins was at the bar. I asked leave to speak and denounced Couthon and Robespierre as vile slanderers. I said that though I had been free to make my escape, I had preferred to offer my head if I were found guilty but that I invoked the justice of the Convention. The Assembly passed a decree referring the consideration of my conduct to a joint meeting of the three Committees. I became calmer, hoping that they would not dare to violate this decree by having me arrested and condemned without a hearing. Robespierre, however, summoned the Committees of Public Safety and General Security to meet the same evening and spent the night demanding my arrest, though to no avail. As he had never before been resisted to his face, Robespierre thought that his plans had been exposed, and the next day he came to the Assembly and read a cunningly contrived speech that he called his last will and testament. It was the death warrant of us all that he believed he was pronouncing as he sought to rally his supporters, but he had a great majority against him. The Assembly even refused to print his speech. Enraged, Robespierre went to read his testament to the Jacobins and made every effort to raise them against the Convention. There was a fire in the mine, and the explosion was near at hand. . . .

(2) Merlin de Thionville[5]

People who like to establish relationships between faces and moral qualities and to discover likenesses between human beings and animals have observed that Danton had the face of a mastiff, Marat that of an eagle, Mirabeau of a lion and Robespierre of a cat. But the type of cat that his face resembled changed as time went by: at first it bore the anxious but gentle appearance of the domestic cat, then the savage look of the wild cat, and finally the ferocious aspect of the tiger cat.

For Robespierre's temperament underwent a remarkable development: it began by being melancholic and ended by being violent. In the Constituent Assembly his complexion was pale and wan; in the Convention it became livid and yellow. For a long time his speeches in the Constituent Assembly were made up of groans; in the Convention he frothed at the mouth as he spoke. The history of his temperament is an important part of his history.

His intellectual faculties were always limited, but fundamentally they were sound enough. He always had few ideas, but they were stubbornly held; little imagination, but a tenacious memory; little flexibility, but he always moved in the same direction. Such qualities are the lot of a melancholic disposition, which makes the brain dry and rigid and slows down and clogs the intelligence. Subsequently, black humor made his mental processes a torment, made terrible phantoms of his ideas and a

---

[5] Antoine-Christophe Merlin (1762-1833), called Merlin de Thionville to distinguish him from his colleague Merlin de Douai, was the deputy for the Moselle in the Legislative Assembly and the National Convention. He voted with the "Mountain" (Robespierre's group) in 1792-4 and was a leading figure of the Thermidorian period. The passage is from Jacob, *op. cit.*, pp. 187-91; trans. G. Rudé (by permission of the Librairie Armand Colin).

fury of his imagination. This is the ordinary destiny of tyrants who are driven to frenzy by fear and to fear by frenzy and whose every day becomes more cruel and more wretched.

He was never a man of talents. He retained no more from the sterile studies of his student days than he did from his practice at the bar. From working on the prize essays set by the provincial academies he had acquired a few ideas, which were philanthropical rather than philosophic. His learning was limited to these. He never had the slightest notion of government, administration or of negotiating terms or treaties. He never had any sense of the finer distinctions between war and the *total extermination* of the enemy, between anarchy and oppression, between the vexatious anarchy of private property and a total lack of government control; moreover, he only knew how to wage war by dint of numbers, to oppress by dint of tyranny and to govern by dint of money.

. . . It is false that he had the honor to love women; on the contrary, he did them the honor of hating them. Had he loved them, would he have been so cruel?

It is false that he loved glory. In truth, when he left school and entered the arena of the bar, he acquired a taste for an audience and for applause for which his earlier training had ill equipped him; but this taste is something quite different from a love of glory. Always greedy for noisy acclamation, what has he ever done to win the votes of honorable men? He always unashamedly loved the clamor that surrounded him, both because he stood in the midst of it and because there was none other so well suited to deafen him.

It is false, too, to say that Robespierre *loved* supreme power: he was incapable of either exercising or of enjoying it. It has been suggested that he was already ambitious to govern at a time when his only ambition was to appear on the rostrum. . . . If he aspired to the trappings of power, it was without any love of power and as a contemptible ruler who could not bear to see it in the hands of others. . . .

Robespierre felt no passions except such subordinate ones as stem from egoism: envy, hatred and the desire for vengeance; and in him these passions were totally divorced from any courage.

Envy was his dominating passion. He only resuscitated *Eternity*[6] because Eternity is invisible and because by directing man's eyes towards heaven he averted them from the earth where he wished only his own voice to be heard. . . .

Robespierre had no talents other than those of his vices, and of these

---

[6] A reference to Robespierre's part in introducing the Cult of the Supreme Being.

he was able to exploit but a few. Sometimes he displayed *oratorical talent,* which is in itself far from being enough to make an orator, and he never displayed the slightest *talent for action.*

His style was always sluggish and diffuse, lacking color and rhythm. The reason is simple: all his ideas were uncertain and confused. . . . To a high degree he possessed the art of perfidious insinuation but totally lacked that of honest persuasion and vigorous conviction. And even his desire to injure long concealed itself behind a fear of causing offense. He attacked only from behind; his shafts were poisoned, but he cast them from so great a distance, and they were so blunted and muffled, that the victim often succumbed without having felt them. At the end of his reign, at the time when he had the courage to make a frontal attack on wretches who did not dare defend themselves, he sometimes spoke as an insolent and cruel opponent but never as one superior to his victim.

Since his death, a writer who has written of him expressed the view that he had a talent for polemic. This, indeed, is one of those qualities to which he was a stranger. It is not that he lacked logic: he had sufficient to organize his ideas, but he lacked the skill and the knowledge required to penetrate the minds of others, to analyze their thoughts and reduce them to their proper value. It is a fact that he never tried his strength against an opponent and that he always evaded the issue in debate and limited his attack to persons rather than to ideas.

In 1790 and 1791, he had great difficulty in gaining access to the rostrum and even greater difficulty in persuading men to listen once he had got a hearing, so obscure and nebulous was he, so fastidious and lethargic in his person. He would never have won the attention of the Assembly if he had not first won that of the gallery; and he would never have won the latter without the prophetic hocus-pocus he indulged in once the news-hacks had acclaimed the truth of his earlier declamations, and especially not without the adulation in which he wallowed before the gallery. . . .

How could Robespierre have been an energetic speaker when he remained paralyzed whenever the moment came for action? Which of us ever saw him in action? I am not speaking solely of the moments of danger when he remained in hiding, but also of the most peaceful situations. It is quite remarkable that this man of whom so much has been said in the past six years, who appears to some to have borne the full weight of the experience of two National Assemblies on his shoulders, has not added a single line to the forty volumes of laws that have issued from these two Assemblies; and even among the revolutionary measures adopted during the last two years there is not one of which he was the author, although he gave his close support to several. . . .

It is events entirely outside Robespierre's calculations that have been responsible for the remarkable fortune of this very ordinary person. It is precisely because he did nothing, while circumstances worked for him, that he acquired this great power for a year, which, in truth, represents a century of crime. If he appears to have been constant in his ideas, it is because he had none. If he appears to have been for long a powerful party man, it is because he was for long a mere party orator. If he appears to have risen above so many men of talent, it is because they overthrew one another in succession and he was the only one who remained standing on his feet in the arena; and he remained standing only because he had neither moved a finger nor walked a step. And if people then fixed their eyes on him, it was that he had forbidden all others to compete, that he had held the rostrum for five years, that he had always said the same thing and that the things he had said, being inspired by hatred, vengeance and envy, had by now unfortunately become so many prophecies. Only once in his life did he try to walk; he took a step without support, without a guide or an attendant, and this step led him . . . to his death.

Some people think that Robespierre will cut quite a figure in history. It is not Robespierre who is remarkable at the present stage of the French Republic; it is the Republic, and not he, that is remarkable. History will say little of this monster and will limit its verdict to the following words:

"In those days so rotten had the condition of France become that a bloody mountebank without talent or courage, whose name was Robespierre, made every citizen tremble under his tyranny. While twelve hundred thousand warriors were shedding their blood for the Republic at its frontiers, he drove her to her knees by his proscriptions. She was still there when the arm of the avenger delivered her from tyranny; and even though she applauded the tyrant's fall, she dared not yet rise to her full height."

(3) Fouché [7]

There was one man in the Convention who appeared to enjoy an unassailable popularity. He was the Artesian Robespierre, a man who

[7] Joseph Fouché (1759-1820), deputy to the Convention and member of the Committee of General Security, and one of Robespierre's bitterest enemies in Thermidor, became Minister of Police under Napoleon. The passage is from Fouché's *Mémoires,* reproduced in Jacob, *op. cit.,* pp. 166-9; trans. G. Rudé (by permission of the Librairie Armand Colin).

combined cunning with pride, envy, hatred and vindictiveness; who had an unquenchable thirst for the blood of his colleagues and whose aptitude, bearing, cast of mind and obstinacy of character equipped him to rise to the most terrible occasions. From the dominating position that he enjoyed in the Committee of Public Safety he aspired, beyond the tyranny exerted by a committee of ten, to the personal dictatorship of a Marius or a Sulla. He needed to take but one step to become the absolute master of the Revolution, which he had the ambitious temerity to wish to control at his will: he needed but thirty more heads, and he had marked them down within the Convention. He knew that I had divined his intention, and so I had the honor of being inscribed on his list of intended victims. I was still on mission when he accused me of oppressing patriots and intriguing with the aristocracy. Recalled to Paris, I had the courage to challenge him in the Assembly to provide grounds for his accusation. He had me expelled from the Jacobin Club where he ruled as a high priest, which was the equivalent of a sentence of death. I did not lose time in arguing about my fate, nor did I hold long discussions in secret meetings with colleagues threatened like myself. I merely told them, among others Legendre, Tallien, Dubois de Crancé, Daunou and Chénier: "You are on the list! You, as well as I, are on the list, I am sure of it!" Tallien, Barras, Bourdon de l'Oise and Dubois de Crancé displayed some energy. Tallien fought for two lives, one of which was then dearer to him than his own.[8] And so he determined to strike down the would-be dictator with his dagger within the Convention. But what a foolish risk to take! Robespierre's popularity would have outlived him, and we should have been sacrificed on his tomb. I dissuaded Tallien from resorting to an isolated act of vengeance that would, while destroying the man, have left his system unimpaired. Being convinced that other means must be found, I went directly to those who shared the government of the Terror with Robespierre, and whom I knew to be envious or fearful of his great popularity. I revealed to Collot d'Herbois, Carnot and Billaud de Verenne the plans of this modern Appius, and to each one in turn I traced so vivid and realistic a picture of the danger of his situation, I exhorted them with such skill and with such success that I was able to instill in them not only mistrust, but the courage to take immediate steps to prevent the tyrant from further decimating the Convention. "Count," I said to them, "the votes within your Committee and you will see that he will be reduced, whenever you are firmly determined, to share an impotent minority with Couthon and Saint-Just.

---

[8] A reference to Tallien's mistress and future wife, Theresa, daughter of the banker Cabarrus.

Refuse him the right to call for a vote and drive him, by the force of your inertia, into isolation." But to what subtle twists and turns and tortuous devices I had to resort in order not to alarm the henchmen and fanatical supporters of Robespierre! Once sure of having sown the seed, I had the courage to defy him on the 20th Prairial (June 8, 1794), on the day when, filled with the ridiculous ambition to solemnly proclaim the existence of the Supreme Being, he dared to declare himself to be both its prophet and its priest before a vast concourse assembled in the Tuileries. As he was mounting the steps of his lofty dais, whence he was to launch his manifesto to the glory of God, I told him in a loud voice (twenty of my colleagues heard me do so) that his fall was near at hand. Five days later, at a meeting of the Committee, he demanded my head and the heads of eight of my friends while reserving the right to bring down another twenty or more at a later time.

What were his astonishment and his anger to find among the members of the Committee an invincible opposition to his bloody designs against the National Assembly! It has already been mutilated more than enough, they told him, and it is time to stop an annual cutting that will end by striking us all. Seeing his majority escape him, he withdrew full of spite and anger, vowing never to set foot again in the Committee so long as his intentions were misunderstood. He immediately summoned Saint-Just, who was with the army; he rallied Couthon to his bloody banner; and, still master of the Revolutionary Tribunal, he could still terrorize the Convention and all those many whom fear reduced to silence. Assured of the support of the Society of Jacobins, of the commander of the National Guard, and of all the Revolutionary Committees in the capital, he flattered himself that with so many followers he would eventually win the day. By thus withdrawing from the center of power, he wished to make his adversaries the target of a general execration, to have them regarded as the sole authors of so many murders, and deliver them to the vengeance of a people that was beginning to murmur at the sight of so much blood. But, being cowardly, mistrustful and hesitant, he was incapable of action and allowed five weeks to go by between the first secret rumblings of dissension and the open crisis that was silently preparing.

I was watching him and, seeing that his supporters had dwindled to a faction, I secretly urged his opponents, who clung to their posts of command within the Committee, to withdraw from Paris at least the companies of gunners who remained devoted to Robespierre and the Commune and to dismiss or suspend Hanriot from his office. The first of these objects I realized, thanks to the insistence of Carnot that it was essential to reinforce the artillerymen serving with the armies. As for the dismissal of Hanriot, this was considered too strong a measure; Hanriot remained and almost spoiled everything, or rather, I must confess, it was he who, on the 9th Thermidor, doomed Robespierre's cause; for his victory lay for a moment in his hands. But what could one expect from a stupid, drunken one-time footman? [9]

The rest of the story is too well known for me to linger over its telling. It is known how Maximilien I perished, a man whom some writers would wish to compare with the Greeks although he had neither their eloquence nor loftiness of spirit. I admit that, in the intoxication of victory, I said to those who attributed to him dictatorial ambitions: "You do him too much honor: he had neither plans nor ideas; far from being able to master the future, he was carried along by an impulse which he was powerless to arrest or to control." But I was then too close to the event to be close to history.

"THE IGNOMINY OF THERMIDOR": ROBESPIERRE VINDICATED BY HIS FRIENDS

(1) Saint-Just[10]

I declare that an attempt has been made to stir up bitterness and discontent in order to provoke members to have recourse to drastic measures; and I trust that no one will expect me to sully my clean hands by lending them to such iniquity. Do not imagine that I had the thought to flatter a man! I defend him because I believe him to be above reproach, but, equally, I would accuse him if he were to act as a criminal.

Let me appeal to your conscience as honest men. Is it not true that a concerted attempt has been made to terrify members to the point where they feared to sleep in their own beds? Insinuations were made that certain members of the Committee [of Public Safety] were threatening them with a bloody fate. Thus hearts were attuned to vengeance and injustice. I vouch that Robespierre has declared himself a firm champion of the Convention and has, in the Committee, shown the greatest reluctance to speak of injuring any of its members.

[9] Hanriot, commander of the Parisian National Guard, prided himself on his sans-culotte origins, being a former minor customs official and the son of a domestic servant.

[10] The extract is from the prepared speech that Saint-Just was prevented from delivering at the riotous session of 9th Thermidor; reproduced by Jacob, op. cit., pp. 141-5; trans. G. Rudé (by permission of the Librairie Armand Colin).

For some time past, Collot and Billaud have taken little part in the Committee's deliberations and appear to be given up to other, more private interests and pursuits. Billaud attends all the meetings, but he does not speak unless it be to make passionate outbursts against Paris or the Revolutionary Tribunal or against the men whose downfall he appears to favor. My complaint against him is that, in the course of a debate, he sits with his eyes closed, feigning sleep, as though his thoughts were on other matters. But for some days now anxiety has taken the place of this taciturn behavior. . . .

Often Billaud repeats with a simulated terror the words: *we are treading over a volcano.* I agree; but the volcano over which we are treading is his own deceit and love of domination. . . .

But if we consider what has given rise to this dissension, it is impossible to justify it in terms of any action dictated by the public interest. No single act of government had divided opinion; not that every measure had been wise without exception, but because the most important decisions, being taken in wartime, had been secretly resolved and put to execution.

One of the Committee's members[11] had undertaken, being deceived perhaps, to insult without reason the man whose doom they sought,[12] in order to goad him to behave thoughtlessly, make public complaints, isolate himself, and noisily defend himself, so that they might later accuse him of provoking the dispute of which others (though refusing to admit it) were the authors. This plan, it seems to me, succeeded.

The victory of Fleurus served to open the road to Belgium. I would wish that justice be done to every man and that victories be honored, but not in such a manner as to honor the government more than the armies, for it is only those who take part in the battles that win them, and it is only those who are in power that can exploit them; so let us simply praise the victories and be silent about one's own particular part.[13]

If everyone had been modest and had not been jealous that one should speak more of another than of oneself, there would be no dissension among us; and reason would not have been outraged to the point where it is imputed a crime for an honorable man to be compelled to defend himself. . . .

When I returned from the army the last time, there were several

[11] Carnot.
[12] Robespierre.
[13] The reference is to Barère, who dramatically announced the armies' victories to the Assembly, while Saint-Just himself was with the army at Fleurus.

familiar faces that I missed. Members of the government were scattered over the frontiers or buried in their offices; and decisions were left in the hands of two or three men entrusted with the influence and authority of the Committee as a whole, most of whose members were dispersed by their missions, or by sickness, or by the accusations brought against others in order to keep them away. It seemed to me that the government had been entirely taken over by two or three men, and I believe that it was during this period of isolation that they conceived the dangerous notion of making changes in the government and of attracting greater authority to themselves.

On my return, as I have said, everything had been changed; the members of the government were not divided but they were scattered, and the few who remained enjoyed absolute power and, in order to maintain it, accused others of aspiring to it.

It was under these circumstances that a plan was conceived to bring innocent men to trial and that an attempt was made to rouse against them suspicions that had no foundation. For my own person, I have nothing to complain of: I was left in peace as a citizen without ambition and one who walked alone, and it was by error and the accident of the vote that I was entrusted with a report that was to commit me to ideas which, I would say, I was ill suited to express. . . .

If you reflect carefully on what took place at your last meeting, you will note the realization of all that I have said. Here we have a man whom hostile treatment drove away from the Committee at a time, in fact, when it was composed of but a handful of men. In seeking to justify his conduct before you, he does not, it is true, explain himself with sufficient clarity; but some allowance may be made for his withdrawal from the scene and the bitterness of his soul. He does not know the cause or the purpose of his persecution; he is merely aware of his misfortune. It is said that he seeks to enslave men's minds: this point I must explain and dispel a fallacy which, if persisted in, would threaten virtue with proscription. What exclusive right do you claim over men's minds, you who believe it is a crime to touch men's souls? Is sensibility a thing of evil?

Are you then at the court of Philip,[14] you who make war on eloquence? An enslaver of men's minds, you say? Who denies you the right, you who think it evil that a man should win the nation's esteem, to attempt to do likewise? There never was a despot, unless it was Richelieu, to whom a writer's fame was a personal affront. . . . And yet today a

[14] Philip of Macedon, father of Alexander the Great.

French citizen is told: *You have not the right to attempt to persuade.*
The member who spoke to you yesterday[15] does not appear to have
pointed clearly to those whom he accused. He has no complaint to make,
and indeed he made no complaint, of the Committees themselves; for
the Committees are, I believe, still worthy of your esteem, and the
misfortunes whose course I have traced to you were born of the
isolation and the excessive authority of a few of their members who
were left in solitary control.

The work of the government was bound to be impaired by the dis-
persal of its members. Couthon is continually absent; Prieur de la Marne
had been absent for eight months; Saint-André is at Fort-la-Montague;
I was with the army; and the rest, who exercised the authority of us
all, appear to me to have attempted to profit by their absence. . . .

One single obstacle yet stood in their way: the Jacobin Club, which
they term the enslaver of opinion. So it became necessary to sacrifice
the most influential of its members. For, while they hatched the plot of
which I have spoken, Billaud-Varenne and Collot d'Herbois have for
some time vented their spleen against the Club; they have ceased to
attend it and to speak there.

If they had succeeded in their plans while the majority of the Committee were immersed in the details of their tasks, a few men would have
ruled; they would no longer have had to fear any trouble from the
orators and would have enjoyed an unchallenged reputation and authority.

There was, then, a conspiracy afoot to usurp all power by sending
some of the Committee's members to the scaffold and dispersing others
in various parts of the Republic, by destroying the Revolutionary
Tribunal and depriving Paris of its magistrates. Billaud-Varenne and
Collot d'Herbois are the authors of this plot. . . .

(2) Levasseur de la Sarthe[16]

Has one, in fact, ever believed or been able to believe that the
Terror was the work of one man or of a handful of men? Could one
possibly calculate its nature and its consequences in advance? I find it
difficult to comprehend! But as this fact, if not believed, has at least

[15] Robespierre.
[16] From Levasseur's *Mémoires,* published in the 1820s. The passage is reproduced in
Jacob, *op. cit.,* pp. 155-7; trans. G. Rudé (by permission of the Librairie Armand
Colin). René Levasseur (1747-1832) represented the Sarthe and voted with the Mountain in the National Convention, 1792-4.

been often repeated, let us reject this shameful, ignoble distortion of
the truth and demonstrate that humanity has not descended to such
depths of ignominy.

Did Robespierre and the Mountain, who have been made the scapegoat for all the Revolution's excesses, deliberately create and develop
the reign of Terror? This is how, in my opinion, the question should be
put, and the facts will give us the answer. First of all, it will surely not
be argued that Robespierre deliberately planned all these demoralizing
excesses, seeing that he constantly opposed them and that their authors
were his bitterest enemies. Among the papers collected by Courtois[17]
one finds various notes drafted by Robespierre that are sufficient to
show the horror that the saturnalian orgies of the Terrorists inspired
in the illustrious member of the Committee of Public Safety. Here we
find him reproaching Léonard Bourdon for having degraded the Convention by introducing the habit of speaking without removing one's
hat; and here he condemns with all the power at his command the
ghastly attempts made by the Commune to establish the public cult of
atheism. On all occasions he reveals himself as the friend of virtue,
religion and decent behavior. The cult of the Goddess of Reason dis-
gusts him even more than the fanaticism of the Catholic priests. He
realizes that a man can be a true republican only if he is steeped in
morality and religion. These are also Saint-Just's ideas and the ideas of
every honest man in the Mountain—that is, of the vast majority of its
members.

But, it is said, behind his elegant façade, Robespierre, in order to pave
the way for his dictatorship, shed blood with indifference, if not with
joy. Owing to his implacable hatred, scaffolds were erected everywhere.

Let us consider the facts. Where were the most odious of all these
crimes committed? At Nantes and at Lyons.[18] Let us see how the friends
and confidants of Robespierre spoke with him of these excesses; and I
quote from the papers assembled by Robespierre's principal accusers. . . .[19]

The two first testimonies that I have cited prove, I believe, beyond
any shadow of doubt that the wild excesses of a few proconsuls, whose

[17] Courtois was the author of a report, based on the private papers of the victims of
Thermidor, which was submitted to the Convention in the late fall of 1794 as an
indictment of Robespierre and his group.

[18] Carrier's *noyades* at Nantes and Collot d'Herbois' *fusillades* at Lyons were among
the most notorious of the acts of the "proconsuls" in suppressing the provincial revolts
against the Jacobin government in the fall of 1793.

[19] Levasseur here quotes from certain passages in Courtois' report which express
the revulsion felt by two of Robespierre's correspondents at the repressive measures
taken by Carrier at Nantes, Collot at Lyons and Tallien at Bordeaux.

activities have sullied the glorious record of the Republic, cannot be attributed to Robespierre and that part of the Committee of Public Safety and the Mountain which voted with him. The last of them proves, too, that in the midst of anarchy men of heart and reason were dreaming of laying the foundations of a happy and orderly system, but one that should be based on complete equality and the most absolute freedom. As Saint-Just said so often, "The Republic must be loved in order to be solidly established." How then should he have wanted to degrade it and to drench it in blood?

Yet certain acts of severity may be ascribed to Robespierre and his supporters. They were all inflexible when they believed that the safety of the sacred cause was being compromised. None of these men recoiled before the consequences to which their principles led them, however deplorable their temporary results might be and however painful might be the acts that they entailed. Thus they struck down the leaders of the Gironde, the Constituents who devised the Constitution of 1791, the rabid associates of Hébert and the corrupt friends of Danton. But there is a vast gulf separating these acts of legal vengeance, whose necessity they believed to be established, from the bloody holocausts that horrified all France; it is the gulf dividing the legal punishment of crime from the murder of innocent men in the bosom of their families. The difference between Robespierre and Saint-Just and men like Carrier, Collot and Le Bon is like that between a just but sternly inflexible magistrate and an executioner stained with the blood that he has been paid to spill.

Robespierre and the Mountain, it has been said, were the instigators of excessive violence. How comes it then that they broke with the vile and stupid demagogues of the Paris Commune? Robespierre and the Mountain, they say, were eager to shed blood. How comes it then that the enemies who overthrew them had at their head Collot d'Herbois, Billaud-Varenne, Carrier, and all the murderers and human tigers of that tragic yet glorious period?

This is not the place to examine Courtois' report against Robespierre and the Republic; but the brief reflections that I here offer to the reader will be so many landmarks to help me to rediscover the ignominy of Thermidor and the baseness of the leaders who divided the government between them after that counterrevolutionary event.

(3) Babeuf [20]

What a difference there was between Danton, the patron of every enthusiast for the Republic of the rich, and those whose every word and deed breathed their love for the common people and for Equality! Danton loved the Republic, but after the fashion of his intimate friend, the butcher Legendre. His conception of a Republic was one in which the revolutionaries would take the place of the princes and great lords, in which Le Rincy should be given to Merlin de Thionville and Comtat-Messaline to the same Legendre.[21] We are as good as Artois and Orleans, these rogues would say, following their master. Yes, Danton would frequently repeat, let each man have his turn. The Revolution is for those who made it. The revolutionaries must take the place of those they have overthrown; like them, they shall have gold, property, palaces, beautiful mistresses and every imaginable delight. Was this the doctrine of the philosopher of Arras [Robespierre]? Let one but listen to his sublime speech of the 17th Pluviôse of the Year II [February 5, 1794], and one will find in it an entirely different conception of the *aim* of revolution: "We desire (he said) an order of things . . . in which THE *PATRIE* ASSURES THE WELFARE OF EVERY INDIVIDUAL and in which every individual proudly enjoys the wealth and glory of the *patrie*." And that is the man who, at the moment when the whole nation is regretting the folly of the path into which it was drawn, is attacked by an individual called Vilain d'Aubigny, a pander to the voluptuaries of our times. With what arguments do such men support their charges? What case does this man make for a legitimate indictment of the youthful but wise Saint-Just, whom he equally slanders and vilifies? This is what he concocts against the two of them: a wretched re-hash of the same atrocious distortions that were spread about in the months following Thermidor and that, one would have hoped, had worn too thin since then to be used again. Urn of Robespierre! Beloved ashes! Come to

---

[20] From no. 34, *Tribun du Peuple*, 5 Nov., 1795; reproduced by Jacob, *op. cit.*, pp. 205-8; trans. G. Rudé (by permission of the Librairie Armand Colin).

Gracchus Babeuf (1760-97), author of the Manifesto of the Plebeians (1795) and promoter of a conspiracy to overthrow the Directory and found a socialist-cooperative commonwealth in 1796; hence often described as a forerunner of Karl Marx. Disillusioned with Robespierre's group over the shelving of the Jacobin Constitution in the fall of 1793, he condemned Robespierre as a "tyrant" and joined in the chorus of vilification of the fallen leader in Thermidor and the months that followed. But his experiences of the Thermidorian "reaction" and the development of his own political ideas led him, by the end of 1794, to revise his judgment of Robespierre and to present him (as in this article) as the would-be architect of an egalitarian society.

[21] The actress Comtat was Legendre's mistress.

life again and confound these empty slanderers. Yet no! despise them and rest in peace, dear bones! The whole French nation rises up to avenge your death. And you, to whom is offered the sacrilegious broadsheet of which I speak, learn to honor the memory of a sage, a great lawgiver and a friend of the human race! And refrain from insulting a man whom posterity will venerate. As for you, patriots, into whose unwilling hands this disgusting pamphlet has been forcibly thrust, what must you do with it? Am I to believe that you will hesitate to fling it into the sewers?

Democrats do not like to hear the Constitution of 1793 spoken of in disrespectful tones; besides, they do not consider it to be the exclusive work of Hérault de Séchelles.[22] While I agree with the author of the *Opinion* that this code neither established nor yet assured the highest degree of social happiness, yet one must admit that it took a great step towards it. It was a solid base, a foundation stone, on which the future perfect edifice of Equality might be built. All the elements and means of improvement were contained and indicated in this single sketch, and it is because they were only too well aware of it that our enemies would stop at nothing in order to destroy it. One sees, too, in the presentation of this great work the application of a thought as bold and philanthropic as that already long conceived in the mind of Maximilien Robespierre. In one of the numbers of his newspaper he blames Solon for having wished only to frame such laws as were "the least bad that the people for whom they were intended could conceive of"; and he adds "that true lawgivers must not adjust their laws to the corrupted tastes of the people for whom they are destined; but they must be able both to frame laws that will regenerate the people by basing them on justice and virtue, and to overcome every obstacle in order to subject the people to them." This, I repeat, is the intention that lies behind the charter of '93, whose principles are far more pure than the French nation which adopted it, even at the time when it was published. Yet those who drafted the charter did not apply Robespierre's maxim in its entirety, no doubt because they deemed it unwise to do so and thought they might arrive more surely at the summit of justice if they proceeded by degrees. Their intentions to reach it were, I believe, genuine enough, and I cannot consent to charge them with cowardice and hypocrisy. The advance that they had planned by short stages might perhaps not have been a bad thing; they had still a long way to go. It is true that their enemies had had thereby time to see the way they were going and to cut off their

[22] Member of the Committee of Public Safety and promoter of the Constitution in the Convention; executed with Danton in April 1794.

route. But who can be certain that a man who insists on driving post-haste will not hurl his carriage over a precipice? Let us not condemn those who sought the good of mankind but who, to achieve it, chose a different route from ours. When Michel Le Pelletier presented his plan for a common education, he also aimed at Equality. And Robespierre had aims of a similar kind when, at the Jacobin Club on April 23, 1793, he won the well merited applause and enthusiastic support of the people after presenting to them his Declaration of the Rights of Man, in which property was thus defined: "The right of every citizen to enjoy that portion of goods that is guaranteed to him by Law; a right that is limited by the obligation to respect" the rights of all other members of society and whose exercise shall be without prejudice to their safety, their liberty, their life and PROPERTY.[23] This definition became my own Manifesto, and that drafting of the Rights of Man and the Citizen was the work of no hypocrite. The epithet may be applied to those who changed that definition and put in its place the equivocal formula that "Property is the right to dispose at will of the fruits of one's industry," etc. Robespierre's Declaration of Rights was altered only in this crucial point; otherwise it appears almost unchanged at the head of the Constitution of '93. So it may be said that, mutilated in this way, it was no longer the same as my Manifesto. Yet I would not, for that reason, have the presumption to challenge Robespierre's right to the claim that it was he who, in the Revolution, was the first to devise a plan for true Equality, an object that, as proved in a hundred passages of his works, long occupied his thoughts. Such is the justice that it behooves me to render to this *tyrant*, whose goods and chattels were sold in early Pluviôse [late January 1795] by the State for the sum of thirty thousand francs in *assignats*, or three hundred francs in coin.[24]

[23] For Robespierre's draft of this Declaration, see pp. 54-57.
[24] At the time Babeuf wrote (November, 1795) the revolutionary paper money (the *assignat*) had fallen to 1 per cent of its nominal value. At the time Robespierre's goods were sold it still stood at about 15 per cent. Three hundred pre-revolutionary *livres* (or francs) were the equivalent of about £25 sterling, or $100.

13
Robespierre in Retrospect

The four judgments that follow were made by three men and one woman who had lived through the Terror and had known either Robespierre himself or some of his close associates. But, though they were contemporaries, theirs were mature judgments recorded twenty, thirty or even forty years after his death.

The first judgment is by Bertrand Barère, who had been Robespierre's colleague for a year on the Committee of Public Safety and had played a leading part in his overthrow. But, unlike his fellow "Thermidorians" Fouché, Merlin and Dubois de Crancé (see Chapter 12), he shows a regard for the fallen leader which is reminiscent of that shown by Brutus for his victim Caesar.

The second is by Filippo Buonarotti, Italian revolutionary democrat, associate of Babeuf in 1796, founder of the Italian Carbonari society, and the author of Conspiracy of the Equals (1829), which had considerable influence on the early French socialist movement. As a young man, he had met Robespierre at Maurice Duplay's.

The third is by Madame de Staël, writer and political hostess, archenemy of Napoleon, and daughter of Louis XVI's minister, Necker. She had met Robespierre at her father's house in 1789.

The fourth (in two parts) is by Napoleon, taken from his reminiscences in captivity at St. Helena. As a young brigadier, Napoleon had himself been a "Robespierrist": he does not appear to have known Maximilien, but he was well acquainted with Augustin and, in consequence, had suffered a short term of imprisonment after the two brothers' execution in Thermidor.

BERTRAND BARÈRE: "A TRUE REPUBLICAN" (1832) [1]

"He was a man without personal ambition, a Republican to his fingertips," said Barère; "his misfortune was to have aspired to a dictatorship, which he believed to be the only means to arrest the spread of evil passions. He often spoke of this to those of us who were concerned with the military operations. We were not blind to the fact that

---

[1] From an interview with Barère in 1832, reported by David d'Angers, a former deputy to the National Convention, and published in Barère's *Mémoires* (1842); reproduced in Jacob, *op. cit.*, p. 201; trans G. Rudé (by permission of the Librairie Armand Colin).

Saint-Just, who modeled himself on a leader more dictatorial than himself, would have finally overthrown him in order to take his place; we also knew that he would have sent us to the guillotine as men opposed to his projects; and so we overthrew him. Since then, I have thought much about this man. I have seen that his dominating passion was to establish a Republican government and that those whom he wished to bring to justice were the men whose opposition stood in the way of the operation of such a government. Would to heaven there were in the Chamber of Deputies today someone to point to those who conspire against our freedom! We were then in the middle of a war, and we did not understand this man. He was a nervous, choleric individual, whose mouth twitched when he spoke. His was the temperament of many great men, and posterity will not refuse him this title!"

When M. David spoke of the proposal to make sculptured portraits of the most illustrious men of the Revolution and pronounced the name of Danton, Barère rose excitedly from his chair and cried with an imperious gesture: "Do not forget Robespierre! He was a man of purity and integrity, a true Republican. It was his vanity, his irascible sensibility, and his unjust suspicions of his colleagues that were the cause of his downfall. . . . It was a great calamity!"

FILIPPO BUONAROTTI: "THE VICTIM OF IMMORALITY" (1837) [2]

The public life of Maximilien embraces almost the whole of the first five years of the French Revolution of the 18th century. During that time, he was in turn writer, magistrate, orator and statesman. In the Constituent Assembly he distinguished himself by views which, though directly opposed to those held by the royalists of the old régime, differed in many respects from the political aims of the leading men within that body; and most of his colleagues professed contempt for the unpalatable consequences that he drew from the principle of national sovereignty.

At the time of the massacre on the Champ de Mars, Robespierre drew up a memorable address, in which he expounded his democratic ideas to the people of France and exposed the sinister pretensions of the *bourgeois* and constitutional-monarchist party. After the carnage, Robespierre alone sustained the flagging spirits of the party of equality which, centered in the Jacobin Club, had almost been destroyed by the defection of the deputies who followed Lafayette to form the aristocratic so-

[2] From Buonarotti's *Observations sur Maximilien Robespierre* (1837); reproduced by Jacob, *op. cit.,* pp. 215-19; trans. G. Rudé (by permission of the Librairie Armand Colin).

ciety of the Feuillants.[3] What Robespierre then believed to be far more important than the destruction of monarchy was the elimination of aristocracy and the firm establishment of equality; and it was because he was convinced that this was not the view of the other revolutionary members of the Assembly that he rejected the plan of some for a Republic and proposed the decree excluding all of them from the incoming legislature; for it was his intention to pave the way for the Republic by developing a sense of civic virtue which would be its surest prop.

Under the Legislative Assembly, he refused the post of Public Prosecutor in order not to be compelled to enforce laws made by the rich against the mass of the people. For despite all that has been said, Robespierre was tender-hearted and humane; he proposed that the death penalty be abolished and other penalties be made less severe. In his private relations he was generous, compassionate and ever willing to serve; but towards tyranny, injustice and immorality he was always stern and unrelenting. . . .

On August 10, 1792, Robespierre was a member of the new municipal council to which the people of Paris had elected him at the beginning of the insurrection that overthrew the monarchy. He took part in the activity and shared the dangers of that episode; and it was he who, when victory was won, led a deputation of his fellow councillors to the Legislative Assembly, which was hesitant and divided, and placed before it the political proposals that the occasion demanded. Soon after, the will of the electors, approved by the people of the capital, brought him from the tumultuous sessions of the municipality to the solemn and even more stormy sessions of the National Convention. There began the most glorious part of his whole political career. At certain periods of history there appear on earth rare mortals whose genius, virtue and audacity astonish the world and change the face of nations: such men were Moses, Pythagoras and Lycurgus; such were Jesus and Mahomet; and such would Robespierre, too, have been if there had been fifty men in the Convention to understand him and to lend him their support. He was a man of the most austere principles and habits: he was temperate, incorruptible, industrious and good. These qualities endeared him to all who knew him well; the family of the carpenter Duplay, among whom he passed the last years of his life, still cherishes his memory and venerates his virtues.

In the Convention, it fell to Robespierre to combat at once the remnants of royalism, *bourgeois* greed and the immorality of public

---

[3] The moderates seceded from the Jacobin Club to form their own *société des Feuillants* at the time of the King's flight to Varennes, in June, 1791.

men. His constant thought was to reform both manners and the social order by creating institutions that would serve as a base for the majestic edifice of equality and the people's Republic. His reward was the immortal glory won for him by a violent and untimely death. In the struggle that he waged with such devotion and fortitude he was sustained by a few members of the National Convention, the great majority of the Jacobins of 1793, and the mass of the people who had awarded him a crown of incorruptibility. The writings which Robespierre has left us are, with the example of his private and public life, further witnesses to his constant preoccupation with the social regeneration to which his life had been devoted. PEOPLE, EQUALITY, VIRTUE: these were the great ideas to which he applied all his legislative energies and talents. . . .

The greatest misfortune was that a gangrene was sapping the vitality of the Convention, where Danton, applauded by the great number of his minions, paraded his love of money, greed for power, indifference to the public interest, and contempt for civic virtue. The Committee of Public Safety believed him to be in the pay of England. Robespierre saw in the vices and intrigues of this faction the last obstacle to be overcome in order to realize the peaceful triumph of equality and democracy. He resolved to destroy it, and in so doing he signed his own death warrant. When integrity and virtue were publicly proclaimed and immorality was declared the enemy of revolution, when egoism and factional intrigue were condemned from the Assembly's rostrum, when dishonest deputies were sent before the Revolutionary Tribunal, the factious enemies of virtue grew pale and devised the most atrocious plans. A reform such as that conceived by Robespierre and his friends is so foreign to the generally accepted ideas of social order that it is not surprising that there should have been added to those who fought it as a threat to their interests and vices others who opposed it from an inability to understand its nature and to reconcile it with old habits and established principles; and it is perhaps to this conservative attitude of mind that must be attributed the rejection of two great measures, a common education and the distribution of *biens nationaux* ("national property") among the people. If we are to trust the revelations made by some of Robespierre's accusers, the intention that he had expressed of modifying the laws of property contributed not a little to swell the number of his enemies.[4]

Robespierre had successively attacked court, nobility, priests, *bourgeois,* the Girondins, the corrupted *Montagnards,* the bloodsuckers and betrayers; now they all leagued against him, if not in fact at least in

---

[4] The reference is to the Laws of Ventôse (see page 51).

spirit and intention. His one support lay in the toiling and suffering people; and they could all too easily be divided, deceived and made defenseless. Who can relate all the tricks and calumnies that were devised to persuade the credulous and timid to turn against a man whom they had formerly admired and flattered? . . .

Every form of counterrevolutionary resentment, whether veiled or overt, fixed on this one idea: the death of Robespierre. Then the spirit of reform and equality took refuge in the Jacobin Club and Paris Commune. Danton's friends took fright and sowed distrust, confusion and alarm among the *Montagnards,* in whose number there were several corrupted representatives. We are inclined to believe that Robespierre, enjoying the trust of the people as he did, might have outwitted his enemies if he had taken a few precautionary measures. But, too trustful in the power of truth, he preferred to leave the Convention to judge men whom he might have crushed by the power of his own oratory. In the Assembly, he exposed the immoral conduct of the factions, the errors of government, and the dangers of the policy that then prevailed. From beginning to end his speech exhaled the purest love of truth and of the people. Far from demanding, as has been claimed, an end of revolutionary government, he counseled that it be maintained, while insisting that it be purged of the rogues and traitors who had crept into its ranks. As for the Terror, he wished, while lightening its burden on the people, to make it both more just and more severe in dealing with aristocrats and enemies of civic virtue. He was overwhelmed by the weight of numbers and by the fury of his foes, whose tumultuous accusations drowned his efforts to reply. With scandalous speed they passed from gagging to arresting him and to declaring him an outlaw. The people who rushed to his support were divided and confused by incredible charges of tyranny, royalism and secret relations with the Bourbons. These accusations are confirmed in the Committees' reports, and their authors have later confessed to the treachery that inspired them.

Robespierre died poor and beloved of all who had occasion to know and to appreciate his virtue. He was the victim of immorality. The people never had a more sincere and a more devoted friend. Great efforts have been made to sully his memory: now he is accused of aiming at dictatorship, and now he alone is held accountable for every necessary measure of severity taken by the revolutionary government. But happy, we say, would France and humanity have been if Robespierre had been a dictator and had been allowed to carry out his great reforms! He never held the power to proscribe and to judge; his only authority lay in his voice. He had withdrawn from the Committee of Public Safety during a time when the Revolutionary Tribunal was imposing large numbers of punishments, but at such moments of crisis the urgency and severity of punishment such as these are accepted and approved by men of the most spotless virtue.

MADAME DE STAËL: "HYPOCRITICAL" (1818) [5]

This Committee was not composed of men of superior talent; the machine of terror, the springs of which had been prepared for action by events, exercised alone unbounded power. The government resembled the hideous instrument employed on the scaffold; the axe was seen rather than the hand which put it in motion. A single question was sufficient to overturn the power of these men; it was—how many are they? But their force was measured by the atrocity of their crimes, and nobody dared attack them. These twelve members of the Committee of Public Safety distrusted one another, as the Convention distrusted them, and they distrusted it; as the army, the people, and the partizans of the revolution were all mutually filled with alarm. No name of this epoch will remain except Robespierre. Yet he was neither more able nor more eloquent than the rest; but his political fanaticism had a character of calmness and austerity which made him feared by all his colleagues.

I once conversed with him at my father's house, in 1789, when he was known merely as an advocate of the province of Artois, who carried to a great height his democratical principles. His features were mean, his complexion pale, his veins of a greenish hue; he maintained the most absurd propositions with a coolness which had the air of conviction; and I could easily believe that, at the beginning of the Revolution, he had adopted sincerely certain ideas, upon the equality of fortunes as well as of ranks, which he caught in the course of his reading and with which his envious and mischievous character was delighted to arm itself. But he became ambitious when he had triumphed over his rival in the arts of the demagogue, Danton, the Mirabeau of the mob. The latter had more genius than Robespierre and was more accessible to pity; but it was suspected, and with reason, that he was not proof against the seductions of money; a weakness which, in the end, always ruins demagogues; for the people cannot endure those who enrich themselves. This is a species of self-denial with which nothing can prevail upon them to dispense.

Danton was factious, Robespierre was hypocritical; Danton was fond

[5] From *Considerations on the Principal Events of the French Revolution* (London, 1818), II, 139-44.

of pleasure, Robespierre only of power; he sent to the scaffold some as counter-revolutionists, others as ultra-revolutionists. There was something mysterious in his manner, which caused an unknown terror to hover about in the midst of the ostensible terror which the government proclaimed. He never adopted the means of popularity then generally in use; he was not ill dressed; on the contrary, he was the only person who wore powder in his hair; his clothes were neat, and his countenance had nothing familiar. The desire of ruling carried him, without doubt, to distinguish himself from others at the very moment when equality in everything was desired. Traces of a secret design are also perceived in the perplexed harangues which he made in the Convention and which, in some respects, recall to our recollection those of Cromwell. It is rarely, indeed, that anyone who is not a military chief can become dictator. But the civil power had then much more influence than the military; the republican spirit led to a distrust of all the victorious generals; the soldiers themselves delivered up their leaders as soon as the least alarm with respect to their fidelity arose. Political dogmas, if the name can be applied to such wanderings of intellect, reigned at that time, and not men. Something abstract was wanted in authority, that everybody might be thought to have a share in it. Robespierre had acquired the reputation of high democratical virtue and was believed incapable of personal views. As soon as he was suspected, his power was at an end.

The most indecent irreligion served as a lever for the subversion of the social order. There was a kind of consistency in founding crime upon impiety: it is an homage paid to the intimate union of religious opinions with morality. Robespierre conceived the idea of celebrating a festival in honour of the Supreme Being, flattering himself, doubtless, with being able to rest his political ascendancy on a religion arranged according to his own notions; as those have frequently done who have wished to seize the supreme power. But in the procession of this impious festival, he thought of walking the first, in order to claim pre-eminence over his colleagues; and from that time he was lost. The spirit of the moment and the personal resources of the man were not calculated for the enterprize. Besides, it was known that he was acquainted with no other means of getting rid of competitors than by destroying them through the agency of the Revolutionary Tribunal, which gave murder an air of legality. The colleagues of Robespierre, not less detestable than himself—Collot d'Herbois, Billaud Varennes—attacked him to secure their own safety; the abhorrence of crime did not inspire them with this resolution; they meant to kill a man but not to change the government.

It was not so with Tallien, the hero of the 9th of Thermidor, nor with

Barras,[6] the commander of the armed force on that day, nor with several other conventionalists who then joined them. They meant, in overturning him, to break with the same blow the sceptre of terror. Thus this man, who during more than a year had signed judgments of death, to an unheard of amount, was seen bleeding on the very table where he was wont to affix his name to the horrible sentences. His jaw was shattered by a pistol ball; he could not even speak in his own defence; he, who had spoken so much for the proscription of others. Might it not be said that Divine justice does not disdain, in inflicting punishment, to strike the imagination of men by all the circumstances which can act upon it the most powerfully?

NAPOLEON AT ST. HELENA: "SCAPEGOAT OF THE REVOLUTION"

(1) As Reported by the Count de las Cases (Dec. 15, 1815) [7]

The Emperor, next proceeding to take a review of different points of the Revolution, dwelt particularly on Robespierre, whom he did not know but whom he believed to be destitute of talent, energy, or system. He considered him, notwithstanding, as the real scape-goat of the Revolution, sacrificed as soon as he endeavoured to arrest it in its course: the common fate, he observed, of all who, before himself (Napoleon) had ventured to take that step. The Terrorists and their doctrine survived Robespierre; and if their excesses were not continued, it was because they were obliged to bow to public opinion. They threw all the blame on Robespierre; but the latter declared shortly before his death that he was a stranger to the recent executions and that he had not appeared in the Committees for six weeks previously. Napoleon confessed that while he was with the army of Nice, he had seen some long letters addressed by Robespierre to his brother, condemning the horrors of the Commissioners of the Convention, who, as he expressed it, were ruining the Revolution by their tyranny and atrocities.

"Cambacérès, who," observed the Emperor, "must be a good authority on subjects relating to that period, answered an inquiry which I one day addressed to him respecting the condemnation of Robespierre, in these remarkable words: 'Sire, that was a sentence without a trial'; adding that Robespierre had more foresight and conception than was

---

[6] Madame de Staël has clearly misjudged the situation here: both Tallien and Barras were terrorists who had been criticized by Robespierre for their excessive severity in repressing counterrevolution in the provinces.

[7] From the *Journal of the Private Life and Conversations of the Emperor Napoleon at Saint Helena* by the Count de las Cases (London, 1823), I, 345-7.

generally imagined. That after he should have succeeded in subduing the unbridled factions which he had to oppose, his intention was to restore a system of order and moderation. 'Some time previous to his fall,' added Cambacérès, 'he delivered a most admirable speech on this subject; it was not thought fit to insert it in the *Moniteur,* and all trace of it is now lost.' " [8]

This is not the first instance I have heard of omissions and want of accuracy in the *Moniteur.* In the reports inserted in that journal relative to the proceedings of the Assembly, there must be a period remarkable for incorrectness; as the minutes of these proceedings were for a time arbitrarily drawn up by one of the Committees.

Those who are induced to believe that Robespierre was at once wearied, satiated and alarmed by the Revolution and had resolved on checking it affirm that he would not take any decided step until after he had read his famous speech. He considered it so fine that he had no doubt of its effect on the Assembly. If this is true, his mistake or his vanity cost him dear. Those who think differently assert that Danton and Camille-des-Moulins had precisely the same views, and yet that Robespierre sacrificed them. To these it is replied that Robespierre sacrificed them to preserve his popularity, because he judged that the decisive moment had not yet arrived or because he did not wish to resign to them the glory of the enterprise.

Be that as it may, it is certain that the nearer we approach to the instruments and the agents in that catastrophe, the greater obscurity and mystery we find; and this uncertainty will but increase with time. Thus the page of history will, on this point as on many others, become the record not so much of the events which really occurred as of the statements which are given of them.

(2) As Reported in Gourgaud's Journal (Dec. 16, 1816) [9]

Robespierre's role in history will always remain obscure. It is certain that Carrier, Fréron and Tallien were far more bloodthirsty than he. Danton left a great many friends, among them Talleyrand and Sémonville; he was a real party leader who was loved by his followers. Robespierre should have had himself appointed dictator, though this was not so easy for him as it might be for a general. Soldiers are not liberty-loving republicans; being accustomed to obey, they are quite happy to see civilians subject to orders like themselves. . . .

---

[8] A reference to Robespierre's speech of 8th Thermidor (July 26, 1794).
[9] From Jacob, *op. cit.,* pp. 210-11; trans. G. Rudé (by permission of the Librairie Armand Colin).

The latter [Robespierre] was overthrown because he wanted to moderate and stop the course of the Revolution. Cambacérès has told me that on the eve of his death he made a magnificent speech in this sense which, however, was never printed. Billaud and other Terrorists, seeing that he was wearying of the Terror and would unfailingly bring them to justice, concerted against him and incited the moderates to overthrow (as they said) the tyrant, but in reality it was to take his place and to intensify the Terror. The people of Paris thought that in removing Robespierre they were destroying tyranny, whereas the purpose of his removal was to make it flourish more luxuriantly than ever. But once Robespierre had fallen, the explosion was such that, in spite of all their efforts, the Terrorists were never able to gain the upper hand again.

Collot d'Herbois committed atrocities at Lyons. It is hard to conceive why he should have thought fit to have five to six thousand persons shot when, in a city of this sort, it would have been more than enough to have executed 50 or 60 leaders.

Carrier wrote to the Convention that the Loire was a beautiful revolutionary tomb. These men were far bloodier than Robespierre. He was a man of principle and probity. But he made a fatal mistake in sacrificing Danton; and he should have exiled Chaumette, Hébert, etc., instead of sending them to the scaffold; yet, at that time, there was no other way to punish than by the guillotine. Danton's party was very large, and it had its revenge in the overthrow of Robespierre.

PART THREE

ROBESPIERRE IN HISTORY

Historians' views of Robespierre have been influenced by four main factors: their country of origin, the time at which they wrote, the sources available to them as historians, and their own social attitudes and political beliefs. It is, therefore, important to look into all four factors when considering a writer's credentials as a chronicler of Robespierre.

In the three following chapters, we have tried to take some account of these points in selecting extracts from a representative group of French and English writers of the nineteenth and twentieth centuries.

14

French Historians of the 19th Century

We have chosen three short extracts that are typical, each in its way, of French historians' attitudes toward Robespierre in the last century. The views of these writers vary considerably, reflecting not only their different party-political affiliations, but their varied experiences and the degree of availability of historical records.

The first of them, Adolphe Thiers, *was a professional politician rather than a professional historian, although he combined both functions in the course of a long and distinguished career. He wrote history as a Restoration liberal during the 1820s; he helped to enthrone Louis-Philippe after the Revolution of 1830; and he re-emerged as a conservative Prime Minister after the overthrow of Napoleon III in 1870. But he was at no time a democrat, and, like Madame de Staël, he considered that the Revolution had taken a wrong turning after adopting the liberal-monarchical Constitution of 1791. So he had little use for Robespierre, whom he described as being "one of the most odious beings that could have borne absolute rule over men."*

The second writer, Eugène Sue, was not a historian but a popular novelist. He had been an advanced democrat in 1848, and he evidently both admired and revered the memory of Robespierre. His views are not particularly original, but they are of interest as being typical of a small group of writers (Louis Blanc was another; also Hamel, Robespierre's first serious biographer) who, during this period, cherished the memory of "the men of 1793."

The third writer, Alphonse Aulard, was the only professional historian of the three and the only one who, by today's standards, would be considered a serious scholar. He was, in fact, the first writer of modern French history who based his work firmly on documentary evidence; and he had the advantage over Thiers, who had to rely mainly on descriptive or narrative records, of having access to the papers of both the Jacobin Club and the Committee of Public Safety. Yet, as a Radical of the Third Republic, he could hardly fail to be a Dantonist and, accordingly, to distrust Robespierre, who he thought to have been moved by petty jealousy and injured pride.

But, despite their widely varying opinions of Robespierre, these writers all had in common that they saw the French Revolution essentially as a battle of ideas and of contending political groups (note Aulard's subtitle), and they all tend to present their subject within this rather narrow political and ideological framework.

ADOLPHE THIERS (1824-5) [1]

Robespierre had vanity, but was not sufficiently great to be ambitious. Covetous of flattery and respect, he feasted upon them, and justified himself for receiving them by declaring that he had no wish to be all-powerful. He was surrounded by a kind of court, composed of a few men, but chiefly of a great number of women, who paid him the most refined attentions. Constantly resorting to his residence, they manifested the most unceasing solicitude for his welfare; they were continually praising amongst themselves his virtue, his eloquence, his genius; they called him a divine creature, and quite exalted above our human nature. A superannuated marchioness was the principal of this proud and bloodthirsty pontiff. Nothing is so certain a demonstration of the public infatuation as the gross admiration of the women. It is they also, who, by their active attentions, their language, and their restless affectation, make it appear ridiculous. . . .

[1] From A. Thiers, *The History of the French Revolution* (London, n.d.), pp. 445, 472-3.

It may be asked, what would have happened if Robespierre had gained the ascendancy? The state of desertion in which he found himself, proves that this could never have taken place. But even had he been conqueror, he must either have yielded to the general feeling, or have ultimately fallen. Like all usurpers, he would have been compelled to substitute for the horrors of faction a calm and mild system. But besides this, the disposition of such an usurper did not belong to him. Our revolution had too great a range to permit that the same man, who was deputy to the constituent assembly in 1789, should be proclaimed emperor or protector in 1804, in the church of Notre-Dame. In a country less advanced and of less extent, as England then was, where the same person might still be tribune and general, and combine the two functions; a Cromwell might be both a party man at the beginning, and a usurping soldier at the conclusion. But in a revolution so extended as ours, in which the war had been so terrible and so overpowering, wherein the same individual could not occupy at one and the same time the tribune and the camp, party men first devoured one another; after them came the military men, and a soldier finally remained the ultimate master.

Robespierre, then, could not act with us the part of a usurper. How came it that he was permitted to survive all those famous revolutionists, so far his superiors in genius and in might? Danton, for example? Robespierre was a man who was incorruptible, and a good reputation is requisite for captivating the crowd. He was without sympathy, and pity in revolutions destroys its possessor. He was possessed by an obstinate and pertinacious pride, and this is the only means of keeping oneself constantly present to people's minds. With these qualifications he necessarily survived all his rivals. But he was of the worst species of men. A devotee without passions, without the vices to which passions are exposed, but yet without the courage, the greatness, and the sensibility which ordinarily accompany them; a devotee living for nothing else than to satisfy his pride and his creed, hiding himself in the hour of danger, coming forth to attract adoration after the victory had been gained by others, is one of the most odious beings that could have borne absolute rule over men, and one would also say the most vile, if he had not possessed a strong conviction and acknowledged incorruptibility.

EUGÈNE SUE (1857) [2]

There are certain paradoxes of history, or rather certain historical lies which, by constant repetition, end by being generally accepted as truth, are considered as undisputable facts and remain for long unchallenged.

This has been the case with the event known as *the 9th Thermidor* (1794).

The following, thanks to royalist and liberal historians, is the view that is most generally held of this occasion:

> The revolution of the 9th Thermidor was carried through by the men of honor and decency in the Convention against the rogues in that Assembly . . . These honorable men, being revolted and horrified by the prolonged reign of Terror under Robespierre's dictatorship, joined together against the tyrant and monster, and plotted his downfall.

Now this is the complete and absolute *opposite of the truth.*

The leaders of the Thermidorian revolution *were the biggest rogues* in the Convention, and the martyrs of that revolution *were the purest and most irreproachable* citizens among the Nation's representatives.

Not only did Robespierre not wish the Terror to be prolonged, but *he was sent to the scaffold because he wanted to end a Terror* that had become not only revolting but absurd; and not only that, but inexpedient, since it had ceased to be categorically demanded by the need to defend the Republic, the Revolution and France against the combined assult of the coalition armies and the scourge of civil war that ravaged three-quarters of our provinces.

Not only did Robespierre exercise no other dictatorship than that which, on brief occasions and on certain questions, was thrust upon him by his outstanding patriotism and civic virtue and by the preeminence of his statesmanlike intelligence. . . . But during the last three months preceding the events of Thermidor, Robespierre, far from being the *tyrant* of the Convention, rarely appeared within it and, with his friends, formed a small minority in the Committees of Public Safety and General Security, whose meetings he hardly ever attended.

Before Thermidor, Robespierre wished to attempt to save the Revolution and the Republic from the evil reputation and the ruin with which they were threatened by the monstrous crimes of the Terrorists of the

[2] From an Ms. of June 1857, published by the *Annales historiques de la Révolution française,* no. 179, January-March 1965; trans. G. Rudé. Reprinted in English translation by permission of the Société des Études Robespierristes.

Convention, men like *Carrier, Collot d'Herbois, Tallien, Fouché, Fréron* and other proconsuls whose extortions, revoluting saturnalia and unmentionable cruelties had roused the indignation of France and Europe.

Robespierre wished to persuade the Convention to issue a warrant against the wretches whose presence befouled its meetings and to send them before the Revolutionary Tribunal in order to suffer the consequences for crimes that had too long remained unpunished. . . . But these Terrorists, seeing themselves threatened, united against him and the Jacobin party the majority within the Convention, which believed that it was itself in danger when, in fact, it had nothing to fear.

The following was the cause of that disastrous misunderstanding which was exploited with devilish skill by the Talliens, Fouchés, Frérons and other brigands:

Robespierre, who was determined to demand a warrant against the Terrorists, committed the fatal mistake, in his speech of the 8th Thermidor, of not making his real intentions sufficiently clear and of allowing vague accusations to hover like a threat over the heads of the different groups in the Assembly. Whereas he intended only to frighten the scoundrels, he struck fear into the innocent as well as the guilty . . . instead of preparing, as he had hoped, the minds of his hearers for the formal proposal that his friend *Saint-Just* was to make at the opening of the session after presenting the full facts and naming the Terrorists against whom the warrant was being demanded. . . .

One last reflection on the 9th Thermidor (in my view it is conclusive and irrefutable):

What was the moral standing of the five immortal martyrs of that fateful day—*Robespierre the Elder, Robespierre the Younger, Couthon, Saint-Just, and Lebas?* Their moral standing, as testified by even their bitterest enemies, was irreproachable!

What was the moral standing of *Collot d'Herbois, Fouché, Tallien, Fréron, Vadier,* and the rest, who succeeded in uniting the Convention against Robespierre and the Jacobins on the 9th Thermidor? These men, according to contemporaries and to the verdict of history, were stained with every vice and with every crime!

Does this not prove that the *journée* of the 9th Thermidor marked the *triumph of the scoundrels* over *the men of honor and integrity?*

Annecy, June 10, 1857.   EUGÈNE SUE.

ALPHONSE AULARD (1901) [3]

Robespierre . . . was universally popular in his lifetime. Every one saw in him the apostle, the initiator of democracy. It was he who, in April, 1791, when he demanded universal suffrage, set politicians the example of speaking of the people in a friendly and respectful tone, with a real feeling of brotherhood and equality. The people had other advocates, it is true, but none who exhibited such a lively and imperturbable esteem for the virtues of the people. The democrat Condorcet thought the people would be good when they were educated; the democrat Marat thought them futile and shallow, and treated them like children; Robespierre believed them to be responsible, reasonable, and virtuous; he even stated that all reason and all virtue resided in the people. He proclaimed that the people were never wrong: this was the theme of his oratory, at the Jacobins and in the Convention. And he was sincere; he really saw the people thus, living as he did in the house of working-folk of irreproachable character, educated and generous— the Duplays. This sincerity, his absolute honesty, and his austerity made him, in the eyes of the people, *the incorruptible.*

His deportment contributed to his popularity. The people liked his costume—that of a small "gentleman at large" of the old times—his powdered hair, and knew that he was glad to avoid the open breast, the red bonnet, of the extreme Jacobin. The people loved his grave and restrained eloquence, his long, cautious periods, and his imperturbably serious accent; his horror of laughter and his academic style.

The poor adored him when they heard him say that the rich were vicious; that with more than 3,000 livres a year it was hardly possible to be honest; that virtue lay in mediocrity.

Virtue! All politics, according to Robespierre, must tend to establish the reign of virtue and confound vice. He reasoned thus: those who are virtuous are right; error is a corruption of the heart; error cannot be sincere; error is always deliberate. There are only two parties: good and bad citizens. Conclusion: all those who do not think as we do must be eliminated from the city; they are evil-intentioned and unsociable people. Let us eliminate the Girondists to-day; tomorrow will be the turn of the Hébertists and Dantonists.

There is a political verity. Whosoever departs from it, be it ever so little, is an enemy of the people. How is this verity, this rigid line, to be distinguished? It can be seen if one is honest. Also Robespierre shows

[3] From *The French Revolution. A Political History 1789-1804* (London, 1910), III, 85-91.

it to the people; you need only follow Robespierre; he is and must be the minister of the Truth, the dictator of Verity.

Such, at the time we are speaking of, were the policy and the popularity of Robespierre.

He assumed an appearance of immobility, and he changed. A monarchist before August 10th, he was a republican after September 22nd; and he followed the movements of the populace far more than he led them. It is for this reason that he seems to us to-day a hypocritical demagogue, and also because he points out the desirable but not the possible; he says what ought to be done but never tells one how to do it.

He loves his country and humanity; he is ready to die for the people. But he adores and displays his *ego*. His hatreds are as eternal and inexorable as those of Mme. Roland. If this magnanimous woman prevented the Girondists from becoming reconciled with the Montagnards, we may say that this magnanimous man prevented the Montagnards from becoming reconciled with the Girondists.

The Girondists had wounded him in his religious conscience. He had not forgotten that in 1792 Guadet had ridiculed him in respect of his Providence. This ridicule was renewed. In the *Chronique de Paris* of November 9, 1792, there appeared a pen-portrait of Robespierre, attributed by some to Condorcet, by others to Rabaut Saint-Etienne:

> He has all the characteristics, not of a religious leader, but of the leader of a sect; he has obtained a reputation for austerity which aims at sanctity; he stands on the benches and speaks of God and Providence; he calls himself the friend of the poor and weak; he obtains women and the feeble-minded as his followers; he gravely receives their adoration and their homage; in times of danger he disappears, but when the danger is past one can see nothing but Robespierre; he is a priest, and will never be anything else.

The Girondists, laughing, seemed to foresee the projected pontificate of Robespierre, which as yet, perhaps, was only a dream of his imagination. His ideal was unmasked. Infuriated, he fought the Girondists to the death, in the name of virtue. He slandered them atrociously. With Marat, he prevented the reconciliation between the parties, which might perhaps have altered the fate of France.

Marat and Robespierre, greatly as they differed in character and ideals, were at this time the representatives, in the Mountain, of the insurrectionary tendency and the violent policy which consisted in the absolute destruction of the adverse party.

Danton seemed to be in agreement with them, but in reality he followed a totally different policy—a policy of conciliation, whose object was to form, with the wiser elements of the Gironde and the Mountain, a third party, which, with the help of the centre, would have had a majority in the Convention and would have governed.

Both in character and ideals, Danton formed a striking contrast to Robespierre.

The foundation of Robespierre's character was a belief in the neo-Christianity of Rousseau, the religion of the *Vicaire Savoyard,* and his supreme but so far secret aim was to make this religion the religion of France. Danton does not seem to have believed in the doctrine of the immortality of the soul; one of those dogmas essential to society, according to his rival. An atheist rather, he declared to the Revolutionary Tribunal: "My dwelling place will soon be in nothingness." If he spoke once or twice of the "God of the universe," of the "Supreme Being," we feel that he meant the "enlarged" God of Diderot. He was no philosopher. He did not, like Robespierre, dream of changing the soul of the nation. Leave the people their priests, but see that the latter do not do too much mischief in the State; spread education; trust to time; and, while waiting, since the mass of the nation is Catholic, do not wound the religious sentiment, even by the separation of Church and State, which, good in itself, would be premature in 1792 and 1793.

Politically Danton had no system, except to let conduct be ruled by reason, or rather reason enlightened by history. He was a democrat but proposed no program for organizing the democracy, except the spread of public education. He never outstripped opinion. He was a republican of the morrow. Since the Republic exists, let us accept it; let us make use of it to save the country and the Revolution. His method is to act from day to day, resolving, in an empirical manner, the immediate difficulties as they present themselves.

First we will expel the Prussians; afterwards, we shall see. The Prussians are defeated, and Belgium is conquered: let us negotiate with Prussia and Austria.

War is declared against England; let us nevertheless negotiate with England. The Brissot propaganda is alarming Europe; let us disown it and suddenly change the foreign policy of the Revolution. Danton was responsible for the decree of April 13, 1793, by which the Convention declared that it would not meddle in the home affairs of any other nation.

At home he was in favour of preventing discord at any price; by concessions, by false appearances at need, by an alliance of the well-meaning men of all parties, with a view to forming a solid and homogeneous Government, which should produce on Europe and the anti-revolutionary factions the impression that the republicans were agreed among themselves; to sacrifice everything, even the truth at times, to the propagation and triumph of this impression; to oppose individual passions with the idea of the native land; not a vague and mystical fatherland, but the actual, tangible France: this was Danton's policy. Hatred and vengeance he ignores. Publicly calumniated, he does not waste time in defending himself. He sacrifices his reputation and his honour; he allows men to call him "the drinker of blood." He believes in the omnipotence of material things and of gold. Not venal, he seems so, and that he seems so is a matter of indifference to him.

His sober, lucid eloquence invites to immediate action; he does not leave his hearers for a moment uncertain as to what they must do and the means of doing it. A man of action and a fighter, his advice is rapid and precise; not based upon principles, but yet conforming as closely as possible to the spirit of the Revolution.

Danton's policy is precisely what in our days is known as "opportunism," if that word be understood in a favourable sense. Danton springs from Mirabeau, as Gambetta proceeds from Danton.

He was not so popular as Marat or Robespierre. His language, stark, abrupt, and simple, and by no means academical, may perhaps have been admired by a few fastidious people; but it lacked the ornateness that pleased the people. The Faubourg Saint-Antoine kept the memory of Robespierre and Marat for many long years, by oral tradition; it soon forgot Danton. Yet he was, in his hour, the great national figure; the head of the national defenses, the herald of patriotism. His period of greatest eminence was September, 1792. It rested solely with himself, although his eloquence was not of a kind to stir the unlettered masses, to win for himself a lasting and widespread popularity, both in Paris and in the departments. But he did not stop to concern himself in the matter; out of sincerity, simplicity, and indifference, he fell into a kind of apathy; there was a lack of sequence in his activities.

These three men, Marat, Robespierre, and Danton, so different in their characters and their attitudes, were the most eminent, most influential members of the Mountain; one might almost say the leaders.

15

French Historians of the 20th Century

In contrast with those of the last century, French histori-
ans of the past sixty years have stressed the social and economic
aspects of the Revolution. They have paid more attention to the
economic legislation of the Assemblies, such as the Maximum Laws
of 1793; above all, they have brought to light the previously "sub-
merged" classes, the peasants and the urban "lower orders" (sans-
culottes). A consequence of this new emphasis has been that the
Third Estate (commons) no longer appears as an undifferentiated
whole with its controls firmly directed from Paris: the "small
people" of the town and villages—the peasants, shopkeepers and
craftsmen—are seen to have held views and to have had social
claims of their own that could not be blindly manipulated or taken
for granted by the men at the center. In consequence, it has be-
come necessary to reconsider the leaders, not only in terms of their
oratorial skill or political ideas, but also in terms of their ability
to reflect, to guide and respond to a vast complex of social forces.
This reappraisal has inevitably had the effect of eclipsing many
of the old favorites among the leaders (Danton and the Girondins
are obvious examples) and to bring others, like Robespierre, to
the front of the stage.

In some cases, this development has been accompanied by a
rather unquestioning acceptance of the "Incorruptible's" virtues:
by Albert Mathiez, for example, who found it necessary to "throw
out the baby with the bathwater" in order to give Robespierre his
due; his piece on Robespierre and religion which we print below is
a case in point. In others, as in the work of Daniel Guérin, the
result has been quite the opposite; and Robespierre is portrayed as
a reactionary villain of the piece who deliberately stemmed the
revolutionary tide in the fall of 1793.[1] This, however, is an extreme
example. More typical of the new trend are the excerpts that we
reproduce from the two most eminent French historians of the
Revolution since World War II, Georges Lefebvre and Albert
Soboul.

[1] Daniel Guérin, *La Lutte de classes sous la première République: bourgeois et*
"bras-nus" (1793-1797) (Paris, 1946).

ALBERT MATHIEZ: ROBESPIERRE AND RELIGION (1910)[2]

The figure of Robespierre has been so much misrepresented during the last twenty years,[3] even by republican historians, that to talk of the "Incorruptible's" religious ideas nowadays may seem a rash undertaking. Robespierre, it is proclaimed, was a narrow intelligence, a man of the ancien régime, a coldly ambitious nature who desired to reign over France by imposing upon the country, through the Terror, a counterfeit Catholicism, a deism glorified into a religion of State.

I cannot hope to study here the whole religious policy of Robespierre backed up by the documents and proofs.

It must suffice to choose one example; to examine precisely what part was played by Robespierre in the establishment of the Cult of the Supreme Being: especially since this is the usual butt of all his detractors.

What do the republican historians hostile to Robespierre say? They contrast the Cult of the Supreme Being with the Cult of Reason. The Cult of Reason, which they praise unreservedly, was, according to them, the Hébertist party's own creation. It was, they say, a pantheistic or even atheistical cult, a means of intellectual emancipation. The Cult of the Supreme Being, on the contrary, they allege to have been invented by Robespierre, in all its details, for the satisfaction of his unbridled ambitions and mystical passions. It was, they say, an attempt at political enslavement and intellectual reaction.

Now, however generally accepted this contract between the two revolutionary cults may be, it is none the less false. Far from having been the intention of a few men, Chaumette, Fouché, Hébert, and Cloots, or even of a party, the Cult of Reason was merely the culminating point in a series of civic festivals, the origin of which goes back to the great Feast of the Federation of July 14, 1790. The Festival of Reason resembled all the preceding ones. The same odes were sung, the same processions went through their evolutions, the same patriotic emotion stirred men's hearts at the sight of the same republican symbols. The new feature of the 20th Brumaire, Year II, the day on which the Commune and the Convention glorified Reason in Notre-Dame de Paris, was not even the place chosen for the ceremony—a cathedral—for churches had already witnessed similar scenes beneath their vaulted roofs. The new feature was this: that the fall of constitutional Catholicism, the secularization of the churches, and the abdication of the priests coincided with this festival.

[2] From A. Mathiez, *The Fall of Robespierre and Other Essays* (London: Williams and Norgate Ltd., 1927). Reprinted by permission of Ernest Benn Ltd., London.
[3] This essay first appeared in the *Annales révolutionnaires* in April-June 1910.

But even the overthrow of the constitutional Church cannot be ascribed to the Hébertist party alone, for the Girondins themselves, such as Pierre Manuel, Guadet and Vergniaud, had worked for it energetically since the days of the Legislative Assembly.

Nor was the solemn abdication of the Archbishop of Paris, Gobel, which gave an impulse to the dechristianizing movement, exclusively the work of the Hébertists; for it arose from the initiative of Pereira, Proli and their friends, the party of the Enragés (rabid extremists) which had its centre in the people's societies in the sections, and caused the Commune and Convention a moment's alarm; and the initiative of the people's societies was seconded by some notoriously moderate men such as Thuriot, Basire and Chabot. The truth is that the Hébertists, Chaumette, Cloots, and Hébert were merely falling into line with the obscure patriots of the sections, the nameless crowd of sans-culottes in the outlying parts of Paris.

Finally—and even M. Aulard, the personal enemy of Robespierre, has had to note this—the Supreme Being did not wait for Robespierre's sanction before being adored in the temples of Reason, by the same right, and at the same time, as Nature, Liberty, the Fatherland and Reason herself. We have a large number of speeches delivered in the temples of Reason. Pantheistic declarations—still more, atheistical ones —are the exception among them. We cannot pretend to know history better than those living at the time, who made history and lived through it; and they made no distinction between the two revolutionary cults, which they call indifferently by the same names. The Cult of the Supreme Being was in their eyes no more than a revised and amended sequel to the Cult of Reason. It was the same cult, the same institution, continued and improved.

It was Robespierre's enemies, the former Hébertists and Dantonists, who, in order to justify their conduct on the 9th Thermidor, tried after the event to travesty their victim as a dictator who made use of the religious idea as a means of domination. It was they who first spoke of Robespierre's "pontificate." But must the "Incorruptible" always be judged on the evidence of his implacable enemies?

One simple observation reduces this slander to insignificance. Never was the alleged dictator more challenged, more opposed, more impotent than on the morrow of the establishment of the Cult of the Supreme Being! On the morrow of the Festival of the 20th Prairial, opposition to him raised its head even in the Committee of Public Safety. The festival itself, by the ease with which it lent itself to a perfidious interpretation of his intentions, fed this opposition, which had other causes than religious disagreements; but these causes were such that his opponents could not avow them all.

Curiously enough, those very historians who can only see the Cult of the Supreme Being through the eyes of the Thermidorians, will only look at the Cult of Reason through those of Robespierre. Carried away by the heat of the struggle against the Hébertists, Robespierre had represented their leaders as preachers of Atheism; and Atheism horrified him, not only because he believed in the social necessity of faith in God, but, above all, because he feared that to preach it to a people ill prepared for it might destroy the very foundations of moral life. Robespierre's fears were exaggerated, his accusations ill-founded. The festivals of Reason were in no wise atheistical. Their organizers, whose ambitions were limited to replacing the Catholic Mass by a civil one, believed that the crowd could not dispense with some sort of worship. They were, for the most part, no more advanced, no more secularists, in our sense of the word, than Robespierre himself; men of all parties had experienced a sort of "moral dismay" (*effroi moral*) at the suppression of every form of worship. This was the expression used by one of them, Baudot, a deputy of the Mountain.

The mistake of the historians further springs from the method, or rather absence of method, with which they have approached the study of a question in which it is already so difficult to be impartial, since it is closely connected with our most intimate thoughts, and the bases of our way of life; up to the present the revolutionary cults have only been studied from the political, never from the religious, point of view. Historians, both of the Right and the Left, have only considered the Cult of Reason from the point of view of a party move. They have confused its history with that of the Hébertists. Similarly, they have made the Cult of the Supreme Being a chapter in the history of Robespierre and his party. They have denied that either of these cults was inspired by the religious sentiment, though they were at least as deeply animated by it as the old churches, which were already fossilized.

The mistake of the historians is to a certain extent comprehensible. The revolutionary cults were not like others. Belief in the supernatural was not the essential point in them. The religion of which they were the tangible expression is a religion without mysteries, revelation, or fetishes, a religion in which the act of faith and adoration applies not to a mystical object, but to the political institution in itself, the Patrie, as they called it—that is to say, to a just and fraternal society swayed by good laws, to the Fatherland conceived as the source and means of happiness, of moral as well as of material happiness. The revolutionary creed, being bound up with the Revolution itself, faithfully reflected the whole political life of that tragic period. The fact that it was actually directed towards a political object is no reason for refusing it a religious character. A faith which takes man as a whole, and raises him above the vulgarities of existence in order to make him capable of devotion and sacrifice, even though it be concerned with a secular ideal, is a faith at least as worthy of respect as all those which have as their object some magic operation.

I am ashamed to insist upon this. But the view according to which Robespierre was the creator of the Cult of the Supreme Being cannot stand examination. The essential point of the revolutionary religion was the adoration of the Republic of Liberty and Equality, novel words of which the prestige was still unimpaired: the rest, the metaphysical side, was merely secondary. No doubt a certain conception of society is bound to be accompanied by a corresponding conception of the Universe. Political convictions act and react upon philosophic convictions, and vice versa. Now the great majority of members of the Convention, and almost all Frenchmen, unanimously believed in God. This did not prevent them from believing in the Fatherland—that Fatherland which meant to them far less their native soil than the ideal society in which the human race was one day to find refuge. By placing the republican cult under the protection of the Supreme Being, Robespierre was doing no more than interpret public feeling, and this was the reason of the enthusiasm which he aroused.

There was not the slightest novelty in the proposition which he submitted to the Convention on the 18th Floréal, Year II; not the slightest tinge of invention, or even of personal initiative. It was not on his motion that the Declaration of the Rights of Man, which is prefaced to the Constitution voted in June 1793, was placed under the auspices of the Supreme Being. . . .

In Floréal, Year II, the Committee of Public Safety had just triumphed, not without difficulty, over the double opposition of the Dantonists and Hébertists, who were executed in Germinal. It was making efforts to prevent the return of the groups against which it had had to struggle for many months past. It was effecting the abolition of ministers, who were replaced by commissions subject to its control. It was placing the representatives on mission in closer subordination to itself, "in order," as Couthon said on the 17th Germinal, "to maintain unity of action between them and recall them all to the centre of government." It was the means of effecting this unity of action which was exercising the minds of the Committee, as well as of the Convention itself.

Now the representatives on mission complained in their correspondence that the measures dealing with worship were lacking in coherence and uniformity. They called for a general decree to regulate the conditions of the dechristianizing process and the establishment of Republican festivals for the whole country. There should be unity not only in the government, but also in its executive measures, and, still more, in men's hearts and minds throughout the country. The Committee of Public Safety decided to accede to the desire expressed so frequently by most of the representatives on mission. On the 17th Germinal, Couthon—not Robespierre; but, for M. Aulard, Couthon and Robespierre are one and the same person, like André Pomme and Robespierre just now—Couthon announced to the Convention that the Committee of Public Safety would shortly propose "a plan for a tenth-day festival dedicated to the Eternal, the comforting idea of which has not been taken from the people by the Hébertists." Couthon's words met with applause. Nobody raised the slightest objection.

In order to understand the joy with which the Convention hailed Couthon's project, we should not only remember that the great majority of the Assembly held deistical opinions, but we should take into consideration the necessities arising out of the religious situation.

At that time dechristianization was already fairly advanced, but not complete. The representatives on mission had requested the priests to abjure their religion, and transformed the secularized churches into republican temples. By the aid of the people's societies, they had endeavoured to replace Sunday by Décadi (the tenth day), and to make the people forget the ancient Mass by means of a civic service. Their measures had not been prearranged. They were somewhat varied in character. In some places rest on the tenth day was made obligatory for ordinary members of the public under penalty of a fine. In others Sunday rest was tolerated. In some places the tenth day was celebrated under the auspices of the people's society, in others the republican cult had the municipal officials as its priests. In some places republican missionaries, usually twelve in number, to recall the twelve apostles of the sans-culotte Jesus, were appointed to preach this gospel in the country districts. In others civic books of ritual were published, services for the decade, or ten-day week, or patriotic weekly devotions (such as Le Décadaire du Haut-Rhin, the Documents de la Raison, etc.). In some places the martyrs of liberty were venerated—Marat, Chalier, Le Pelletier and Brutus—in others this veneration was regarded as superstitious. Baptisms, marriages and burials were generally carried out with a lay ceremonial; but this ceremonial varied. The task was to remove

these differences, to regulate and organize the republican worship
which had so far grown up haphazard. It had also to be in some
measure legalized. The Republican Calendar, instituted in October 1793,
was a mere skeleton. Every tenth day had to be consecrated to some particular civic ceremony. It was necessary to distinguish national festivals
from the ordinary tenth-day celebrations. There was room for reducing
all these uncoordinated and desultory experiments to some system.
Catholicism, men said to one another, would not be definitively van-
quished unless it was replaced by a corresponding system, equally well
coordinated, uniform and well regulated.

For several months past the Committee of Public Instruction had been
repeatedly requested to draft a decree which should introduce into the
celebration of civic festivals the order which they lacked. The Committee set to work. In Ventôse, Year II, Mathieu, a deputy for Oise,
presented a completed draft on behalf of the Committee. He proposed
to institute, on the one hand, five national festivals consecrated to the
memory of the outstanding dates of the Revolution: July 14, August 10,
October 6, January 21, May 31; and, on the other hand, as many special
festivals as there were Décadis in the year. Each of these tenth-day
festivals should be "placed under the auspices of the Supreme Being,
and consecrated to one particular virtue." It should consist of speeches
and hymns, to take place in the "temples of Reason," and of military
and athletic exercises. Schoolmasters should be obliged to bring their
pupils to them.

The Convention gave Mathieu's report a hearing, and decided that
his project should be submitted to the Committee of Public Safety, which
should carry it into effect. It was indeed for the government to say the
last word on a matter of such importance. By the 17th Germinal Couthon
announced, as we have seen, that the Committee of Public Safety had
taken cognizance of Mathieu's project, and was going to devise means
for carrying it into effect.

This simple record shows that, contrary to M. Aulard's assertions, it
was not Robespierre who proposed the establishment of the Cult of
the Supreme Being on his own initiative. Robespierre's enemies are left
with the resource of claiming that the Convention, which ordered the
Committee of Public Instruction to prepare a scheme for the tenth-day
festivals, the Committee, which acted on these instructions, Mathieu,
who handed in his report in the name of the Committee, and Couthon,
who gave it the support of the Committee of Public Safety, were mere
marionettes manipulated by the Pontiff from behind the scenes.

To the historian who takes his stand upon the documents, and is not inspired by hatred, the matter presents itself in a perfectly natural light. The Committee of Public Safety entrusted Robespierre with the report which had to be presented on the subject of the project drawn up by Mathieu, because, for several months past, Robespierre had been entrusted with all reports concerning general policy.

Robespierre confined himself to appropriating Mathieu's project almost without a change, but he prefaced it with a long report, in which he defined and justified the aim which the Republic was trying to achieve by the institution of national festivals. Here again, he did no more than recall, in a systematic form ideas current at the time, which had frequently been voiced since the famous memorandum on public instruction composed by Talleyrand in the latter days of the Constituent Assembly; but he added importance to these well-worn ideas by his marvellous language and wonderful sincerity. He was never greater. His speech was listened to amid a truly religious silence, only interrupted from time to time by frenzied applause. This speech has all the force of a testament: not the testament of one man, but that of a whole generation, the generation which created the first Republic, and believed that by the Republic they were regenerating the world.

GEORGES LEFEBVRE: ROBESPIERRE'S POLITICAL IDEAS (1933) [4]

Robespierre no doubt owes to Jean-Jacques Rousseau the fact that he became the most famous of the outstanding leaders of French democracy; but he also owes it in part to his own character and social origins. Son of a lawyer of modest means and orphaned at an early age, he had a brilliant career at the Collège Louis-le-Grand, but he had been dependent on a scholarship and, from 1781 onwards, he had to earn his living when he returned to Arras. He has been represented as a lawyer without briefs and without resources. But, if this were so, how could he have gained admission to the Academy of Arras? How could he have stood up to local challenge within the Rosati? [5] Or how, at the age of 31, would he have been elected as a deputy for the Third Estate of Arras to the Estates-General of 1789? The truth is that while earning his living in an honorable fashion, he yet remained poor. But do not let us have illusions about this term "poverty," which occurs so often in his speeches and writings. To be poor, in Robespierre's sense of the

[4] From G. Lefebvre, "Sur la pensée politique de Robespierre," in *Études sur La Révolution française* (Paris: Presses Universitaires de France, 1954), pp. 95-8; trans. G. Rudé. Reprinted in English translation by permission of the publisher.
[5] Literary and debating society of Arras.

word, is not to wallow in the sort of abject squalor that wears a man out prematurely and gradually degrades him; it is, on the contrary, to find enjoyment in providing for one's needs by one's own labor, yet finding personal contentment without seeking luxury or idleness.

It is evident that, to remain faithful to this principle, as Robespierre was, to restrain one's desires and to resist temptation to do otherwise, especially after being embarked on a political career, required character and, moreover, a temperament which, in some respects at least, harmonized with such an ideal. Being chaste and sober, of a taciturn and melancholy disposition, and delighting, above all, in the enjoyment of a family or of a small circle of friends, Robespierre was quite naturally attracted by Rousseau's teachings. It has been said that he was nothing but a *petit bourgeois*. This is true enough and accounts in some measure for his popularity. The French *petite bourgeoisie,* which made up the bulk of the Jacobin and *sans-culotte* party, saw mirrored in him its own honesty, its serious endeavor, its moral and social respectability, and its mistrust of excessive wealth and unrestricted luxury.

Having spent so drab a boyhood and a life so fraught with toil and austerity, Robespierre conceived a high opinion (it was, you might say, a kind of pride) of his intellectual and moral qualities, and he came to adopt the principle that neither birth nor wealth should be the measure of a man's talents, dignity or rights; and this is of course a fundamental tenet of democracy. In the Estates-General and the Constituent Assembly, therefore, he did not confine himself to defending the Revolution against the privileged classes and to demanding the liberation of all the oppressed, such as actors, Jews, and the Negro slaves in the colonies. In the eyes of the common people, he appeared, more particularly, as the representative of political democracy. The Constituent Assembly, to which the Third Estate had mainly sent comfortable or rich *bourgeois* as its delegates, showed itself to be almost as hostile to the poor as to the aristocracy; and having no intention of introducing universal suffrage, it had restricted the vote to those who paid taxes. From 1789 onwards, Robespierre never ceased to combat this system of discrimination with powerful arguments; and, in my view, none is more cogent than that, in a society founded on the inequality of wealth, universal suffrage is one of the few means that may serve to counterbalance the power of money.

But, it may be argued, Robespierre was not a republican in 1789; he only became one, tardily, in 1792. This is true enough. But it was his attitude to this problem that made it possible for him to underline with such emphasis the deeper significance that a Republic has for us. In the strict sense of the word, a Republic is a government whose leaders are elected and not hereditary. But elected by whom? The Republic of Venice was then an aristocratic Republic; that of the United Provinces and several of the cantons of Switzerland were governed by urban patriciates. Even in the United States, which, in 1789, attracted everyone's attention, suffrage was not universal, and government was in the hands of Virginian planters whose wealth was derived from the labor of slaves. Robespierre did not want any such Republic. He would have preferred a monarchy in which suffrage was universal to a Republic that was in the pocket of aristocrats and men of wealth. That is why, when, in 1792, Frenchmen, hearing of Louis XVI's treason in summoning the Germans to put his subjects back under the yoke, determined to overthrow him, Robespierre proposed that the Republic be simultaneously proclaimed. And so he is, in our eyes, not only the most renowned of the apostles of democracy, but of the Republic as well; for the Republic, such as we conceive it, is not only a form of government but a system whose object is to realize equality and one that would have little sense if it were not both democratic and socially egalitarian. He might have said, like Michelet: "Unless all men, and the most humble among them, have entry to the city, I prefer to remain outside."

The question is whether the acquisition of political rights is by itself enough to give men an effective entry and if certain social conditions are not required to assure them of these rights. Robespierre believed, in fact, that the inequality of fortunes may reduce these rights to a mere hollow sham. Not only is he the historic leader of political democracy, but of social democracy as well. But let us not be misled by the use of this term: there is no question of his being a socialist. A socialist is one who allows of no other private property than the fruit of a man's personal labor, as represented by consumers' goods, and who demands that the means of production, land, machinery and raw materials, the means of communication, banks and commercial undertakings be transformed into public property. Neither Robespierre nor any other Montagnard ever put forward such a program. It is true that, in 1793, they nationalized a part of the nation's economic life by requisitioning and controlling prices. But this was a wartime measure, such as that we imposed, with other belligerents, between 1914 and 1918. Even in peacetime, an economic crisis may force a government to resort to similar expedients. There is no sound reason for believing that the Montagnards had any intention of perpetuating the maximum legislation once the war was over.

Nevertheless, Robespierre thought, with Rousseau, that not only nature but private property such as we know it lay at the roots of social inequality. And if this inequality goes beyond a certain point, political democracy becomes a sham, because the wage earner loses all independence without even being conscious of it, for the press and other means of propaganda, if not also education, fall into the hands of those who employ him and who tell him what to think. In Robespierre's view, therefore, our form of private property is an evil; but it is an evil that cannot be avoided. "I can hardly believe," he told the Convention on April 24, 1792, "that it took a revolution to teach the world that extreme disparities in wealth lie at the root of many ills and crimes; but we are not the less convinced that the realization of an equality of fortunes is a visionary's dream."

What, then, was his social ideal? A society of petty producers, each owning a piece of land, a small workshop, or a shop, enough to feed his family, and exchanging his produce directly for that of his neighbors. Here is reflected his dual concern for morality and social justice. The man who lives by his labor without being indebted to anyone is the one he terms a poor man. His one-man production and his tiny property assure him of personal independence; but to acquire this property and maintain it requires a degree of initiative and the personal qualities of labor, frugality and thrift.

Those who speak contemptuously of this ideal as being "petty bourgeois" fail to observe that such was in 1789 the ideal of the French country laborer and urban worker. The criticism made of the Revolution by the landless peasants was not that it had not created collective ownership, but that it had not distributed to each one of them a piece of land; what the workers complained of was not that the Revolution had failed to build large factories, but that, in abolishing the guilds, it had not made it possible for them to set up as small masters on their own. Robespierre's ideal corresponded to the economic conditions of his day; for the *sans-culottes* he stood as a symbol of a genuine social democracy and today, although conditions have completely changed, I am convinced that for many Frenchmen he appears in a similar light.

But how could the ideal be realized? Should one rely on complete economic freedom and *laissez-faire?* Experience teaches that men, already unequal by nature, if left to themselves, become increasingly unequal through inheritance and speculation; thus the perversion of political democracy becomes inevitable. That is why Robespierre and the Montagnards restored to republican thinking the notion of *social* rights, according to which the national community, being on the one hand the condition and the guarantee of individual rights and having, on the other, no other intelligible object than the maximum well-being or (as they said) the greatest "happiness" of all, is vested with the right to control the organization of property and labor. This is what Robespierre expressed in his speech of April 24, 1793, that I have already cited, a speech made at the time when the Assembly was discussing the new declaration of the rights of man and citizen that was to serve as a preamble to the Republican constitution. "In defining liberty as the first of human needs and the most sacred of the rights that a man holds from nature, we correctly said that this right was limited by the rights of others. Why have you not applied the same principle to property, which is a social institution? . . . You have drafted numerous articles in order to insure the greatest freedom for the exercise of property, but you have not said a single word to define its nature and its legitimacy, so that your Declaration appears to have been made not for ordinary men, but for capitalists, profiteers, speculators and tyrants." He proposed therefore to add to it the 4 articles that have been so frequently quoted: "1. Property is the right of each and every citizen to enjoy and to dispose of the portion of goods that is guaranteed to him by law. 2. The right of property is limited, as are all other rights, by the obligation to respect the property of others. 3. It may not be so exercised as to prejudice the security, or the liberty, or the existence of our fellow men. 4. All holdings in property and all commercial dealings which violate this principle are unlawful and immoral." The following year, his friend Saint-Just summed up this doctrine, in his *Institutions républicaines,* in the arresting phrase: "The independence of all men must be insured."

Only in such a way can political democracy attain its full validity. It is its duty to intervene in order to maintain a relative degree of equality, by reconstituting petty property as economic evolution tends to destroy it, and to prevent the creation of a monopoly of wealth and the proliferation of a dependent proletariat by laws on inheritance, a progressive income tax, and by the establishment of small properties. At a time when the main task was to provide for the peasants, the Republic was not lacking in the means, as it had the lands of the clergy and the *émigrés* at its disposal. In March 1794 (Ventôse of the Year II), Saint-Just further proposed to distribute free of charge to the poor the properties of the "suspects," the enemies of the Revolution. These famous Laws of Ventôse, the extreme form of social democracy in France, were never applied. But, even before this, Frenchmen without property had acquired the right, under the Constitution of 1793, to demand work or assistance from the Republic. It was the Montagnard Convention which adopted the principle of a free medical service and disablement and old age pensions. And as education can become the most cherished privilege of wealth unless the community guarantees it to all, the Assembly put it within reach of the people at large by creating a common school that was free at every stage.

Such is the tradition that Godefroy Cavaignac[6] continued when he reformed the Republican party after the Revolution of 1830.

ALBERT SOBOUL: ROBESPIERRE AND THE POPULAR MOVEMENT (1964) [7]

In the final analysis, the 9 Thermidor constitutes a tragic episode in the conflict of classes within the former Third Estate. But, to place it in the right perspective, we need to remember that the Revolution was fundamentally a struggle between the European aristocracy and the Third Estate as a whole. In this struggle, it is hardly surprising that the French bourgeoisie should have played the leading role. The Revolutionary Government, founded upon an alliance between the Montagnard bourgeoisie and the Parisian sans-culotterie, had been given the task of defending the Revolution against the aristocracy both within France and beyond her frontiers. As far as the Montagnards were concerned, it was perfectly natural that the Revolution should have placed the bourgeoisie in control of the nation's destiny; but, in any case, this was not the immediate problem. Solely concerned with victory, the Montagnards—particularly the Robespierrists—realized that the Third Estate would have to remain united as it had been in 1789. This explains the alliance with the sans-culotterie which made possible the installation of the Revolutionary Government during the summer of 1793. It also explains why this Government—at least until the spring of 1794—should have been so anxious to arbitrate between the interests of the bourgeoisie and the popular movement; to share the necessary sacrifices between them; and to intervene immediately either of them threatened to undermine the policy of national defence. It was a question of directing the entire resources of the nation for war.

On the basic issues—hatred of the aristocracy and the will for victory—the Parisian sans-culottes wholeheartedly supported the Revolutionary Government: the measure of this support can be judged from the fact that on 13 Vendémiaire and 18 Fructidor, setting aside their own legitimate grievances, many of them assisted the Thermidorean bourgeoisie

---

[6] Republican leader of the 1830s, and elder brother of the General Cavaignac who crushed the Paris workers' insurrection of June 1848.

[7] From A. Soboul, *The Parisian Sans-Culottes and the French Revolution 1793-4* (Oxford: The Clarendon Press, 1964), pp. 249-54. Reprinted by permission of the publisher.

to crush the counterrevolution. But differences of opinion on other vital issues rapidly alienated the sympathy of the Parisian sans-culotterie; and although these differences can be traced to the consequences of the war, they nevertheless reveal, quite clearly, the incompatible interests of two distinct social categories.

On the political level, the war created the need for an authoritarian régime. The sans-culottes showed that they were fully conscious of this by playing an important part in the creation of such a government. But it soon became apparent that the democratic ideas favoured by the Montagnards and the sans-culotterie were not designed to meet the particular problems which arose: this was especially true of the kind of democracy practised by the sans-culotterie which, moving spontaneously towards the exercise of direct government, was incompatible with the conduct of a war. The sans-culottes had asked for a strong government to crush the aristocracy; they never considered the possibility that, in order to do this, it would be forced to discipline the popular movement.

In addition, the political ideals of the sans-culotterie, vaguely defined during the revolutionary insurrections, did not tend to further the interests of liberal democracy as interpreted by the bourgeoisie, but those of popular democracy. Control over their elected representatives, the right of the people to revoke their mandate, certain procedures such as those of voting aloud or *par acclamation,* proved that the sectionary militants had no intention of accepting an empty and formal type of democracy. Their struggle succeeded in giving practical expression to what had originally been only an idea; they saw the Republic as the embodiment of the democratic ideal. For the really politically-minded sans-culotte, liberty and equality had not been offered to the people once and for all in 1789; they were principles which had to be reconquered from day to day—liberty becomes liberation, equality, social acquisition. This was the only way in which the happiness of every citizen (*le bonheur commun*), universally recognized as the aim of society, could be realized. This process cannot be explained simply by the unfolding of events during the Year II: it was a fundamental contradiction between the Parisian sans-culotterie and the bourgeoisie, between sectionary militants and the Revolutionary Government.

From an economic and social point of view, the contradiction was equally insurmountable. Robespierre and many other Montagnards had repeated that the country could not be governed in time of war as in peace, a statement which was not only politically, but economically valid. The Revolutionary Government, equally dependent upon both sides, was forced to arbitrate between the conflicting interests of the *possédants,* prepared to support the government, and the wage-earners, instrumental in bringing it to power.

It was only with considerable reluctance that the members of the Committee of Public Safety—firm adherents of a liberal economic system— agreed to pursue a policy of controls and fixed prices. It was only the realization that they could not harness the resources of the nation for war without a controlled economy that finally convinced them of its necessity as a temporary measure to be discarded once the war had ended. The revolution which they controlled was still, despite its increasingly democratic character, a bourgeois revolution. As such, it would have been absurd to fix the price of manufactured goods without fixing wages which ultimately decided what their cost price would be. The government found that it had to maintain a certain balance between the owners of business and manufacturing concerns, whose support was indispensable, and the wage-earners.

A controlled economy was also neccessary if a complete collapse in the intrinsic value of money was to be avoided. In order to prevent the *assignat* from becoming absolutely worthless, despite the inevitable inflation (the possibility of a complete devaluation of money in the middle of a war was not seriously considered), the government was forced to impose a maximum on wages as well as on manufactured goods. If it had agreed to a rise in wages, this would inevitably have led to a rise in the price of supplies vital to the war effort, since the government had decided not to interfere in private ownership or profits—a policy which can only be explained in the light of a bourgeois revolution. The Committee of Public Safety accepted price-fixing as a means of realizing a policy of national defence financed by the State without releasing an "infernal" spiral in prices, profits and wages which would, in turn, have resulted in uncontrollable inflation—the *assignat* would have been ruined and the Revolutionary Government swept from power.

This policy depended upon the continuation of the alliance between the Montagnards and the sans-culotterie, and, although it adversely affected the interests of the bourgeoisie—even the Jacobin bourgeoisie— by restricting economic freedom and placing a ceiling on profits, the latter, at least, were prepared to play their part in the defence of the Revolution and accepted the dictatorship of the Committees. But, apart from war supplies bought by the State and fodder requisitioned from the peasantry, craftsmen and shopkeepers—Jacobins included—evaded the provisions of the maximum. A conflict with the wage-earners was inevitable.

The sans-culottes, suffering from the effects of inflation and the shortage of food supplies, still looked at the problem from the stand-point of a relationship between wages and prices as they had done under the *ancien régime*. Their campaign for price-controls and requisi-tioning does not reflect their concern for national defence so much as their interest in providing themselves and their families with sufficient food. As for the workers, they were naturally anxious to take advantage of the relative shortage of labour to demand higher wages without bothering to consider the effect upon prices. From the autumn to the spring of the Year II, when the sans-culottes were in control of the capital, or, at least, feared by the Convention, they were successful in these demands: the Hébertist Commune, disregarding the law, refused to intervene. The government decided that it was time to act.

After Germinal, the Revolutionary Government reviewed the problem of the declining profits of manufacturing concerns, caught between the maximum on the one hand and an illegal rise in wages on the other. Numerous decrees by the Committee of Public Safety authorized a rise in the price of goods compared with the scale fixed by the maximum of Ventôse, despite the law. But these higher prices would have had no real effect if wages had continued to rise. The result was the decree of the Robespierrist Commune on 5 Thermidor enforcing the *maximum des salaires*. Although this decree was only to be introduced in the capital, the Committee of Public Safety—in view of the approaching harvest—had asked the districts to decree what amounted to a similar drop in wages for agricultural workers as early as Prairial. By depriving the wage-earners of the advantages which they had so recently acquired, the Commune appeared to be departing from the mediatory policy which had previously been adopted by the government. The controlled economy of the Year II, which was not based upon class differences, be-came unbalanced: after Thermidor, the whole structure collapsed.

It is clear that in a fundamentally bourgeois society the system of arbitration introduced by the Committee of Public Safety would be bound to favour the *possédant* class more than the wage-earners; the former being in a position to compensate for losses sustained as a result of price-fixing by producing for a private market. If it had been at all possible, the Robespierrists would probably have been only too happy to redress the balance. There can be little doubt that artisans and shopkeepers would have been less hard on the consumer if, assured of an adequate supply of raw materials and food supplies, their sales had guar-anteed them a reasonable profit. *Compagnons* and artisans had always maintained that, in order to safeguard their right to live, prices should bear a direct relationship to wages: they might well have resigned themselves to the maximum if only they could have been sure of receiving the basic necessities of life.

But the Revolutionary Government simply did not have the means of regulating the law of supply and demand for manufactured goods and vital food supplies: production methods and transport facilities had not yet been modernized by the capitalist concentration, rationalization, and mechanization of industry. The government had to work within the framework of an out-moded economic structure; war further aggravated the problem of keeping the nation supplied. Insurmountable difficulties arose when the economic system of the Year II was introduced to meet the demand for livestock and farm produce. The interests of the peasantry had also to be taken into consideration. Even the regular supply of bread was affected by inadequate means of transport, coupled with the absence of any form of concentration in the milling trade— one of the problems which capitalism would eventually solve.

The Revolutionary Government decided, therefore, that the best it could do in these circumstances was to keep the population of Paris supplied with bread, without going so far as to organize rationing on a national basis. As for the rest, local authorities and consumers had to make what arrangements they could to see that producers and merchants observed the provisions of the maximum. Requisitioning was reserved solely for the benefit of the army. The Parisian sans-culottes, discovering that this arrangement did not appear to be working in their favour, demanded a rise in wages and resorted to strike action: the Committees, faithful to the tradition of the *ancien régime,* declared such action to be illegal. Thus, at the root of the fundamental contradiction which had arisen between the Revolutionary Government and the popular movement responsible for bringing it to power, lay the failure of an artisanat economy to adapt itself to the demands of a full-scale national war.

16

English Historians and Robespierre

English historians have, in their views of Robespierre, been subject to the same sort of pressures—national, social and political—as the French; in addition, they have been influenced by the changing fashions in France.

At first, Robespierre was seen quite simply as a "bloodthirsty monster": so he appears in a 133-page pamphlet, published in Lon-don in 1794 under the title of The History of Robespierre, Political and Personal; *and "the tyrant" and "malevolent genius" reappear in Helen Maria Williams'* Memories of the Reign of Robespierre *in 1795. John Adolphus'* Biographical Memories of the French Revolution *(London, 1799) also dismisses Robespierre with a num-ber of epithets.*

The more serious study of Robespierre began in the 1830s, first with Sir Archibald Alison's History of Europe during the French Revolution *and William Smyth's* Lectures on the History of the French Revolution *but, more particularly, with the works of John Wilson Croker and Thomas Carlyle. Carlyle's portrait, which we reproduce, is shrewd, sometimes compassionate, but generally ma-licious: Robespierre's austere "incorruptibility" did not accord with his conception of a "hero." Croker, though far the more conserva-tive of the two (he condemned Thiers'* History *as a gross piece of whitewashing of the Jacobins and the Terror!), is surprisingly perceptive in his treatment of the crises of 1792 and 1793; like Napoleon, he believed Robespierre had been made the scapegoat of the villainies of others.*[1]

The midcentury saw two interesting studies by James Bronterre O'Brien, including his Dissertation and Elegy on the Death of Maximilien Robespierre *(1859). Reflecting the views of O'Brien's fellow Chartists and the socialists of his day, it is an uncritical eulogy; and, in order to present his hero in the most favorable light, he is compelled to absolve him from all responsibility for the Terror, to which O'Brien, as an advocate of "moral" and not "physical force," was resolutely opposed.*

With Lord Acton's Lectures *(delivered at Cambridge in the*

[1] See J. W. Croker, *Essays on the Early Period of the French Revolution* (London, 1857), especially pp. 299, 302-3, 352-6, 358-9, 363-4, 399-400, 420.

*1890s), from which extracts follow, we return to a far more hostile
view of Robespierre. As an old-style Whig who distrusted democracy, Acton saw him as a dangerous demagogue and called him
"one of the most hateful characters" in history. Yet he has doubts
as to Robespierre's responsibility for the grosser excesses of the
Terror.*

*J. M. Thompson's biography, first published in 1935, closely
reflects the revolution that had taken place in Robespierre studies
in France since World War I. Yet Mathiez' obvious influence is
tempered by the author's own liberal-radical views; and Robespierre's "deterioration" after 1793 is in some measure, at least,
attributed to the abandonment of his earlier liberal views.*

Finally, by way of contrast, I add a piece of my own.

THOMAS CARLYLE (1837) [2]

[In the Jacobin Club, early 1792]

But the chief Priest and Speaker of this place, as we said, is Robespierre, the long-winded incorruptible man. What spirit of Patriotism
dwelt in men in those times, this one fact, it seems to us, will evince:
that fifteen hundred human creatures, not bound to it, sat quiet under
the oratory of Robespierre; nay listened nightly, hour after hour, ap-
plausive; and gaped as for the word of life. More insupportable individual, one would say, seldom opened his mouth in any Tribune. Acrid,
implacable-impotent; dull-drawling, barren as the Harmattan wind. He
pleads, in endless earnest-shallow speech, against immediate War, against
Woollen Caps or *Bonnets Rouges,* against many things; and is the Tris-
megistus and Dalai-Lama of Patriot men. Whom nevertheless a shrill-
voiced little man, yet with fine eyes and a broad beautifully sloping
brow, rises respectfully to controvert; he is, say the Newspaper Reporters,
"M. Louvet, Author of the charming Romance of *Faublas.*" Steady, ye
Patriots! Pull not *yet* two ways; with a France rushing panic stricken
in the rural districts, and a Cimmerian Europe storming in on you! . . .

[In the National Convention, November 1792]

Pause of deep silence: a lean angry little Figure, with broad bald
brow, strode swiftly towards the tribune, taking papers from its pocket:
"I accuse thee, Robespierre,"—I, Jean Baptiste Louvet! The Seagreen
became tallow-green; shrinking to a corner of the tribune: Danton cried,
"Speak, Robespierre; there are many good citizens that listen"; but the
tongue refused its office. And so Louvet, with a shrill tone, read and
recited crime after crime: dictatorial temper, exclusive popularity, bully-
ing at elections, mob-retinue, September Massacres;—till all the Con-

---

[2] From *The French Revolution* (London, 1906), pp. 489, 626, 778-9, 806-7.

vention shrieked again and had almost indicted the Incorruptible there on the spot. Never did the Incorruptible run such a risk. Louvet, to his dying day, will regret that the Gironde did not take a bolder attitude and extinguish him there and then.

Not so, however: the Incorruptible, about to be indicted in this sudden manner, could not be refused a week of delay. That week he is not idle; nor is the Mother Society idle; fierce-tremulous for her chosen son. He is ready at the day with his written Speech; smooth as a Jesuit Doctor's; and convinces some. And now? Why now lazy Vergniaud does not rise with Demosthenic thunder; poor Louvet, unprepared, can do little or nothing: Barrère proposes that these comparatively despicable "personalities" be dismissed by order of the day! Order of the day it accordingly is. Barbaroux cannot even get a hearing; not though he rush down to the Bar and demand to be heard there as a petitioner. The Convention, eager for public business (with that first articulate emergence of the Trial just coming on), dismisses these comparative *misères* and despicabilities: splenetic Louvet must digest his spleen, regretfully forever: Robespierre, dear to Patriotism, is dearer for the dangers he has run. . . .

[In March 1794]

Danton meanwhile has been pressingly sent for from Arcis: he must return instantly, cried Camille, cried Phélippeaux and Friends, who scented danger in the wind. Danger enough! A Danton, a Robespierre, chief-products of a victorious Revolution, are now arrived in immediate front of one another; must ascertain how they will live together, rule together. One conceived easily the deep mutual incompatibility that divided these two: with what terror of feminine hatred the poor sea-green Formula looked at the monstrous colossal Reality and grew greener to behold him; the Reality, again, struggling to think no ill of a chief-product of the Revolution, yet feeling at bottom that such chief-product was little other than a chief windbag, blown large by Popular air; not a man, with the heart of a man, but a poor spasmodic incorruptible pedant, with a logic-formula instead of heart; of Jesuit or Methodist-Parson nature; full of sincere-cant, incorruptibility, of virulence, poltroonery; barren as the eastwind! Two such chief-products are too much for one Revolution. . . .

[On 10th Thermidor, July 28, 1794]

Robespierre lay in an anteroom of the Convention Hall while his Prison-escort was getting ready, the mangled jaw bound up rudely with bloody linen: a spectacle to men. He lies stretched on a table, a deal-box his pillow; the sheath of the pistol is still clenched convulsively in his hand. Men bully him, insult him: his eyes still indicate intelligence; he speaks no word. "He had on the sky-blue coat he had got made for the Feast of the *Etre Supreme*"—O Reader, can thy hard heart hold out against that? His trousers were nankeen; the stockings had fallen down over the ankles. He spake no word more in this world.

And so, at six in the morning, a victorious Convention adjourns. Report flies over Paris as on golden wings; penetrates the Prisons; irradiates the faces of those that were ready to perish: turnkeys and *moutons,* fallen from their high estate, look mute and blue. It is the 28th day of July, called 10th of Thermidor, year 1794.

Fouquier had but to identify, his Prisoners being already Out of Law. At four in the afternoon, never before were the streets of Paris seen so crowded. From the Palais de Justice to the Place de la Révolution, for *thither* again go the Tumbrils this time, it is one dense stirring mass; all windows crammed; the very roofs and ridge-tiles budding forth human curiosity, in strange gladness. The Death-tumbrils, with their motley Batch of Outlaws, some Twenty-three or so, for Maximilien to Mayor Fleuriot and Simon the Cordwainer, roll on. All eyes are on Robespierre's Tumbril, where he, his jaw bound in dirty linen, with his half-dead Brother and half-dead Henriot, lie shattered; their "seventeen hours" of agony about to end. The Gendarmes point their swords at him, to show the people which is he. A woman springs on the Tumbril, clutching the side of it with one hand, waving the other Sibyl-like, and exclaims: "The death of thee gladdens my very heart, *m'enivre de joie.*" Robespierre opened his eyes. "*Scélérat,* go down to Hell, with the curses of all wives and mothers!" At the foot of the scaffold, they stretched him on the ground till his turn came. Lifted aloft, his eyes again opened; caught the bloody axe. Samson wrenched the coat off him; wrenched the dirty linen from his jaws; the jaw fell powerless, there burst from him a cry—hideous to hear and see. Samson, thou canst not be too quick!

Samson's work done, there bursts forth shout on shout of applause. Shout, which prolongs itself not only over Paris, but over France, but over Europe, and down to this generation. Deservedly, and also undeservedly. O unhappiest Advocate of Arras, wert thou worse than other Advocates? Stricter man, according to his Formula, to his Credo and his Cant, of probities, benevolences, pleasures-of-virtue, and suchlike, lived not in that age.

A man fitted, in some luckier settled age, to have become one of those incorruptible barren Pattern-Figures and have had marble-tablets and funeral-sermons. His poor landlord, the Cabinetmaker in the Rue Saint-

Honoré, loved him; his Brother died for him. May God be merciful to him and to us!

LORD ACTON (1895-9) [3]

With Danton and his following we reach the lowest stage of what can still be called the conflict of opinion and come to bare cupidity and vengeance, to brutal instinct and hideous passion. All these elements were very near the surface in former phases of the Revolution. At this point they are about to prevail, and the man of action puts himself forward in the place of contending theorists. Robespierre and Brissot were politicians who did not shrink from crime, but it was in the service of some form of the democratic system. Even Marat, the most ghastly of them all, who demanded not only slaughter but torture and whose ferocity was revolting and grotesque, even Marat was obedient to a logic of his own. He adopted simply the state of nature and the primitive contract, in which thousands of his contemporaries believed. The poor had agreed to renounce the rights of savage life and the prerogative of force, in return for the benefits of civilization; but finding the compact broken on the other side, finding that the upper classes governed in their own interest, and left them to misery and ignorance, they resumed the conditions of barbaric existence before society and were free to take what they required and to inflict what punishment they chose upon men who had made a profit of their sufferings. Danton was only a strong man who wished for a strong government in the interest of the people and in his own. . . .

A month later, June 8, the Feast of the Supreme Being was held with all the solemnity of which Paris was capable. Robespierre walked in procession from the Tuileries to the Champ de Mars, at the head of the Convention. As the others fell back, he marched alone with his hair powdered, a large nosegay in his hands, wearing the sky-blue coat and nankeens by which he is remembered, for they reappeared in the crisis of Thermidor. He had attained the loftiest summit of prosperity and greatness that was ever given to man. Not a monarch in Europe could compare with him in power. All that had stood in his way during the last five years had been swept to destruction; all that survived of the Revolution followed obedient at his heels. . . .

Experienced observers at once predicted that Robespierre would not last long. He lost no time in devising a precaution equal to the danger.

[3] From Lord Acton, *Lectures on the French Revolution* (London, 1910), pp. 226-7, 286-9, 299-300.

He prepared what is known as the law of the 22nd of Prairial, which was presented by Couthon and carried without a division on June 10, two days after the procession. It is the most tyrannical of all the acts of the Revolution and is not surpassed by anything in the records of absolute monarchy. For the decree of Prairial suppressed the formalities of law in political trials. It was said by Couthon that delays may be useful where only private interests are at stake, but there must be none where the interest of the entire public is to be vindicated. The public enemy has only to be identified. The State despatches him to save itself. Therefore the Committee was empowered to send whom it chose before the tribunal, and if the jury was satisfied, no time was to be lost with witnesses, written depositions, or arguments. Nobody whom Robespierre selected for execution would be allowed to delay judgment by defence; and that there might be no exception or immunity from arbitrary arrest and immediate sentence, all previous decrees in matter of procedure were revoked. That article contained the whole point, for it deprived the Convention of jurisdiction for the protection of its own members. Robespierre had only to send a deputy's name to the public accuser, and he would be in his grave next day. The point had been so well concealed that nobody perceived it. Afterwards, the deputies, warned by the great jurist Merlin, saw what they had done, and on June 11, they stipulated that no member should be arrested without leave of the Convention. Couthon and Robespierre were not present. On the 12th, by threatening that the Committees would resign, they caused the decree of the previous day to be rescinded, but they assured the Assembly that it was superfluous, and their design had been misunderstood. They maintained their text and gained their object; but the success was on the other side. The scheme had been exposed, and the Convention had resisted, for the first time. The opposing deputies had received warning, and showed that they understood. From that moment they were on the watch, and their enemy shrank from employing against them a clause the validity of which he had denied. He gave them time to combine. Over the rest of the nation he exerted his new power without control. The victims increased rapidly in number. Down to the middle of June, in fourteen months, the executions had been about 1200. In seven weeks, after the law of Prairial, they were 1376; that is, an average of 32 in a week rose to an average of 196. But the guillotine was removed to a distant part of the city, where a deep trench was dug to carry away such quantities of blood.

During this time the Tribunal was not acting against men actually in public life, and we are not compelled to study its judgments as if they were making history. Whilst inoffensive people were suffering obscurely, the enemies of the tyrant were plotting to save themselves from the dreadful fate they saw so near them. Nothing bound them together but fear and a common hatred for the obtrusive dogmatist at the head of affairs; and it was not evident to each that they were acting in the same cause. . . .

Robespierre was carried to the Tuileries and laid on a table where, for some hours, people came and stared at him. Surgeons attended to his wound, and he bore his sufferings with tranquillity. From the moment when the shot was fired he never spoke; but at the Conciergerie he asked, by signs, for writing materials. They were denied him, and he went to death taking his secret with him out of the world. For there has always been a mysterious suspicion that the tale has been but half told and that there is something deeper than the base and hollow criminal on the surface. Napoleon liked him and believed that he meant well. Cambacérès, the arch-chancellor of the Empire, who governed France when the Emperor took the field, said to him one day, "It is a cause that was decided but was never argued."

Some of those who felled the tyrant, such as Cambon and Barère, long after repented of their part in his fall. In the north of Europe, especially in Denmark, he had warm admirers. European society believed that he had affinity with it. It took him to be a man of authority, integrity, and order, an enemy of corruption and of war, who fell because he attempted to bar the progress of unbelief, which was the strongest current of the age. His private life was inoffensive and decent. He had been the equal of emperors and kings; an army of 700,000 men obeyed his word; he controlled millions of secret service money and could have obtained what he liked for pardons, and he lived on a deputy's allowance of eighteen francs a day, leaving a fortune of less than twenty guineas in depreciated assignats. Admiring enemies assert that by legal confiscation, the division of properties, and the progressive taxation of wealth, he would have raised the revenue to twenty-two millions sterling, none of which would have been taken from the great body of small cultivators who would thus have been forever bound to the Revolution. There is no doubt that he held fast to the doctrine of equality, which means government by the poor and payment by the rich. Also, he desired power, if it was only for self-preservation; and he held it by bloodshed, as Lewis XIV had done, and Peter the Great, and Frederic. Indifference to the destruction of human life, even the delight at the sight of blood, was common all round him and had appeared before the Revolution began. The transformation of society as he imagined, if it cost a few thousand heads in a twelve-month, was less deadly than a single day of Napoleon fighting for no worthier motive than ambition. His private notebook has been printed, but it does not show what he thought of the future. That is the problem which the guillotine left unsolved on the evening of July 28, 1794. Only this is certain, that he remains the most hateful character in the forefront of history since Machiavelli reduced to a code the wickedness of public men.

J. M. THOMPSON (1935) [4]

It is unfortunate, for a fair judgment of Robespierre, that most of the descriptions of him handed down by historians came originally from men who, either by conviction or by policy, were his enemies, and that they were first published at a time when it was fashionable to blacken his memory. Nevertheless, it is possible to reconstruct a sufficiently life-like figure from descriptions which, however prejudiced, are at any rate contemporary.

Robespierre was a short man, not more than five feet three inches tall. Of slight build, he carried a small head on broad shoulders, and walked briskly along, holding himself rather stiffly, as though on guard against the nervous spasms which occasionally twisted his neck and shoulders, and showed themselves in the clenching of his hands, the twitching of his features, and the blinding of his eye-lids. His hair, naturally of a light chestnut colour, was carefully curled and powdered. His broad, rather flat face, short nose, weak green-blue eyes, and pale pock-marked complexion, sometimes lost their smug mildness in a harsh utterance, or a dangerous glance, of feline ferocity. He dressed neatly, almost foppishly, in a fashion that protested against republican carelessness; and the black suit of the lawyer was soon replaced by a striped or dark blue tail-coat, with high collar, wide lapels, and large buttons, worn with undemocratic breeches, and stockings of Lyon silk; on his head, a three-cornered hat; and always, when reading, a pair of 'preservers' (spectacles), which he was in the habit of pushing up onto his forehead—a disconcerting gesture—when he wished to look anyone in the face. His habitual expression seemed to his friends melancholy, and to his enemies arrogant; sometimes he would laugh with the immoderateness of a man who has little sense of humour; sometimes the cold look softened into a smile of ironic and rather alarming sweetness.

As a speaker, he had learnt to soften the tones of a normally rough

⁴From J. M. Thompson, *Robespierre* (Oxford: Basil Blackwell, 1939), pp. 585-92. Reprinted by permission of the publisher.

and shrill voice, and to moderate his Artois accent; but his utterance remained weak; and his power as a speaker, even in his eloquent moments, lay less in the manner of his delivery than in the seriousness of what he had to say, and the deep conviction with which he said it. With all the tricks, and more than his share of the commonplaces of the rhetorical tradition of the eighteenth century, as he had studied it at College, and practised it at the bar, Robespierre was able to sway the professional and shopkeeping audiences of the Jacobin Club as no other politician of his time could do. There is nothing absolute in eloquence: it is the art of using words to create opinions or acts; and it is judged by its success in producing an intended effect upon a given audience. Robespierre would have been as unconvincing in the House of Commons as a Welsh revivalist in a University church; but in the Assembly, or in the tribune of the Jacobin Club, he was one of the world's great orators.

Robespierre's detractors have been prodigal with the charge of hypocrisy. But a hypocrite is one who professes to be something which he knows he is not, the pretender to a title to which he is aware he has no claim. Robespierre can be represented as a hypocrite only by those who cannot or will not understand the real state of his mind. If anything is certain about him, it is that he was not so much anxiously trying to reconcile, as triumphantly certain that he had succeeded in reconciling, apparent opposites—belief in liberty with a policy of intimidation, love of the people with a suspicious distrust of individuals, dislike of the death penalty with wholesale executions, hatred of militarism with a national war, and a belief in an overruling Providence with a vindictive and merciless Inquisition into the conduct of his associates. His conscience may have been twisted, but it was all of one piece. He may have unconsciously cheated himself: he never consciously cheated others. Honest as to principles he never questioned, he was equally honest as to the exceptions that made them inapplicable. A stupider man would have died for liberty, or peace; a cleverer man would have become a mere opportunist. Robespierre, guided by something lower than logic, but higher than the instinct of self-preservation, kept himself intact and incorrupt, nearer than any other man to the brain and heart of the Revolution.

Most of what was good in him may be summed up in three words— Democrat, Prophet, and Puritan. He sincerely believed, all his life, in the wisdom and goodness of the common people; believed in it at a time when the fashion was to look for enlightenment and virtue from above, not from below; and believed in it, not as a consoling phrase from the pulpit, but as a political axiom, issuing in manhood franchise, equal justice, and the administration of property as a trust for the poor. Again, as he clung to his first principles of liberty and equality, even at moments when, for the best of reasons, he was forced to compromise them, so he refused to be diverted by the opportunism of government from pursuing his vision of a republic founded on virtue and sustained by religion; and the crowd, not understanding what he meant, but feeling that there was something fine afoot, climbed nearer to the summit of the Revolution than the cynics who sneered at him as a wordy ideologue. Puritanism is never popular, particularly in the country of Calvin; and there was an unpleasantly Genevan flavour in Robespierre's moral preaching and practice. But this, which might have been intolerable in a peaceful society, was forgiven, in a time of commotion and civil war, for the consistency with which 'the Incorruptible' stood out against temptations of money and office which were corrupting every rank of political power. 'He was a man of purity and integrity,' confessed Barère on his death-bed, 'a true and sincere republican.' 'No one knows better than I,' said Souberbielle, 'how sincere, how disinterested, how absolute was his devotion to the republic.'

Such were the qualities which won for Robespierre the admiration, and sometimes almost the worship, of people who knew him only by his public reputation, or by his speeches. In the more difficult sphere of private relationship, with its often drastic revaluations of character, respect for Robespierre's principles was balanced, if not outweighed, by dislike of his personal qualities. A cramped and unhappy childhood, a professional career impeded by prejudice and tactlessness, and a political experience of almost ceaseless opposition and intrigue, had left him, by the time he tasted power, jealous, suspicious, and vindictive. He was not a coward; but his caution in face of danger, and his underhand methods of attacking an enemy, had the appearance of it. He was not naturally cruel or bloodthirsty; but patriotism and Puritanism made him ruthless in the shedding of blood. He was no wicked tyrant, oppressing for personal ends, but that much more dangerous character, the conscientious Inquisitor, torturing the body that he might save the soul. Many such have been kindly men, who returned from a séance of rack and thumbscrew feeling that their work had been well done, and faced the world with a smile. Robespierre, said Lakanal, 'was a man full of good qualities, and gifted above all with great sweetness of character' (*douceur*), and an old man visited by Hamel in 1866 still remembered 'the distinction of his manners, his extreme politeness, and his affability.'

This, it may well be said, is the portrait of a man framed for opposition, and out of place in government; and Robespierre himself was sadly aware of it. The story of his life has recently been described as 'a study in deterioration';[5] and there is some justification for this view in the obvious contrast between Robespierre's professions of 1789 and his acts of 1794. But the change that came about was not due to the surrender of any of the citadels of conviction or character, but to intentional, and, as he supposed, temporary withdrawals of the front line, 'for strategical purposes.' He did not believe less in liberty, because he muzzled the anti-patriot press; nor more in capital punishment, when he urged the execution of the king. He had, no doubt, a lawyer's flair for justifying evasions of the law, and applied it to moral problems in such a way as to give rise to the suspicion of casuistry; but it would not be fair to charge him with anything so crude as the belief that the end justifies the means. Intimidation was, to him, not merely a cause of virtue, but its inseparable counterpart; and virtue not merely an effect of intimidation, but its living fruit. It was his original creed that the common people— that is, the classes least corrupted by wealth and power—are essentially wiser and better than their 'superiors.' His aim was to give them power and wealth, but not in sufficient quantities to infect them with the consequential disease. To secure this, virtue must be led by the hand, government checked by safe-guards, and breaches of the law relentlessly punished. There was, in this scheme of life, no before and after, no separation of means and end, no probationary or transitional period. The Robespierrian Utopia was all of one piece. Such inconsistencies as might appear, during the approach to it, were due to the atmosphere in which it was forced to grow, not to any inherent weakness. The thing itself was as single and sincere as the mind and character of its author. If, then, there was 'deterioration,' it was not because Robespierre turned aside from some heavenly vision that he had once enjoyed, but because, clinging to it all his life, he was driven to clothe it in the forms of maturer experience, to re-express the ideas of 1789 in the language of 1794. This does not mean that he never expected to be able to do away with terrorism; for, though he had moods of pessimism in which he doubted whether the interests of the rulers would ever be identified with those of the ruled, there were other times when he hoped, by popular education, good laws, and liberal institutions, to bring the Revolution to a happy issue, in a virtuous and enlightened republic. But he did

[5] By Reginald Somerset Ward in *Maximilien Robespierre. A Study in Deterioration* (London, 1934).

not often put such hopes on record; he left no Political Testament; and it is uncertain how far he felt himself able to look ahead.

Statesmanship implies more than political idealism. Robespierre had something of Mazzini in his outlook: had he anything of a Cavour's insight into the realities of a political situation? If his advice had been taken in 1789-90, and the Declaration of Rights had been embodied in a really democratic constitution, would there have come about such an alliance between the king and the people as might have saved the throne, and defeated the counter-revolution? It is more than doubtful. The middle classes were right in this belief that the common people were unfit for political power; and Robespierre himself was to find that it was one thing to champion their rights in Opposition, and quite another thing to hold them to their duties in the government of the country. Again, if Robespierre's advice had been followed in 1791-92, could France either have kept out of war, or have waged it more successfully? He was right in foreseeing defeat, and in dreading a military dictatorship; but his policy of distrust, and his insistence that military commands should go to patriots rather than proved soldiers, had a sinister effect upon the discipline and efficiency of the army. The six weeks' dictatorship of the Commune in 1792, a foretaste of Robespierre's ideal state, produced, along with a genuine outburst of patriotic fervour, an unscrupulous rigging of the elections, and an abominable series of massacres. In the matter of the king's trial and execution Robespierre showed a clear-sightedness and ruthlessness which lacked only one thing—the certainty that he was not aiming at merely a party success, but at an act of national justice. The overthrow of the Gironde in June, 1793—another stroke of Robespierrian policy—was necessary for the safety of the country, and the proscription of the party leaders which followed was justified by their resort to civil war; but it is hard not to lay part of the blame, for all this bitterness, upon the inquisitorial methods of the Jacobin 'purge,' which made it increasingly difficult for anyone to work for the country, unless he belonged to the straitest sect of Robespierrism. When, finally, Robespierre found himself the reputed head of a dictatorial committee, his statesmanship was put to the supreme test—and failed. For a year, indeed, the country was more effectively organised and disciplined than by any ruler between Louis XIV and Napoleon. But it was done at a terrible cost. An ignorant and provocative foreign policy gave the Revolution the habit of war, and increased the danger of Robespierre's own bugbear, a military dictatorship. Terrorism, the weak man's remedy for disorder, became a drug the strong man could not do without, till it destroyed just those elements of virtue and good sense to which Robespierre had hoped to appeal; whilst the failure of Jacobinism to provide an economic programme ruined its credit with the common people, and rendered it helpless in face of a vulgar coup d'état. Robespierre was never a dictator, and part of his failure must be put down to personal qualities which made him unfit for leadership or power; but there is enough evidence that he was at once too visionary, too narrow-minded, and a man of too little worldly experience or tact to be a statesman.

Where, then, did his greatness lie? In the thoroughness with which he embodied the main ideas and experiences of the Revolution, from the enthusiastic liberalism of 1789, through the democratic aspirations of 1792, to the disciplined disillusionment of 1794. At every turn of events he was there, ready like a Greek chorus, with appropriate comments; ready, like a Jewish prophet, with denunciation and warning; ready also, like any demagogue, with flattery of the people, and promises of a political millennium. Through it all, he was as sincere, as solemn, and as self-questioning as his master, the model of Jacobinism, Jean-Jacques Rousseau; fundamentally impracticable, perhaps, as he had been; and an unwilling example of the ultimate savagery of an appeal to the laws of nature.

More than this. Robespierre's place in history hardly rests upon anything that he was, or thought, or said, except in so far as he was impersonating the Revolution. However pure his conduct, and pleasant his manners, his personality was cold and unattractive. However eloquent his speeches, they seldom went outside the commonplaces of republican oratory; they contain ideas which have borne fruit in later reforms and revolutions, but they provide little permanent food for thought. The praise that might justly be accorded to the one republican leader who professed to identify government with the rule of morality is silenced by the reflection that he also identified it with the regime of the Revolutionary Tribunal, and of the guillotine. But so long as the French Revolution is regarded, not as the 'suicide of the eighteenth century,' but as the birth of ideas that enlightened the nineteenth, and of hopes that still inspire our own age; and so long as its leaders are sanely judged, with due allowance for the terrible difficulties of their task; so long will Robespierre, who lived and died for the Revolution, remain one of the great figures of history.

GEORGE RUDÉ (1958) [6]

. . . As we have seen, there have been few men whose claim to greatness has been more strenuously denied by their critics. Hypocrite, petty despot, bloodthirsty tyrant, doctrinaire fanatic—these and other epithets have been freely applied to Robespierre. Even the one praiseworthy quality that has seldom been denied him—his "incorruptibility" —has been so presented as to suggest that he was something less than human.

Nothing, perhaps, has contributed more to the legend of Robespierre's hypocrisy than the contrast between his personal appearance and the part that he played in history. The prim, fastidious figure; the meticulous attention to sartorial elegance; the powdered hair, the neat cravat and stockings of best Lyons silk; the cold manner and didactic tone; the twitching eyelids behind polished lenses; the absence of any "common touch" in either word or gesture—not only is the picture less attractive than that suggested by the gay abandon and breezy vulgarity of Danton or the rugged charm and insolent urbanity of Mirabeau; many have also found it ill-suited to a man who, day in and day out, paraded his devotion to democracy and inspired and directed the Terror in the proclaimed interests of the poor and humble. More cogently, it has been asked, how is it possible to trust the sincerity of a man who condemned capital punishment at one stage and yet sent the King—and countless of his former subjects—to the guillotine at others? Who condemned war in 1791-2 yet condoned and vigorously prosecuted it in 1793 and 1794? Who swore friendship to Danton and Desmoulins, only to sign their death warrants shortly afterwards?

Yet the charge is generally undeserved. In each case, it can be argued that the decision taken was determined by a firm and consistent attachment to political principle. To Robespierre, the sovereignty of the people, the triumph of the Revolution in the interests of the small proprietors (though not of the wholly dispossessed) was all-important: this theme is constant and runs through all his speeches and actions from June 1789 to Thermidor. In 1791, the war was condemned—not on pacifist grounds, but in the belief that it would strengthen the Court and counterrevolution; after August 1792, this particular danger no longer existed. Objection to the death penalty was abandoned because he believed that the King's survival after abdication would create a tangible center for aristocratic intrigue. Similarly, the liberal of 1789-91 gave way to the

[6] From "Robespierre," *History Today,* May 1958, pp. 221-9 (slightly adapted). By permission of the editors.

protagonist of "revolutionary government" not by virtue of any deeply rooted devotion to "totalitarian" principles, but because he had become convinced, by the experience of military defeat, treachery, inflation and "federalist" disruption, that the Revolution could not go forward on any other basis. The sacrifice of Danton was, of course, a different matter; but it is hardly to Robespierre's discredit that he should have put what he believed to be the safety of the Republic before the ties of personal friendship.

Nor can one reasonably doubt the sincerity of his democratic professions. No other deputy fought so hard, and even courted ridicule in the process, to make a reality of the Declaration of the Rights of Man and, in the first place, to remove the distinctions drawn by the Constituent Assembly between "active" (voting) and "passive" (nonvoting) citizens. But formal political equality was not enough; the nation's representatives, he insisted, "should debate in the presence of the whole French people." Officials and deputies, far from enjoying unlimited immunity, must be continuously subject to the salutary pressure of public criticism and, if need be, condemnation. Such was the conviction underlying the great "purges" carried out, at Robespierre's instigation, in the Jacobin Club from 1791 onwards and his creation, in 1794, of a special police department of the Committee of Public Safety to deal with the misdemeanors of government officials.

But how, it may be asked, can one reconcile these professions with the suspension (decreed at his and Saint-Just's request) of the liberal-democratic Constitution promoted by the Jacobins themselves in June 1793? Had this been intended all along and was this Constitution merely a "blind" to cover up the new rulers' dictatorial designs? We shall never know the certain answer to this question, as neither Robespierre nor his closest associates lived long enough to be given the chance of restoring a more liberal system once the national danger was over. Yet it may be argued that the dangers then facing the Republic from both within and without could not have been averted by any other means. So, at least, it seemed at that time to the main body of "moderates" in the Convention who—despite the hallowed precepts of Montesquieu and Rousseau—readily agreed to suspend elections and invest a Revolutionary Government drawn from the Assembly itself with almost unlimited authority "for the duration."

What of the charge that he was a bloodthirsty fanatic, whose reign of Terror was cut short only by the timely and resolute action of his opponents? The accusation seems plausible enough, for was not the law of 22nd Prairial (June 10, 1794), which substituted the tempo and procedure of the court-martial for the hitherto more liberal and leisurely methods of the Revolutionary Tribunal, drafted by Robespierre and Couthon in person and pushed by them through the Convention? And did not the guillotine in Paris work at double or treble speed precisely during those last nine weeks leading up to Robespierre's own fall and execution?

True enough, yet the case is not proven. The law of 22nd Prairial, with all its dangerous innovations, met with general approval (there was a perpetual fear of prison outbreaks) and was opposed by a minority in the Convention, not so much because it limited the accused's opportunities for defense as because it appeared to infringe the cherished right of the Assembly to refuse to hand over its own members to justice. But a far more important consideration is that the decisions of the Committee of Public Safety were collectively taken and that all its *arrêts*, whether relating to police, military operations or to internal administration, were signed by those members who happened to be in attendance. Though Robespierre and Saint-Just had a special responsibility for the Committee's police department, the instructions that emanated from it were as likely to be signed by Carnot, Barère, or other of their enemies in Thermidor as by any of the "Triumvirs" themselves.

Besides, for all his severity, Robespierre was a discriminating judge: he showed greater clemency to the seventy-three Girondin supporters who protested against the purge of June 1793 than did most of his Jacobin colleagues. His brother Augustin, with his full approval, emptied the prisons of the Franche Comté of those unjustly sentenced by "Hébertist" extremists; and he himself publicly condemned the excesses of Collot and Fouché at Lyons and of Carrier at Nantes—a condemnation that drove these "proconsuls," in self-protection, to conspire to destroy him in Thermidor. Napoleon, for one, believed that an important reason for Robespierre's overthrow was that he had plans to relax the harsher rigors of the Terror.

Like many of the Revolution's leaders, Robespierre was profoundly influenced by Rousseau; it is said that he kept a copy of *The Social Contract* in his bedroom at Maurice Duplay's. From Rousseau he derived much of his political thought and much of the vocabulary and imagery in which it is clothed. From him, too, he drew his belief in the social utility of a civic religion stripped of superstition and also his ideal of a republic of small and "middling" property owners and craftsmen, uncorrupted by their wealth or destitution. This conception lies at the back of much of his talk of "corruption" and "virtue," which became almost an obsession with him towards the close of his career. In Rousseau, again, he found justification for his belief that though the sovereign people were good and could basically do no wrong, they might be temporarily misled and suborned by a perversion of the "general will." Hence his readiness to believe that the food rioters of 1793, whose actions he deplored, could have been led to act as they did only as the result of an aristocratic plot. Hence, too, his overconfident belief that political morality and attachment to the Revolutionary government in 1794 were one and the same thing.[7]

Do such facts justify the charge that he was a doctrinaire fanatic whose every action was determined by an inflexible attachment to abstract principles? The proposition is hardly a tenable one, as it ignores the instinct for political realities and the capacity for practical statesmanship that Robespierre displayed in the course of a succession of revolutionary crises, and never more than as the chief architect and guiding spirit of the Revolutionary government of 1793-4.

Why, then, did he fall so ignominiously and why did his career end so abruptly in bitterness and defeat? Because, I believe, it proved impossible in the long run to reconcile his high social ideals with the political possibilities that lay at his and his associates' command. Above all, his attempt to found a republic of small proprietors, being an anachronism, proved incapable of realization. The Revolutionary government fell apart not so much from dissension at the top—this was a symptom of a deeper crisis—as from the sheer impossibility of harmonizing the rival claims of *bourgeoisie* and *sans-culottes*. In June 1793, he had called for the support of the people to curb the "egoism" of the rich. Concessions to popular demands had followed: among them, the control of food prices and the enactment of severe laws against hoarders and speculators. But, in the spring of 1794, the clamor of property owners and producers, whose support was increasingly necessary for the conduct of the war, induced the Committee to relax controls and to sacrifice the small consumers and wage earners. As a result, Robespierre and his companions fell between two stools, and no one was satisfied. It was the *bourgeoisie* that overthrew him; but the *sans-culottes* stood by and refused to intervene. So, in the last resort, he fell victim to his own ideals as much as to the machinations of his enemies.

[7] For a fuller discussion of this point, see M. G. Hutt, "Robespierre, the Incorruptible," in *The Listener,* January, 1959, pp. 205-7.

Afterword:
The "Mystery" of Robespierre

We have seen that historians have been strongly divided in their estimation of Robespierre; but all, with the exception of those who have been committed to uncritical praise or denunciation, have left as many unsolved questions about him as they have found certain answers. Croker wrote of him as "the most mysterious figure" of the Revolution and found his "latter conduct . . . obscure and unaccountable". Acton, too, writes of the "unsolved problem" of Robespierre's ulterior aims "left by the guillotine." Napoleon spoke to Las Cases at St. Helena for the "obscurity and mystery" that enveloped the drama of Thermidor. Thompson found it hard (though he made a gallant effort) to account for the change that took place in his subject between 1792 and 1794. Others have left a different set of question marks: When, and why, did Robespierre begin to think in terms of a dictatorship? Why did he become obsessed with "virtue" in 1794? Why did he stay away from the Committee of Public Safety in the summer of 1794 and then play into the hands of his enemies by his oblique denunciations in his last speech to the Convention? Why did he hesitate to call to his aid the 3,000 troops drawn up at the City Hall on the night of 9th Thermidor in response to the Commune's summons?

To some of these questions we shall never have entirely convincing answers. They depend too much on finding the right document (which probably does not exist) or on the revelation of hidden motives that lie beyond the historian's reach. Did he boycott the Committee's meetings because of injured pride, of a distaste for unpleasant encounters, or in order to take stock of events and prepare for another day? Did he challenge his enemies within the Convention (against Saint-Just's advice) because he was confident of a greater measure of support, or because he was deliberately courting martyrdom? Did he refuse to give firm orders to the troops because he refused to challenge the lawful authority of the Convention, or because he knew that the game was up and had no further spirit for the fight? But these are relatively minor "mysteries," and the fact that they will probably remain unsolved is not of any great moment.

Far more important for our ultimate judgment of Robespierre are the larger questions: Why was the liberal Constitution of 1793 laid aside and supplanted by the Revolutionary government of the "Year II"? Why were the rival "factions" of Dantonists and Hébertists destroyed? What were Robespierre's intentions in the summer of 1794: to reinforce or to relax the Terror? To these important questions, as we have seen, historians, like contemporaries, have given quite conflicting answers, and it is certainly too much to hope that these "mysteries" will ever be cleared up to everybody's satisfaction.

However, Napoleon may have been wrong when he claimed that "the uncertainty" (he was, of course, talking only of the "mystery" of Thermidor) would be likely to increase rather than diminish "with time." This is not so much because Robespierre is likely to cease to be a controversial —and therefore a "mysterious"—figure, but because the new focusing of recent research and the experience of the past hundred or more years can help to correct the often one-sided impressions of historians even where the documents themselves are silent. The new emphasis on the social aspects of the Revolution has helped to throw light on Robespierre's own social and political ideas: we have seen this in our extract from Georges Lefebvre. Besides, Lefebvre's own work on the peasants and Soboul's on the Parisian *sans-culottes* have not merely enriched our knowledge of these classes, but, by showing how they obtruded onto the political scene, these works have added a new dimension to the struggle of parties. It thus becomes reasonable and possible for the historian of the 1960s, where (unless he were a Marx or a Tocqueville) it was not possible for one of the 1860s, to explain such episodes as the adoption of price-controls (Law of the Maximum) or the elimination of the "factions" in terms other than of doctrinaire fanaticism, a purely personal antipathy, or the long-cherished ambitions of power-hungry men.

Again, our own and others' experience of the past half-century, in particular, helps us to throw light into some of the more obscure corners of 1793-4. It was not from any personal hostility to his teacher, Aulard, that Mathiez began to build up Robespierre and to deflate Danton. But from his experience of the corruption, financial scandals and profiteering of the France of the World War I and prewar period, he began to see Danton as the typical venal politician of the Third Republic; while Robespierre's "incorruptibility," in contrast, took on an added lustre. Equally, the wartime controls exercised by the belligerents on both sides led him to look afresh at the Convention's Maximum laws, and he saw how they developed from a combination of the pressure from the streets and the imperious demands of a "revolutionary" war.

Although Mathiez may have overplayed his hand, his reasons for looking at these matters afresh were perfectly sound, and they are a healthy reminder that historical acts should not be treated in a political vacuum. Several historians of Robespierre and the Revolution have done precisely this: by discussing the problems and attitudes of politicians in isolation, they have tended to divorce the decisions and activities of governments and groups, or (say) Robespierre's preoccupation with "virtue," from the wider context of war and civil war and the rival pressures of popular revolt and counterrevolution. This is particularly true of nineteenth-century historians like Acton and Croker and is even true, at times, of Thompson.

These considerations are particularly relevant to such questions as the decision to lay aside the liberal Constitution and form a "revolutionary" Government "for the duration." We cannot know for sure whether the Jacobin leaders would have returned to the democratic-liberal principles of June 1793 once the emergency was over: they perished before the promise could be put to the test. We can only speculate on the answer, and our conclusion will be strongly colored by our own political leanings and our sympathy or aversion for Robespierre and Saint-Just. But we can find reasonable evidence to support the view that the resort to Revolutionary government was not a long premeditated act. For one thing, it ran counter to the teachings of the "philosophers": all previous revolutionary Assemblies had been careful to preserve the "separation of powers" and a strong legislature and a weak executive. We can also learn something from our own study or experience of subsequent wars and revolutions. In our century, "total" war, quite apart from revolution, has bred centralization of government, strict controls, rationing and food-cards irrespective of the political ideas of the men in power. But "total" war, accompanied by revolution (as in France in 1793), has bred, in addition, counterrevolution, terror and counterterror; and this again does not have to be explained in terms of the predilections of individual leaders. Moreover, similar experiences teach us that terror creates its own professionals who cling tenaciously to their craft (whether they be of the Right or the Left), and the fact that "professionals" of 1794 like Fouché, Collot and Carrier had begun to see the Terror almost as an end in itself does not justify us in tarring Robespierre with the same brush. Admittedly, we cannot be any more certain than Napoleon was that he would have taken immediate steps to dismantle it once that last surgical operation had been performed. But we may feel disposed to give him the benefit of the doubt.

It is perhaps not surprising that in some countries—in France, for example, and in some countries of Eastern Europe—these problems have not appeared as intractable as they have in Great Britain and the United States. This is not because historians in those countries have a

greater wisdom, nor is it simply that they have a different political outlook; but they have certainly had a closer acquaintance with war *and*
revolution. Even if we are not particularly anxious to share that experience, we may perhaps find it easier to understand Robespierre and his
problems if we are willing to learn some of its lessons, even at second
hand.

Bibliographical Note

There has been a rising interest in Robespierre as a world-historical figure in the past half-century, particularly since the series of modern revolutions began with the Russian Revolution of 1917. New books about him or relating to him have appeared in several European countries: in Russia, Austria, and East Germany, as well as in France and Italy; in South America and Japan. For a discussion of Robespierre as seen by historians in a number of countries (including France, England, Belgium, Spain, the U.S.A., Hungary, Germany and Russia), the student who reads French is referred to *Actes du Colloque Robespierre* (Société des Etudes Robespierristes, Paris, 1967), pp. 165-238. As very little of this work has been translated into English (and much of it not into French), it will have to be largely ignored in this Note.[1] Unfortunately, too, remarkably little of the best work on Robespierre, written at any time, or of his writings and speeches, has been published in English (as will be evident from the footnotes to this volume); so it will be necessary to include in this Note some of the basic works in French as well as the work of English and American historians.

A ten-volume edition of the complete works of Robespierre is still in the process of preparation by the Société des Études Robespierristes in Paris. Volume IV: *Les journaux, Le Défenseur de la Constitution,* edited by Gustave Laurent, appeared in 1939; and since 1950, four further volumes (VI-IX) have appeared, jointly edited by M. Bouloiseau, A. Soboul and the late G. Lefebvre. Unfortunately, the most important volume of all—Vol. X, which is due to include all the speeches made since September 1793—has not yet been published. Other collections of extracts from Robespierre's speeches in French are to be found in: A. Vermorel, *Oeuvres de Robespierre* (Paris, 1865); H. Morse Stephens, *The Principal Speeches of the Statesmen and Orators of the French Revolution, 1779-1795,* 2 vols. (Oxford, 1892); and Jean Poperen, *Robespierre. Textes choisis,* 2 vols. (Paris, 1957). In addition, speeches or extracts are to be found in some of the collections of documents relating to the Revolution as a whole: e.g., in Buchez and Roux's *Histoire parlementaire de la Révolution française,* 40 vols. (1834); and in A. Aulaud's *La Société des Jacobins,* 6 vols. (1889-97) and *Recueil des Actes du Comité de Salut Public,* 26 vols. (1889-1923).

[1] Mention must, however, be made of the bicentenary volume dedicated to Robespierre, published in the German Democratic Republic in 1958: W. Markov, ed., *Maximilien Robespierre, 1758-1794* (Berlin: Rütter & Loening, 1958; rev. edition, 1961), with an introduction (in French) by G. Lefebvre and articles (in German) by French, English, Italian, Polish, Hungarian, Czech, German, American and Russian historians.

For historians' views of Robespierre (in addition to the special number of the *Annales historiques* mentioned above) see Lord Acton, *The Literature of the Revolution* (Appendix to his *Lectures on the French Revolution*, 1910); G. P. Gooch, *History and Historians of the Nineteenth Century* (1931); G. Rudé, *Interpretations of the French Revolution* (London: Historical Association, 1961), and, above all, the 35-page Introduction to J. M. Thompson's *Robespierre* (Oxford, 1939). For views of Robespierre by his contemporaries, see Louis Jacob, ed., *Robespierre vu par ses contemporains* (Paris 1938), of which ample use has been made in the present volume. There are also contemporary sketches of him (some reproduced in this volume) in *The Correspondence of William Augustus Miles, 1789-1817*, 2 vols. (London, 1890); in J. M. Thompson, ed., *Witnesses of the French Revolution* (Oxford, 1939); and in B. C. Davenport, ed., *A Diary of the French Revolution by Gouverneur Morris*, 2 vols. (London, 1939).

Among biographies of Robespierre in French, one of the earliest and longest is E. Hamel's *Histoire de Robespierre*, 3 vols. (1865); but, like James Bronterre O'Brien's *Life and Character of Maximilien Robespierre* (1837) and his *Dissertation and Elegy on the Life and Death of Maximilien Robespierre* (1859) in English, it is a solemn piece of hagiography rather than a critical work of history. In fact, the English-speaking reader may reasonably confine his attention to a number of recent French biographies, such as G. Walter, *Robespierre*, 3 vols. (1936-40); J. Massin, *Robespierre* (1956); and M. Bouloiseau, *Robespierre* (Que sais-je? series, 1957). But he should also consult some of the numerous studies of Robespierre by his great rehabilitator, Albert Mathiez, such as *La Conspiration de l'Etranger* (1917), *La Corruption parlementaire sous la Terreur* (1918), *Robespierre terroriste* (1921), *Autour de Robespierre* (1925), *Girondins et Montagnards* (1930), *Etudes sur Robespierre* (1958), and the collection of essays translated into English as *The Fall of Robespierre and Other Essays* (London, 1927). Reference may also be made to G. Lefebvre's *Etudes sur la Révolution française* (1954) for portraits of Danton and Robespierre; and students should read A. Soboul's *The Parisian Sans-Culottes and the French Revolution, 1793-4* (Oxford, 1964) and his article "Robespierre and the Popular Movement of 1793-4," in *Past and Present*, May 1954. For a critical study of Robespierre from a "Trotskyist" viewpoint, see D. Guérin, *La Lutte de classes sous la première République: bourgeois et "bras-nus"* (1793-1797), 2 vols. (1946).

In addition, specialists may wish to consult the index of the *Annales historiques de la Révolution française*, or the general histories of the Revolution by G. de Staël (1818), A. Thiers (1824-5), F. A. M. Mignet (1915), J. Michelet (1847-53), Louis Blanc (1847), A. Aulard (1910), J. Jaurès (1901), A. Mathiez (1927), G. Lefebvre (1962, 1965) and A. Soboul (1962), from some of which (de Staël, Thiers, Aulard) passages have been reproduced in this volume.

As we have noted, the work done on Robespierre by English and American historians has been scanty and much of it undistinguished. Of that done in the last century, only one piece is still of some interest: J. W. Croker's 130-page essay on "Maximilien Robespierre," which first appeared in the conservative *Quarterly Review* in 1835 and was republished in the author's *Essays on the Early Period of the French Revolution* in 1857. For other 19th-century work the student may perhaps confine himself to consulting the general histories or published lectures of Thomas Carlyle (1837), William Smyth (1846), G. H. Lewes (1849), H. Morse Stephens (1886, 1891), and Lord Acton (1910).

More recent biographies of Robespierre in English include Hilaire Belloc's *Robespierre. A Study* (1901) and C. F. Warwick's *Robespierre and the French Revolution* (New York, 1909); but both have been outdated by recent research. A work that gives a stronger impression of having kept up with the times (though not with historical research) is Reginald Somerset Ward's *Maximilien Robespierre. A Study in Deterioration* (London, 1934). However, its claim to be a "psychological" study is somewhat vitiated by its crude anti-"popular" prejudices, and it probably tells us more about the author himself than about his subject. A more respectable attempt to place Robespierre in a history of political ideas is made by J. L. Talmon in *Origins of Totalitarian Democracy* (London, 1952).

By far the most complete and perceptive biography of Robespierre in English—and perhaps the best in any language—is J. M. Thompson's *Robespierre*, 2 vols. (Oxford, 1935); rev. edition, 1 vol., 1939), which is essential reading for every student. There is a shorter biography by the same author entitled *Robespierre and the French Revolution* (London, 1952); and there is a useful portrait in his *Leaders of the French Revolution* (Oxford, 1928).

Among recent articles, mention may be made of A. Cobban, "The Political Ideas of Maximilien Robespierre during the period of the Convention," *The English Historical Review*, January 1946; G. Rudé, "Robespierre," *History Today*, May 1958; and M. G. Hutt, "Robespierre, 'The Incorruptible,'" *The Listener*, January 29, 1959.

Finally, students are advised to read R. R. Palmer's *Twelve Who Ruled. The Year of the Terror in the French Revolution* (Princeton, 1941), which is the only scholarly account in English of the collective work of the men who ruled France between July 1793 and July 1794.

Index